INTEGRATING EASTERN EUROPE INTO THE GLOBAL ECONOMY

International Studies in Economics and Econometrics

VOLUME 25

The titles published in this series are listed at the end of this volume.

Integrating Eastern Europe into the Global Economy: Convertibility through a Payments Union

by

Jozef M. van Brabant

SPRINGER SCIENCE+BUSINESS MEDIA, B.V.

ISBN 978-94-010-5586-4 ISBN 978-94-011-3578-8 (eBook)
DOI 10.1007/978-94-011-3578-8

Printed on acid-free paper

To Miyuki - for her alone

Preface

This book is designed as a modest contribution to the ongoing deliberations about how to ease the fairly tight constraints on the external payments of many countries of the eastern part of Europe. In the first instance, this inquiry is addressed to those that have embarked on wide-ranging systemwide reforms. External constraints have been markedly hampering the introduction of market-oriented economic mutations, thereby raising the cost of transition far above levels expected at the outset of the present wave of uniquely restructuring the countries involved.

I explore here several angles of this discussion. But three stand out. One is the disintegration of the postwar framework for economic cooperation in that part of the world. Another is the disarray brought about by incisive economic transformations in the area. Finally, various national, regional, and international interest groups are at work there, hoping to mold somehow the drift of the reform, or at least key components thereof, in their own "image." In the process it is often forgotten, as Ralf Dahrendorf (1990, p. 41) so pointedly remarked that "[a]ll systems mean serfdom, including the 'natural' system of a total 'market order' in which no one tries to do anything other than guard certain rules of the game discovered by a mysterious sect of economic advisers."

It is my firm belief that the reforming countries should be able to profit from restructuring their intragroup trade in line with prevailing (but only partially utilized) comparative advantages and foster dynamic comparative advantages as well. To make such process a coherent part of the drive to open up these long-protected economies to constructive international competition, restrictions on economic intercourse among the reforming countries themselves need to be removed as expeditiously as possible too. This was the motivation behind an earlier attempt (Brabant 1990c) to examine the political economy of the transition in a broader framework, but one set specifically against the backdrop of western assistance efforts. This study is a logical sequel thereto, but it is far narrower in scope and, in some respects, more technical.

The debate on the reconstruction of intragroup facilities, after the demise of the postwar economic order in the east, heated up considerably in 1991. The renewed interest in the reforming countries, on the part of regional and international organizations, academics, banks, transnational corporations, and others created an atmosphere that was conducive to the convening of numerous meetings at various levels of sophistication on one aspect or another of the transition. Needless to say that none of them has produced much by way of clarifying the bulk of the critical down-to-earth daily issues confronting those managing the reforms. In fact, many have simply resulted in more muddle on a number of transition issues. Certainly one of these forms the core topic of this book.

On many an occasion in 1991, I was invited to present my views on union formation among the reforming countries. In the process, my stance elicited countless comments and suggestions, some formal but most rather informal, that in one way or another have shaped my present conviction on the matters at hand. My debt to critics, friends, detractors, and the phalanx of would-be specialists is, I hope, carefully interwoven with the arguments defended in this volume. I say "hope" with circumspection for, as many others in the field, I have been chasing a rapidly moving target. Writing a book under the circumstances was not easy. I trust that putting my ideas down in their full context may help to clarify matters. Although it would be churlish on my part not to acknowledge with gratitude my undeniable debt to the brainstorming and doubts that all these contacts have afforded over the past year or so, I hasten to add that no single individual or institution should be held responsible for any of the opinions expressed here.

Finally, although this monograph was written in my "spare" time, while employed by the United Nations, I wish to emphasize most emphatically that the opinions expressed here are mine and do not necessarily reflect those that may be held by the United Nations at large or its Secretariat in New York in particular.

I would be remiss if I did not explicitly single out Miyuki, who has been the involuntary midwife of yet another step-child, for a special word of thanks and another promise that long-neglected chores will be mended "soon" again. For that, and much more, I dedicate this volume solely to her.

Jozef M. van Brabant
Ossining, NY, 15 April 1991

Table of contents

Abbreviations

Bank	International Bank for Reconstruction and Development
BIS	Bank for International Settlements
BLEU	Belgian-Luxemburg Economic Union
BTPA	bilateral trade and payments agreement
CEEU	Central European Economic Union
CEPU	Central European Payments Union
CMEA	Council for Mutual Economic Assistance
Comecon	Council for Mutual Economic Assistance
CPE	centrally planned economy
CSCE	Conference on Security and Cooperation in Europe
CSFR	Czech and Slovak Federative Republic
DE	developing economy
DME	developed market economy
EBRD	European Bank for Reconstruction and Development
EC	European Communities
ECA	Economic Cooperation Administration
ECU	European currency unit
EES	European economic space
EFTA	European Free Trade Association
EMS	European Monetary System
EMU	economic and monetary union
EPU	European Payments Union
ERP	European Recovery Program
FDI	foreign direct investment
FRG	Federal Republic of Germany
FTO	foreign trade organization
Fund	International Monetary Fund
GATT	General Agreement on Tariffs and Trade
GDP	gross domestic product
GDR	German Democratic Republic
GNP	gross national product
IBEC	International Bank for Economic Cooperation
IBRD	International Bank for Reconstruction and Development
IIB	International Investment Bank
IMF	International Monetary Fund
LIBOR	London Interbank Offered Rate
ME	market economy
MFN	most-favored nation
MFT	state monopoly of foreign trade and payments

MPE	modified planned economy
NIE	newly industrializing economy
NMP	net material product
ODA	official development assistance
OECD	Organisation for Economic Co-operation and Development
OEEC	Organisation for European Economic Co-operation
OIEC	Organization for International Economic Cooperation
pb	per barrel
PET	planned economy in transition
PHARE	*Pologne/Hongrie: assistance à la restructuration économique*
Rb	ruble
SDR	special drawing right
SEI	socialist economic integration
SOE	state-owned enterprise
TNC	transnational corporation
TR	transferable ruble
TRP	transferable-ruble price
U.N.	United Nations
UNECE	United Nations Economic Commission for Europe
WMP	world market price
World Bank	International Bank for Reconstruction and Development
WTO	Warsaw Treaty Organization

List of tables

Introduction

Eastern Europe[1] has been passing through an unprecedented wave of political and institutional transformations since mid-1989. Many more, some very incisive, changes are on the current policy agenda. The newfangled political leadership in these countries is very ambitious as regards the speed and scope of the coveted mutations. This attitude is being fortified by self-styled policy advice being counseled - even administered - with increasing frequency by an emerging phalanx of new experts on Eastern Europe. As John K. Galbraith (1990, p. 51) recently put it rather acerbically, but no less pointedly:

> In my view, some, and perhaps much, of the advice now being offered the Central and Eastern European states proceeds from a view of the so-called capitalist or free-enterprise economies that bears no relation to their reality. Nor would these economies have survived if it had. What is offered is an ideological construct that exists all but entirely in the minds and notably in the hopes of the donor. It bears no relation to reality; it is what I have elsewhere called the primitive ideology.

I agree with this undoubtedly harsh assessment.

Regardless of the intrinsic wisdom of these stances, there is no doubt at all that any meaningful societal reform can be carried out only through painful adjustments. Likewise, the brunt of the burden cannot but be borne by these countries themselves. Certainly, external assistance can ease matters somewhat and an east-west cooperative reform strategy may shorten the adjustment phase. Even under the most auspicious circumstances, however, the burden is bound to be substantial, protracted, and painful. Not only that, there is no guarantee of success. This uncertainty applies to the original time frame envisaged by reformers. It holds equally, if not more, for any costing figure that may be hazarded by the new leadership or approved through a social consensus, possibly reached through the newly established democratic process. As regards speed, comprehensiveness, sequencing, and transparency, the differences among

[1] In what follows, Eastern Europe denotes Bulgaria, Czechoslovakia (officially Czech and Slovak Federative Republic or CSFR), Hungary, Poland, Rumania, and the Soviet Union. Occasionally, I use the concept for the first five countries, in which case the context makes it clear that I have that subgroup in mind. Whenever reference is to the period before 3 October 1990, the German Democratic Republic (GDR) is, of course, included. However, many of the issues revolving around the former GDR's role in intragroup cooperation have not all completely vanished with the country's submersion into Germany. But with post-unification references, I shall make it explicit whenever the ex-GDR's links in the context of the new Federal Republic of Germany (FRG) are being envisaged.

genuine reforms that envisage laying the firm foundations for any type of market economy (ME) can only be a matter of degree.

This volume looks at one paramount aspect of the adjustment effort, namely the multiple dimensions of the *problématique* revolving around the emerging external-payments constraints. Central is how these nitty-gritty obstacles to marketization could be overcome through a cooperative strategy with western economic assistance in combination with individual as well as joint efforts of the reforming countries themselves. It is useless, however, to confine the investigation to economics *per se*. Related mutations in the politics and ideology of Eastern Europe - and indeed east-west relations - must be factored into the analysis to obtain a proper perspective on what is possible in the economic domain and can politically be implemented without eroding the very foundation of the emerging democratic culture.

That is to say, the core of the investigation here is set by the aspiration of policy makers in Eastern Europe to enact market-oriented reforms as a precondition for the full integration of the economies in transition into the world economy. I draw the backdrop to the rationale for this focus in Section 1. Next I investigate critical aspects of the foundations for moving toward the market in a multiparty system. Section 3 examines intragroup economic cooperation that should, in fact, be fully heeded in searching for a solution to the chronic problems of balancing external payments in these countries. Next I briefly sketch the backdrop to some of the research that led to this volume. In this context, I argue in Section 5 the case for adopting a structured approach to the creation of some payments facility. This also analyzes whether the current approach to providing western assistance could be mobilized to alleviate Eastern Europe's external-payments problems. The last section provides a succinct overview of the volume.

1. Backdrop to the payments constraint

Several of the smaller members of the Council for Mutual Economic Assistance[2] (CMEA[3]) countries of the group, identified in this volume as the

[2] I shall be concerned chiefly with Eastern Europe as defined. In addition, the CMEA had three other active full members (Cuba, Mongolia, and Vietnam); one inactive full member (Albania); one associate member (Yugoslavia); nine cooperants (Afghanistan, Angola, Ethiopia, Finland, Iraq, Mexico, Mozambique, Nicaragua, and Democratic Yemen - now again Yemen); and a variable number of invited observers, chiefly the other socialist countries (China, Laos, and North Korea), developing countries, and representatives from international organizations. Occasionally, I shall also refer to the possible role of Yugoslavia in the new Eastern Europe for reasons detailed in Chapter 1.

[3] I prefer this acronym to the admittedly more euphonic, but politically loaded and inaccurate, abbreviation Comecon.

planned economies in transition or PETs - no pun intended - are now envisaging or have already embarked upon genuine market-oriented reforms. Many are hoping soon to find common ground in the "European economic space (EES)." In the process, until its formal demise in mid-April 1991, the CMEA had for long been on an elusive course in search of a new mission. During most of the time spent writing this volume, the organization appeared utterly moribund, but it simply would not vanish from the debating table. Few of its members, at least in Europe, supported radical CMEA reform short of fully eroding the residual vestiges of socialism and integration still embodied by that organization. Similarly lukewarm support for reviving - and redirecting on the basis of market-conform criteria - economic cooperation at least among the more radically reforming countries is evident. These attitudes cannot be cogently explained in a rational economic discourse. Rather, most of Eastern Europe deems it impossible to make a strong dash for market-oriented reform in the context of intensive intragroup ties without there first being further incisive political and economic changes primarily in the Soviet Union.

Whereas political achievements in Eastern Europe since late 1989 have been breathtaking and the further sociopolitical aspirations of many of these countries far-reaching, economic realities argue strongly in favor of a more sober approach, especially in the short to medium run. Before the reforming economies can fully fuse themselves into the economic community of Western Europe, or the world economy for that matter, at levels of living that they aspire to preserve and are willing to protect, major changes in economic structures need to be undertaken. This will have to be sought in the first instance in each country individually through an ambitious revamping of the entire framework of domestic economic decision making. The role of the state in the economy will eventually become that of a central coordinator, rather than detailed orchestrator, of what is to be produced and sold by whom; consumed and saved; and how workers should divide their time between leisure and work. Most of these issues should be devolved to firms, private as well as others, that are financially fully autonomous. Other tasks should be entrusted to individual economic agents, subject to socially approved rules, for instance, on labor organization. This may require the formation of proper trade unions that, perhaps in conjunction with the government as arbiter between employers and employees, can ensure the social peace and fair compensation for labor without stifling capital formation and productivity growth. Property relations in such a market-oriented economy will need to be restructured as well, although that does not necessarily call for privatizing the bulk of state assets, if outright sale or divestment is thereby implied (Brabant 1990c, pp. 120-38; 1991b, c, l).

The kind of reform that most of Eastern Europe presently envisages can realistically be managed only through the wholesale revamping of the entire framework of economic decision making. This will have to be sought in the first instance in each country individually. But it also needs to be fostered in the regional concert of these countries. There are many reasons for this. A core determinant, certainly in the immediate future, derives from the need to ensure that the proper policies, institutions, and policy instruments are put in place to enable these reforming countries to exploit their reciprocal static and dynamic comparative advantages. Doing so through the transition to competitive markets is being considerably complicated by prevailing constraints on maintaining buoyant intragroup levels of trade and payments. The lack of effective cooperation among these countries is in some cases emanating from active resistance against even-level efforts. Rather than buttressing the reform sentiment and assisting the wholesale societal mutation under way, these uncooperative policy stances are hampering the transformation process in a number of respects. This is unfortunate, given the weak commitment to real transition.

2. Consensual transition policies

Perhaps the most fundamental transformation - a veritable revolution in a number of respects - in Eastern Europe since 1989 has been the rapid erosion of the supreme role of the Communist Party which had formerly been uncontested (Dahrendorf 1990). The central position of the Party was not, of course, confined to the political process as it extended through all layers of societal relations. As János Kornai (1990a) has so passionately stressed, the starting conditions for the PETs are societies, where public ownership has dominated for over forty years, enabling an almighty bureaucracy with uncounted tentacles (Winiecki 1990, 1991) to reach throughout society into the life of virtually every citizen. Under the circumstances, sovereignty of the individual; autonomy and private property; business, political, and intellectual freedoms; the institutions of democracy; and the rule of law were suppressed for decades. Although the role of the Communist Parties throughout Eastern Europe has been considerably whittled by the movement toward constitutional governance, powerful legacies of the erstwhile monolithic "system" continue to pervade these countries. In coming to grips with them, political and emotional issues get inextricably intertwined with the niceties of economic analysis and rationality as to the best ways to reach certain objectives. Many more, some very incisive, changes can, therefore, be anticipated over the coming years.

Indeed, the current policy agenda in the majority of these countries is exceedingly ambitious as regards the speed and scope of the coveted mutations in politics, societal relations, and economic affairs. But even the transition in economic institutions, policies, and policy instruments is by no means an autonomous process over which domestic policy makers have full control. For one thing, these countries have the ambition to become rapidly integrated in the international economy. Also, they are seeking sizable economic, financial, technical, and other assistance from abroad in various forms. Finally, some are pursuing these far-reaching transformations at a time of substantial indebtedness to a variety of international actors.

Even without the external limits to autonomous transition that reformers must be prepared to heed, domestic policy flexibility is also constrained by there being actually less than full consensus on what the transformation should entail, thereby imparting uncertainty into the environment for transition. This lack of unanimity ranges from political decision making, over the attainment of a social consensus on reform, to having at least a coherent conception of what the coveted ME for any particular country should be all about. Disagreement at any of these levels is bound to restrict the autonomy - hence the speed and the determination - with which the economic transition can be pursued.

Frequently, advice to managers of the transition in Eastern Europe, which has become ubiquitous, tends to gloss over the fact that politics in the west is often about comfort, as John K. Galbraith recently put it, rather than the bewildering agenda for societal transformations that have been challenging policy makers in the east. That discussion is not, of course, facilitated by the lack of adequate institutions through which consensual arrangements can be hammered out. In mature MEs, these are essential in channeling and directing, and often cramping, the implementation of programs aiming at societal changes and indeed the more general activities of government.

As noted, any meaningful societal transformation can be carried out only through painful adjustments. As regards speed, comprehensiveness, sequencing, and transparency of the transition, the differences among countries can only be a matter of degree. But the environment within which these measures can be sought and implemented may vary markedly. This consists of three main components: (1) political consensus on the need for economic transition, (2) social consensus on the magnitude and distribution of the costs of adjustment and at what speed this burden can be absorbed, and (3) consensus on the broad components of the ME that policy makers seek to establish.

Regarding political consensus, as Bronisław Geremek, a key actor in the political transition in Poland, put it in *Gazeta Wyborcza* (as quoted in *Financial Times*, 27 December 1990, p. 8), "The prospects for freedom are secure; but those for democracy remain uncertain." Indeed, arriving at a solid majority view on the transition with the minority abiding by the selection process achieved under the changed societal conditions has been vexing. For one thing, the political transformation in most countries was achieved without there being a fair political contestation. That process was in essence set off by agreements reached between the political opposition and the Party-*cum*-Government in power to resolve the widespread anti-establishment leanings of the former rather than based on a concrete political package of positive changes. Whereas in most countries that process eventually led to freely contested popular elections, such has not yet taken place in all countries, notably in Poland.

Without there being an unambiguous agreement on consensual decision making at the highest political level, including through the emerging democratic institutions, it is all but in vain to embark on incisive reforms that are credible and, at the same time, can be adhered to for sufficiently long to make a difference. These features apply regardless of the level and range of external assistance that policy makers feel they can count on.

This uncertainty pertains to countries where the consensual decision making of the emerging democratic process is not yet in place, yet the inherited political structures are no longer accepted by all actors. It is also relevant for countries where the democratic process has now been firmly endorsed, but it is not yet so strong as to prove irreversible and sufficiently robust to withstand setbacks that may be incurred, say, while carrying out sizable economic transformations. Indeed, in some countries there are deeply rooted ethnic or regional revendications that must be sorted out before a credible agreement on nationwide economic reform, let alone other elements of reconstructing society, can be solified. Key is the degree to which sufficient popular support can be mustered. This might be easier to ensure if political decision makers enjoy a comfortable popular majority (as in Czechoslovakia and Poland), perhaps reached through the newly introduced electoral processes, as compared to countries where decisions are still taken by leaders whose mandate has not yet been validated at the ballot box or whose visions of the transformation process are not easily reconciled with the pursuit of marketization in a pluralistic environment.

If the political process has selected an unambiguous majority for one or more parties with a distinct profile, the debate on economic transition can at least be focused within that majority. But that does not necessarily guarantee that it will quickly opt for one reform package - witness the drawnout debate on reform in Bulgaria and Rumania, for example. Nor does it necessarily find a buttress at the grassroot level once the concrete implications of several dimensions (such as inflation, unemployment, and erosion of economic and social security) of the economic reform take shape. This uncertainty is bound to be far larger for countries that still lack a solid political consensus on reform. It is likely to be especially pronounced when the debates are being waged by remnants of the political structures that dominated Eastern Europe for over forty years. Political stalemate is then likely to paralyze the process of economic reform and many other aspects of the agenda for remaking these societies.

Even if there is a political consensus that has broad popular support, it is by no means a foregone conclusion that the transition of these societies will necessarily be shaped by the salient features of the ME. The political majority for now may harbor particular preferences, including for electoral purposes, that encumber market-oriented reform as the longer-term goal of the transition. It bears to note in this connection that the PETs have to cope with current problems as well as with the design and implementation of the transition. The choice between doing the latter while downplaying the former is not one that economists called upon to draft the contours of a transition process can decide. It is up to the political processes in place to ensure that this choice is made in a pluralistic manner. Although the economist cannot take on this role, any blueprint of the transition must heen the prevailing political realities.

The process of transition is yet more complex than the already enumerated steps. Even if there exists broad political consensus on market orientation that is buttressed by the population at large, in spite of the adverse implications that are bound to emerge at least in the short run, policy makers are not always autonomous in designing reforms and implementing them. Because these countries are already in the multilateral framework for trade and payments, the room for domestic maneuver, for example, with foreign-trade and -exchange reforms may be confined.

Finally, the commitment in principle to strive for democratization and marketization of Eastern Europe has also elicited considerable intellectual, institutional, financial, and organizational support from abroad. The PETs' reform process should preferably be fully dovetailed with the assistance that outsiders may be disposed to grant. This does not mean that there would be no room for the self-interest of donor countries to assert themselves, certainly in determining the amount and composition of assistance. Nonetheless, it would be extremely helpful if external assistance could be formulated and dispensed so as to maximize gains for the reform from the resources that outsiders are willing to appropriate, while at the same time donors and their electorate are reassured that credible progress with the transformation is being registered.

Once the bulk of the political ramifications of economic transition have been satisfactorily weathered, conceptually the next condition for moving toward the setting of a full-fledged ME is reaching a social consensus. Indeed, there is no assurance at all that the envisaged changes reached at the political level will elicit a social consensus. Even if attained, there is no guarantee that it can be maintained once the process of adjustment gets under way and its various costs become tangible. Even if there is in principle convergence of opinion on moving away from administrative socialist planning to the coordination of decisions through market-based institutions, instruments, and economic policies, the depth and scope of popular support for the political factions in power remain to be plumbed with respect to the magnitude, speed, and distribution of adjustment costs associated with market reforms.

Even in the oldest democracy, where majority decision making is not in doubt, there is uncertainty about changes in policy that society at large might subscribe to. Indeed, implications of policies for, say, the pace of inflation, the magnitude and dispersion of unemployment, cutbacks in subsidies or government services, or other perceived negative drawbacks of policies have frequently led to a reconstitution of government through the democratic process. This is, in fact, the essence of a popular mandate. There is no reason to believe that the resilience of the eastern societies to immiseration in the short run, whatever the longer-term benefits of marketization in a pluralistic environment may be, is any more solid than what it is in mature MEs. It probably is much less robust than that.

There is, therefore, a need to spell out the initial conditions within which reforms are formulated and carried out, and to assess to what extent other features of the startup determine the social consensus. Similarly with respect to the requirements for maintaining consensual support during the transition to the agreed objective. Of particular importance in this connection is whether it is true that sociopolitical and economic chaos mandate speedier policies toward creating the market on a broad front right away than would otherwise be the case, the sort of choice between "shock therapy" or "big bang" adjustment policies, on the one hand, and the more gradualist approach to the transformation. If such a consensus exists, there is no guarantee that this mandate can be sustained as the multiple costs of adjustment become felt. Because these are necessarily unequally distributed, apparent reversals in reform policies or setbacks in the implementation of the transition package may occur that are perfectly logical, given the social and political context within which societal transformations must perforce be pursued.

In the meantime, however, the institutions, instruments, and policies of central planning cease to function and there is no replacement in sight. All kinds of informal coordination mechanisms, usually typical of the underground economy, emerge. The perceived inequities thereby generated cannot but eventually become destabilizing. Open inflation and sizable unemployment, whatever its officially measured indicators might intimate, in conjunction with disenchantment with the incomplete reform processes, may set the stage for the adoption of "shock therapy" or the "big bang" transition in the short run. Whether this will then provide an impetus to reaching the social and political consensus necessary to address the technical issues of the economics of transition remains to be seen, however.

Finally, if the political leadership has a firm platform for moving toward the market and believes it can muster popular support for forging ahead, the paramount task is the formulation of a clear-cut blueprint for market-oriented reform. This may be easier to achieve in PETs that have had prior experience with administrative decentralization and modest market orientation. Some experimentation with freeing up price formation, linking domestic with foreign prices through a surrogate exchange rate, devolving the banking sector into at least two tiers, foreign-exchange auctions, redefining property rights, and related elements of the market environment are potentially of special importance. The breadth of the adjustment and the uncertainty of its success are likely to be a multiple of what they are elsewhere.

The above suggests that there are at least two key constraints on speed and comprehensiveness, hence sequencing, of the transition. One is the degree of social consensus reached in particular on the amount of the adjustment cost to be borne, how quickly this can be absorbed, and how equitably it should be distributed over the various layers of society. Another is that there are severe administrative constraints to how quickly the governmental structures in place can proceed with shifting to the ME environment, provided that it is well defined. At the very least, this suggests that key features of the transition need to be sculpted to reflect country characteristics. Although there is not one single path to the creation of effective markets, the alternatives are necessarily limited in both time and scope. Further, the very existence of choice as regards speed, comprehensiveness, and sequencing depends on the macroeconomic conditions prevailing in the country about to launch its particular transition. Putting it in stochastic terms, credibility of the transition package depends on maximizing the joint probability of realizing the various interrelated components of the transformation.

3. Regional cooperation and economic reform

For several practical purposes, each of the PETs remains quite dependent on intragroup trade and payments. In this, the lingering dysfunctional effects of the transferable-ruble (TR) trade and payment regimes are hampering reconstituting this interlinkage on a solid economic last. This holds also for the transition in early 1991, at least in principle, to world market prices (WMPs) and convertible-currency payments. Too many resentments prevail and are poisoning the atmosphere within which these countries must seek to reform the framework governing their mutual cooperation. Activating meaningful economic reforms and safeguarding achievements bought at a high social cost in the presence of market-averse intragroup relations is not at all an easy task. The transition in orienting individual economies toward competitive markets is being considerably complicated by prevailing constraints on maintaining buoyant commerce. These strictures could be loosened by making available, under some conditions, a payment mechanism that does not compel an abrupt switchover from settlements in TRs to convertible-currency payments - perhaps the epitome of the shortage economy in Eastern Europe.

As noted, the core focus of this volume is the short- to medium-term constraints on managing Eastern Europe's external balances with some degree of flexibility with two main purposes. One is the restructuring process itself. As noted, this refers to domestic economic reform and the imbalances it may give rise to. It also includes the effects of seminal shifts in the TR trade and payment regimes. The other envelops problems of adjusting external sectors that stem from fluctuations in the global economy.

To illustrate the point, let us consider the symplified settlement process for oil. Transferable ruble prices (TRPs) for crude traded within the CMEA used to be patterned, at least in principle, after average WMPs of the preceding five years. Thus, TRPs in 1989 were in principle derived from WMPs observed in 1984-1988. Average annual WMPs were in theory translated at the average annual exchange rate of the TR quoted by the CMEA's settlements bank - the International Bank for Economic Cooperation (IBEC). To the degree that actual WMPs expressed in TRs at the official exchange rate exceeded those observed on average during the reference period, nominal TRPs tended to be inferior to the corresponding current WMP, and *vice versa*. Shifting CMEA pricing from TRPs to WMPs, under the circumstances, could not but impose a cost to close the gap separating currently applicable TRPs from prevailing WMPs. If in addition, WMPs during the switchover period drift upwards, the magnitude of adjustment grows too but its precise size can only partially be anticipated. This is precisely the situation that Eastern Europe faces, after the regime switch in 1991. But I hasten to add that the actual calculus of TRPs and WMPs, and indeed the precise nature of the regime mutation, is vastly more complicated than the above simple comparison of price levels (Brabant 1987b).

The second focus of this volume is one that has kept my attention for many years: economic integration in Eastern Europe. It is undoubtedly true that the CMEA in many of its incarnations is quite dead (Brabant 1990c, pp. 15-19; 1991a, e, i, j). But the plug of the rapidly eroding life-support system especially for what the organization could have stood for in some other meanings has not yet been pulled. This applies most obviously to actual and prospective trade and payment relations. In fact, on simple economic grounds there is no reason to sever these links at all cost.

Among the economic arguments is the trade patterns that would be economically warranted if the countries could channel their foreign commerce on the basis of comparative advantages. For that to emerge, the countries must first and foremost put in train policies, institutions, and policy instruments that enable them to scrutinize such trade-offs on simple economic grounds, and thus to ascertain precisely their static comparative advantages through ordinary commercial decision making. Surely, such a more efficient allocation of resources, including notably in external sectors, would force down intragroup trade to zero only by sheer fluke. Under normal circumstances, there must be considerable opportunities for independent firms to engage in profitable trade, provided they are entitled - and enabled - to explore just that on their own account. Simple commercial decision making to maximize profits has not been a guiding beacon of trade in Eastern Europe, including the present PETs, for the past forty years. The rationale for the PETs' attitude is bewildering, but it owes a good deal to the peculiar planning, trading, and payment systems that Eastern Europe wedded itself to with the adoption of the status of centrally planned economy (CPE) in the late 1940s; of course, the USSR had done so already twenty years earlier. In this reluctance, I include all efforts that some of these countries undertook by way of administrative reform. For brevity's sake, I refer to the economies that pursued administrative streamlining mainly since the 1960s as modified planned economies (MPEs). In seeking to explain the frequent disregarding of economic motives behind the chosen patterns of external trade and payments, ideology cannot be ignored. The way it codetermined the roots of the perceived need to provide fraternal economic assistance in the broad sense must be invoked. In establishing trading patterns with many CMEA and other socialist countries, this confounded at the very least foreign affairs, ideology, politics, economics, and issues pertaining to development assistance. As a result, it became simply impossible to sort out what was intrinsically profitable from relations possibly justified on other grounds.

In addition to exploiting static comparative advantages, domestic resource-allocation processes could be considerably streamlined with a view to supporting more buoyant growth in the area as a whole and each PET individually. This cannot but give rise to dynamic comparative advantages among these countries as well as other partners, of course. These emanate from shifts in supply resulting from structural change. They also crystallize because of the emerging transformation of demand patterns stemming from marked fluctuations in incomes, incentives, and expectations. At the very least, such modifications should dam the depth and breadth of the economic recession, not to mention reverse sociopolitical cynicism, that may be unwittingly engineered in the process of economic reconstruction. One important determinant of such a recession under the most favorable policy circumstances arises from the sluggish supply response for some time after the inauguration of economic reform.

I am, of course, fully aware that any advocacy of regional economic cooperation in Eastern Europe has been received none too positively in recent years. Objections have been raised from many quarters and on many aspects of the proposal. Most observers reject any intragroup integration efforts after the seminal political and societal transitions in Eastern Europe. Some treat such advocacy as an emanation of professional obtuseness, to put it mildly; the more aggressive, self-styled advisers unceremoniously label any push in favor of deepening and widening regional economic collaboration an act of mental folly.

I think I can well understand the stance taken by the new political leaders of Eastern Europe. Their attitude can be gauged from other angles than what should emanate from within the economic arena. But the position argued by numerous academic economists and other scholars on the matter has baffled me for quite some time. There are two major components to this puzzle. One derives from the well-known rationalization of regional economic integration as a second-best policy choice. The other finds its rationale in a discourse on how best to capitalize on static comparative advantages and to foster economic progress with a view to building up dynamic comparative advantages too. But the position taken is often based on a highly questionable reading of what the CMEA was and, even more, of what Eastern European economic collaboration more generally has meant to the various countries. Even greater doubt is cast by myopic views on what the principal focus of such intragroup economic cooperation *could* be all about.

I hope to make my position crystal clear in the course of this volume by utilizing two main props. One is built around the well-known second-best arguments on regional union formation among competitive economies in a static sense. The other bundle of arguments in favor of reviving intragroup trade and economic collaboration, but now principally based on economic grounds, utilizes the existing static comparative advantages as initial inducement. These could be fortified by also vigorously exploiting the benefits that will be accruing from the dynamic comparative advantages induced by positive economic reforms.

The peremptory rejection of Eastern Europe as a viable trade horizon for these countries to explore is very difficult to grasp on economic grounds. Certainly, Eastern Europe's potential for mutually reinforcing the pace of growth comes nowhere near that of the most vibrant global markets. Yet, even if Eastern Europe were to be a "poor man's club" (Portes 1990, Sachs 1990), these countries must have static comparative advantages, only some of which have thus far been exploited. This has arisen in part because of policies, institutions, and policy instruments - the cooperation mechanism, if you wish - that were not very conducive to maximizing the potential gains to be reaped from international commerce and external economic cooperation more generally. A revamping of the trade and payment regimes on economic grounds would certainly lead to a different level, commodity composition, and geographical orientation of trade. But it would manifestly not cut out trade altogether. It might in fact lead to a significant expansion of commerce among the smaller Eastern European countries, given that in the past their trade was primarily really interlinked in radial fashion with the needs and potential of the Soviet economy as axis. It has traditionally also been heavily concentrated on the exchange of fuels and raw materials for investment goods. Furthermore, economic reforms that generate factor-productivity growth should open up opportunities for building up comparative advantages. The Belgian-Luxemburg Economic Union (BLEU) or Benelux after World War II might provide a useful example, as argued in more detail in Chapter 3.

4. Backdrop to the proposal to create a payments union

In addition to diagnosing the key problems with external payments and the potential for intragroup economic integration, the volume's third main concern is a technical one. It inquires into the usefulness of formulating a cooperation mechanism with multiple purposes. The principal one is twofold. It should enable these countries to come to grips in a flexible manner, given the prevailing circumstances, with the obstacles emanating from their intragroup economic intercourse. Impediments to a swift and radical reform, to the extent possible, must be removed so that there will be only minimal need for the PET leadership to back down on their commitment to seeking market-oriented reforms and buttressing multiparty decision making. At the same time, it would provide another prop to encourage regional or subregional integration on simple economic grounds. Of course, such a technical mechanism must necessarily be constructed around the avowed reform intentions, to which one further nudge toward convertibility is provided. It should be supervised from the outside. Finally, it should by its very nature and managerial acumen be of short- to medium-term duration. By virtue of it being a stopgap, it could not possibly offer a satisfactory guideline to the longer-term development strategy on the basis of which these countries will prospectively be able to generate their growth momentum and enhance their prosperity. Eventually, convertibility at least for current-account transactions would be an extremely useful instrument in integrating these emerging MEs into the global economic concert. It should also be an explicit aim of instituting radical market-oriented reforms. This provides a very constructive target for western assistance.

From early 1990, I have been pressing my case for innovating some payment mechanism with outside assistance to alleviate obstacles to clearing the conventional intragroup trade of Eastern Europe that embodies an economic rationale at least during the process of transition. That is, *no* attempt to maintain trade that is unprofitable from the microeconomic point of view should even be contemplated. But I see every reason to try to support commercial exchange that is warranted on economic grounds now, although possibly not in the future, when some components of structural reform will have been realized.

For trade that cannot now be cleared, given the constraints on balancing external payments, there could be only four solutions. One would be simply to cut out the bulk of the traditional external demand and supply through drastic deflationary policies, and incur the enormous domestic adjustment cost that would be implied. A second avenue would be rapid trade diversion to the west, regardless of its sociopolitical costs, including the transitory economic recession that might thereby be engendered. The latter could conceivably be averted through structural-adjustment loans either from the official multilateral organizations or contracted in commercial markets perhaps with government guarantees. This could work if the absorptive and adaptive capacity of the Eastern European countries in the 1990s were to be noticeably better than in the preceding two decades. Otherwise, borrowing would only postpone the adjustment effort, in the process further piling up foreign debt. Finally, room could be explored to maintain the conventional trade and payments of these countries, as defined earlier, while introducing rather rapid modifications in trade and payment mechanisms. Those transformations may in time erode some of the presently existing comparative advantages. In this connection, a facility to manage external payments, properly conceived and managed, would be a highly constructive device. It would help to nurse along the process of marketizing these economies. In addition, it would permit them to take advantage of the better sides of past CMEA relations. Moreover, it would contribute to the integration of the PETs into the world economy. Finally, it would also stimulate moving forward toward currency convertibility.

Such a constructive mechanism could take several forms. One way of sinking solid anchors for accomplishing the above tasks with minimal disturbances to established economic relations would be through a payments union. With that in mind, I felt in early 1990 that it might be useful for east and west alike to set up a Central European Payments Union (CEPU) preferably in conjunction with the radical transformation of CMEA cooperation that had then just been promised as the outcome of the January 1990 CMEA Council Session. For a while, there were prospects for "marketizing" the CMEA as well and rather quickly, notably for the PETs. Because of the situation in early 1990, I envisaged such a CEPU essentially for Czechoslovakia, the GDR, Hungary, and Poland. I had included the GDR because it was the second largest CMEA partner with a key role in the formation and maintenance of the machine park of the rest of the CMEA and the modalities of the then just announced intention to seek rapid economic and monetary union between the two Germanies were still on the drawing board. I argued that a CEPU for these countries might usefully be created in conjunction with a Central European Economic Union (CEEU), which could form an integral component of a constitutional CMEA reform. Initial versions of these ideas were published anonymously in two major publications of the United Nations (U.N.)[4] and one circulated in my name (Brabant 1990b). These proposals have led to sharp criticism and considerable controversy. Further defusing this criticism is another purpose of this volume. I hope to have rendered my arguments much more cogent here than in the various papers that I have produced in sequence to persuade one group or another of observers and decision makers of the desirability of creating a payments facility for Eastern Europe. Even so, I see the need to deflect in a coherent fashion most of the more onerous types of critiques that my proposals have elicited. I shall do so in Chapter 7.

5. Toward convertibility through a payments union

As noted, the brunt of the adjustment burden will have to be borne by the reforming countries themselves. There is simply no alternative. But the depth of the economic and social hardships to be weathered in the process can be contained and their magnitude spread out over time and in an acceptable manner with properly targeted western economic assistance. The latter's support for the transition in the countries that are committed to democratization and marketization is critical. Because the volume of aid earmarked by the west is necessarily limited, the question arises of how best to foster the transition (Brabant 1990c, pp. 139ff.) notably toward currency convertibility.

There are several ways in which currency convertibility could be brought about. Barring untoward circumstances, a gradual approach with preset policy

[4] As usual, individual contributions to core U.N. publications must perforce remain anonymous since all such documents are, in fact, issued under the responsibility of the Secretary-General. The more complete version of the proposals for a CEPU and CEEU written in conjunction with the staff of the United Nations Economic Commission for Europe (UNECE) is in UNECE 1990, pp. 147-50. A truncated version of the logic of moving toward such a form of assistance is in UNWES 1990, p. 98. Unfortunately, heavy-handed editing of drafts for the latter publication made the proposals all but unrecognizable.

commitments on the part of national and international decision makers provides the least costly way for most countries. Those that are emerging from utter chaos or that have a built-in proclivity for setting off hyperinflationary tendencies and leading to economic contraction may wish to proceed differently from the options seemingly preferred by countries that are still capable of sustaining slow growth with moderate inflationary pressures. This could formally be enacted by setting up a payments union for countries that are committed to market-oriented reform and pluralistic decision making. Such a facility would necessarily be temporary, geared as it by nature and design must be to transitional payment needs. But it could provide a critical avenue that will enable these countries eventually to compete effectively in world markets, hence to integrate themselves into the global economic context, with minimal disruption to social and economic stability.

The emerging crisis around the problems that PETs have in balancing their external payments has multiple origins. Two principal forces stand out, although they cannot be separated logically and analytically in all details. One consists of the consequences for external payments of domestic and regional economic reforms. This includes the multiple repercussions of the shifts in economic structures that are bound to emerge as a result of efforts to place these economies on a stabler economic last. Among the consequences to be reckoned with are also those emanating from abandoning the traditional TR trade and payment regimes in favor of conditions that are "more normal" in the global context. The second group of problems envelops the more usual pressures on convertible-currency imports. These are due to adverse terms-of-trade shifts and intrinsic limits to earning convertible currency from traditional exports. These drawbacks are significantly exacerbated by two other developments, however. For a while in late 1990, most critical was the massive change in the global terms of trade resulting from the third oil shock at a time that the PETs began to be compelled to procure growing volumes of oil from nonsocialist markets and their ability to increase export revenues remained rather limited at best. Also the emerging recession in the western economies will have palpable consequences for convertible-currency export earnings by the PETs. It will also have implications for the ability and willingness of western countries to aid the PETs in various forms, not just direct financial transfers.

Of course, in practice both principal causes emanating from the need for structural adjustment will have to be addressed simultaneously. My main analytical concern in this connection here is how these countries could weather the repercussions of the first set of issues through some western assistance. It assumes that with the resolution of the crisis in the Persian Gulf the WMP of oil will soon stabilize at around $20 per barrel (pb). This would also compress the depth and duration of the economic recession in MEs.

Arguing the case for western assistance in progressing toward currency convertibility is the core of this book. This plea falls logically into three different parts. The first is essentially a diagnosis of the key problems that are currently hemming in growth and economic transformation in these countries. Among the many problems, the constraints on balancing external payments undoubtedly constitute an important set of policy concerns. Second, these problems can be resolved by these countries themselves, if at all, through a deep economic recession or by borrowing abroad as they did in the 1970s and 1980s. Moreover, western financial assistance alone cannot forestall such an undesirable turn of economic fortunes. Hard work is required by these countries themselves individually as well as in their regional concert. Ways in which their competitive position can be strengthened *vis-à-vis* both Eastern Europe and the global economy need to be actively explored. This brings me to the third core issue, namely the creation of a regional payments union to facilitate the broader transformation of these countries.

Of course, borrowing in western financial markets could provide the funds to sustain current-account deficits for a while. But would private banks be found willing to lend again on a substantial scale to Eastern Europe, including the heavily indebted countries like Bulgaria, Hungary, and Poland? I doubt that this is realistic at this stage. There is some room to mount financing resources from the official multilateral agencies and to obtain government guarantees for commercial lending. But there are stiff limits to these resources. Even if it were feasible to raise the necessary funds, borrowing as occurred after the oil crises of the 1970s without firm macroeconomic policy commitments can only raise debt levels. In essence, it would amount to a fairly simple repetition of the course then pursued, as if policy makers and the international community had learnt next to nothing from that calamitous experience. Attaching realistic strings to such loans and seeing to it that commitments are honored are hardly tasks for private bankers when dealing with sovereign borrowers. Yet without these two conditions, massive lending does not strike me as a commendable way to assist the radically reforming countries of Eastern Europe. Raising debt levels without undertaking the structural change required to service those debts against a reasonable horizon would be the worst outcome of the present opportunities for reformulating policies and revamping institutions and policy instruments in these countries. A recession sometime in the future would be the only outcome.

Certainly, the key arguments developed here are primarily concerned with the potentials of Eastern Europe. The same applies as regards the formation of some, deliberately modest policy recommendations on what can be done to assist the PETs. In this, my search is in the first instance motivated by what benefit these countries themselves. However, the world is becoming increasingly interdependent. Buoyant economic growth in Eastern Europe derived from economically justified resource-allocation criteria cannot but spill over into more potent commercial and financial relations with other countries as well. This will be a boon in the first instance to Western Europe and indeed the integration process taking place there. It may be hoped that the positive impacts cannot but spill over to Eastern Europe too. Europe will be remade in the process, not just through a burst of brisk political fervor but by laying solid economic bridges, among other instruments. This will hopefully create a more favorable setting to reconceptualizing the ways and means of supporting global economic management. Reaching this goal could not but enable the developing world too to profit in time from the unprecedented changes that have been crystallizing on the European continent. But these fruits can be consummated at best in the medium to long run.

6. Organization

The volume is organized into eight chapters. I start off in Chapter 1 with a broad overview of the prevailing socioeconomic situation in Eastern Europe. This treats the core issues of the current policy agenda of the economies in transition, including the drift of the reform debate. It also examines the major obstacles that are presently hindering swift progress with the transition or that loom on the horizon. The latter will crop up especially if efforts to shift gears fail to materialize soon. Success would mean easing the prevailing constraints on external payments that have been gathering force since early 1990. A broad picture is sketched regarding the external-payments problems with respect to the group as a whole as well as other countries, developed market economies (DMEs) and developing economies (DEs) alike. In this I include DEs with which Eastern Europe has traditionally maintained bilateral-clearing arrangements. The nature of the western-assistance efforts and how they may affect the external position of the reforming countries will be explored only briefly. All I hope to accomplish is to set the framework for subsequent exploration.

The core adjustment obstacles facing the PETs derive in some measure from the disintegration of the CMEA and the sudden switchover in TR trade and payment relations. These were initially slated for full introduction in early 1991. But impromptu alterations in the CMEA framework going in that direction had already earlier commenced and strengthened rapidly from early 1990 on. These issues form the subject of Chapter 2. The focus here is on the repercussions of changing intragroup relations toward WMPs and convertible-currency payments under various scenarios of the expected shocks. But a brief review of related CMEA issues and the recent, in paramount respects still ongoing, reform debate needs to be drawn too. Especially important is the correct gauging of the stark differences between the orthodox TR trade and payment regimes and those envisaged to be adhered to from now on. These have palpable implications for sustainable levels of economic activity in the area in the short to medium run that must be sorted out too. A distinction is drawn among trade and payments for essential inputs (especially fuels and raw materials), manufactures (especially those in support of the existing transportation and capital infrastructure), and consumer goods on the basis of both existing and expected comparative advantages.

High-level policy debates on CMEA reform have had a long and checkered history. Professional recommendations on what to do with regional economic integration, certainly in ways in which it would diverge from the orthodox path toward socialist economic integration (SEI) envisaged in the last two decades, had an even longer and more varied history. Chapter 3 focuses specifically on the recent discussions on what to do with economic relations that used to be subject to the TR trade and payment regimes and efforts to produce integration through production specialization. Making effective use of the opportunities for trade and cooperation among the reforming countries themselves on the basis of economic incentives and potentials is crucial in charting the longer-term development course of Eastern Europe. Policy measures being embraced since early 1990 (such as the imposition of sizable customs duties, the forceful cutting of potential exports to the TR area, the conversion of imbalances at *ad hoc* exchange rates of dubious economic merit, and the ruthless revaluation of the domestic currency in terms of the ruble) are not conducive to stimulating buoyant intragroup economic cooperation or buttressing domestic reforms for that matter. Some are in fact dysfunctional in the sense that they debilitate the exports of firms that under more normal economic conditions would be justified, even if only marginally. How economic union could assist the reforming countries in capitalizing on their static and dynamic comparative advantages so as to provide critical supports for domestic reform and the ambition to integrate in world markets forms the central argument here.

Effective marketization of integrated economies that participate in the global economic framework cannot be assured without some measure of currency convertibility. There are many possible paths toward convertibility. Many different forms of moving toward convertibility for current-account transactions in Eastern Europe could be envisaged. Some have been tried out or are being actively considered by one country or another. Chapter 4 explores four such variants. These include the big bang (such as in Poland), the more gradual movement toward current-account convertibility (such as Hungary), the creation of a market with a parallel currency (as considered in the Soviet Union), and gradualism through the creation of a payments facility. Why I feel the latter road to be the preferred one in the case of Eastern Europe, or pivotal parts thereof, is the central questions around which the architecture of this chapter is configured. The more general merits and drawbacks of a regional payments union will be specified in some detail here too.

A payments union has many technical facets that need to be clarified. Chapter 5 is devoted to these thorny issues. These include questions on quotas, what to do with the existing debt and pre-union current-account imbalances, the clearing authority, credit tranches, asymmetry in allocating currency payments and credits to creditors and debtors, the exchange rates utilized for transactions, the capital fund, the kind of surveillance required and how it can best be exercised (although these topics are dealt with at length in the next chapter), duration of the agreement, and so on. In other words, this chapter examines key elements of the mechanics of setting up a payments union and operating the settlements procedures that participants agree upon. Some can only be hinted at because concrete details can crystallize only through compromise negotiations among national and international decision makers. Others can be conceptually detailed and their implications hypothetically assessed with a view to gaining insight into the paramount obstacles to be overcome.

A payments union can be successful only if imbalances are manageable and, at the same time, members promote with determination the rapid emergence of a more rational trade pattern and market-clearing domestic prices linked to effective WMPs. A payments union should not directly be concerned with domestic reform. Given the context in which such a scheme for Eastern Europe would be set up, however, a clear understanding on basic markers of promoting market orientation and commitment to essential ingredients of trade liberalization are necessary preliminaries to making a payments union with western technical and financial support work. In the case of the PETs, this is being significantly complicated because it is essentially unpredictable what the nature and size of future imbalances among the participants of the payments union will be. It is therefore impossible to determine a nearly accurate magnitude and formulate a clear assessment of the types of technical problems such a union might have to tackle in the context of continuing reform in Eastern Europe. To overcome these problems without getting bogged down by political or diplomatic traps, some authority associated with the clearing scheme must exercise strong surveillance. Its nature and the commitment in principle of participants to abide by the agreed-upon rules need to be clearly set forth prior to the inauguration of the payment scheme. Chapter 6 addresses the multiple issues.

The creation of economic facilities for the reforming countries of Eastern Europe is not, of course, without risks. If not operated and monitored with a firm hand and vision, such facilities might unduly delay feasible adjustment. This would clearly be counterproductive for a variety of reasons. Against this backdrop, the proposals that I have advocated to come to grips with the constraints on external payments of the PETs in particular have met stiff resistance. Some criticisms have been well taken, reflecting essentially weaknesses inherent in any cooperative payment scheme because it is by its nature discriminatory. Other arguments invoked must be attributed to views that I do not at all share. In any case, such goals should not be pursued in the context of a transitional payments union, which is designed simply to improve gradually the convertibility of intragroup transactions. These issues are discussed at some length in Chapter 7.

A successful payments union will make itself redundant approximately within the time horizon originally agreed upon. How the advocated economic and payments unions will facilitate the further integration of Eastern Europe into the global economy, especially in the all-European context, forms the main subject of the final chapter. Initiatives enunciated from within the European Communities (EC) and recently also from within the European Free Trade

Association (EFTA) are evaluated against the possibilities and aspirations of the Eastern European countries individually and as a group (Havel 1990, Kostrzewa and Schmieding 1990, Krenzler 1990, Lamb 1990). These are set against the backdrop of the processes known as "1992" and efforts to create the EES, essentially an integrated European economy that would function like in a mature federation of states with checks and balances, such as in the United States. But macroeconomic management in a united Europe, including through the Eurofed, may well take on its own flavor.

The conclusion provides a succinct summary of the principal arguments advanced in this volume with a view to buttressing the main thesis: Advocacy of the eminent desirability of Eastern European economic and payments unions. They would measurably facilitate the transition of these economies to flexible market operations by easing temporary problems encountered in balancing their external payments. They would strengthen the foundations for progressing steadily along the ineluctable road toward currency convertibility at least for current-account transactions. At the same time, they should accelerate the integration of the PETs into the world economy in general and Europe in particular.

1

The prevailing socioeconomic situation

The truly revolutionary changes in the political mold of Eastern Europe since the latter half of 1989 have been very impressive. For over forty years in the case of Eastern Europe and over seventy in the case of the Soviet Union, these had been societies where life in general was dominated by prescriptions handed out bureaucratically through a singleminded monoparty and its associated privileged functionaries - the omnipresent *nomenklatura* (Winiecki 1991). By arrogating to itself nearly all commanding heights in society, and hence most of the flows of information and influence that mattered, the Communist Party through its comprehensive control over institutions held a formidable grip on these societies. The pervasive feeling of helplessness among wide layers of the population encouraged apathy and cynicism. These deleterious characteristics were exacerbated by the fact that, for many years after World War II, the self-styled vanguards of Eastern Europe remained under the singular influence of the founding fathers of the Soviet Union as interpreted by that country's own unrivaled *nomenklatura*, ideologists, and indeed opportunists.

In spite of the deeply rooted bureaucratized system, in less than one year key elements of these stereotypes of communist regimes were thrown over board. The six Eastern European countries in the process set up multiple political parties and, on the whole, held fair democratic elections in early 1990. As far as the composition of its parliament is concerned, Poland remains a singular exception for unusual circumstances. For the GDR, its moving toward democracy took a sudden turn in 1990, first as a result of economic, social, and monetary union with the FRG and on 3 October 1990 by the country being completely absorbed into the (re)unified Germany. Elsewhere in most cases fledgling parliamentary systems are now in place. With a bit of luck, especially in the external environment, these fragile foundations for societal decision making will slowly, but hopefully steadfastly, solidify into more genuine democratic cultures. Upon the foundation of democracy can the broad restructuring of these countries be undertaken, almost literally from the ground up. The other components of societal reforms have been much more difficult to graft onto democracy, however. There are many reasons that help to explain this state of affairs. Some could have been predicted at the outset of the transition. Others stemmed from untoward developments.

This chapter highlights the paramount features of the overall socioeconomic situation in Eastern Europe at this juncture. In the first two sections I discuss the parlous, in some cases precarious, state of these economies as they attempt to transform themselves. Next I summarize the drift of the reform debate in Eastern Europe. Details on the multiple problems encountered in balancing external payments with respect to both the former CMEA group and third parties are set forth in a nutshell in Section 4.

1. Problems of changing Eastern European societies

The twin component of political transition, with its attendant implications for societal stability, is the dismantling of the system of central planning. Undertaking this remolding, after forty years of grinding through detailed planning and its political, managerial, and administrative support subsystems, has been far more cumbersome and time consuming than had been imagined by most participants in and observers of the revolutions of 1989. The magnitude and scope of what needs to be done have also far exceeded the expectations of many experts. Some had naïvely built their suggestions on the premise of there being a near *tabula rasa* in these "regained" societies.

Whereas the political will to move decisively and quickly toward market-geared policy making is generally prevalent, at least in the PETs, the means to alter existing economic systems from the ground up have proved to be exceedingly limited. The legacies of centrally planning economic affairs for institutions in the broad sense and their attendant societal markers - namely the behavior and expectations of economic agents - are numerous and pervasive. They include lack of familiarity with how markets really operate; the absence of a broad middle class that could take over management from the *nomenklatura* and administrative decision makers; a generally missing managerial and entrepreneurial culture, which has instilled risk aversion in wide layers of society; expectations of individuals that, though suffering in terms of unemployment, inflation, and the erosion of liquid assets would have to be taken in stride, the scope and magnitude of the reforms would on the whole preserve the benefits that had been taken for granted under communism; the absence of the institutions, legal bases, financial infrastructure, and the other organizational wherewithal of MEs; and the need to set in train a coordination mechanism through orthodox macroeconomic policies to take the place of what central planning was originally intended to accomplish in the CPE environment.

Perhaps most troublesome has been the determination of the size and scope of the adjustment burden with some degree of realism. No less complex has been finding a suitable approach to hammering out a consensus on how quickly this cost should be absorbed and how best to distribute it among the various layers of society. It has been quite clear for some time that any drastic change in the policies and institutions typical of the CPE environment would require painful sacrifices. But the probable dimensions thereof have become somewhat more transparent only in recent months. Regardless of the magnitude of western assistance and the imagination of the new leadership in the area, sizable cuts in levels of living of wide layers of the population will have to be factored into the transition equation, not just at one point of time but stretching over several years. How quickly this process should be completed and how much attention should be devoted to equity, perhaps by installing a broad "social safety net," are questions that the newly constituted societies have found to be very slippery and divisive indeed. But the initial phases of the transition could hardly have been navigated without involute questioning.

As if the domestic obstacles to socioeconomic transitions by themselves were not sufficiently daunting, the effort is being strongly buffeted by various groups of reformers having firm, but divergent, convictions on the fundamental objectives, speed, and tactics of transformation. Also, unfortunate external developments are proving to be quite intractable. In several countries, there now reigns a widespread sense of hopelessness and helplessness in coming to grips with newly emerging policy issues. This is fueling the pervasive powers of cynicism and apathy that were temporarily set aside at the height of the euphoria of the political revolutions of late 1989 and early 1990. One external shock has been emanating from within the collapsed CMEA and the replacement of its traditional TR trade and payment mechanisms. Another area of serious external disturbances will need to be faced. It consists of two forces. One is the deterioration of Eastern Europe's terms of trade with the west. The other can be captured under the notion of a revenue loss that may soon be incurred on account of the economic recession in the United States spilling over notably into Western Europe. Another is the more general difficulty in any case of diverting significant volumes of Eastern Europe's exports from eastern markets and domestic supplies mainly to Western Europe. Put in a different context, it is the inability of the PETs to quickly reallocate resources for the production of convertible-currency exports at prevailing levels of purchasing power that aggravates and deepens the adjustment burden.

For the most part, the PETs could not have done very much about the unanticipated global economic fluctuations set off by the crisis in the Middle East. That "augmented third oil shock" consisted of the superimposition onto the third global oil shock of 1990 of the effects of switching TRPs to WMPs and TR payments to convertible-currency settlements beginning in 1991. This threatened to build up into a major drain on convertible-currency reserves, thus sharply curbing trade flexibility in Eastern Europe. In any case, the settlement of the war in the Persian Gulf may alleviate this addition to the already sizable domestic transitional problems these countries have to weather in any case.

It is regrettable that the new leaderships have not shown greater insight and forbearance with respect to the traditional mutual economic ties that their countries maintained for over forty years. Certainly, the inefficiencies embedded therein should no longer be condoned. Agreeing on the need to eradicate the economically unwarranted specialization is quite a different matter from willfully destroying commerce or ignoring the potential benefits of exploiting their reciprocal comparative advantages. Inhibiting economic agents from specializing in areas that have not so far been fully investigated because of inadequate policies, institutions, and policy instruments is also a poor policy stance.

The economic transformation of CPEs into PETs, and the latter into fully market-based economies, has several dimensions. One is in the microeconomic sphere, essentially placing enterprises on a hard budget constraint and holding management responsible for observing certain rules on asset valuation, possibly through privatization. As I shall argue below, privatization should be understood in its broad connotation, namely the removal of the government (both politicians and bureaucrats) from the decision making about the allocation of the service streams emanating from the capital stock and resource allocation more generally. Of course, the separation between government and the formulation of economic policy reaches wider, for instance, into monetary and fiscal policies. But the matters at stake are only tangentially related to the hard-core aspects of privatization. The intersection is nonempty because economic policy and government actions determine the arena within which privatization and private enterprise must be pursued. The macroeconomic framework in place and the coordination of microeconomic decisions that it seeks set the basic determinants of success with private enterprise. Other determinants issue from individual actions of owners or managers acting on behalf of clear owners.

In addition to these current problems, the transition is very much compounded by the multiple needs to come to grips with legacies from central planning. This has shadings that have to do with economic administration, including the prospective role of planning offices and ministerial bureaucracies, and how more appropriate economic institutions, instruments, and policies could be substituted for those essentially anchored to central planning as it evolved for nearly four decades in Eastern Europe and six in the Soviet Union. There are also inherited imbalances, including possibly a monetary overhang and sizable external debts, that will have to be worked off at the start of the transition. It has another component, namely the need to restructure these economies into competitive entities that can hold their own in the global economy. Such restructuring can be undertaken only over time. Under the best of circumstances, it can be sought only by idling and scrapping capacity, which will imply capital costs but also temporary and possibly even structural unemployment. Coping with the human dimensions of the restructuring and transition efforts generally ranks - at least it should rank - high on the agenda of most policy makers of the PETs, given the nature of these societies (Dahrendorf 1990; Garton Ash 1989, 1990; Havel 1989, 1990; Konrád 1984).

2. The current socioeconomic situation in Eastern Europe

Based on what policy makers perceived to be their main tasks after the first hesitant steps toward reform taken right after the momentous political changes of late 1989, the outlook for growth in 1990 throughout Eastern Europe was not at all uplifting. By the end of the first quarter of 1990, aggregate output, as measured by net material product (NMP), was anticipated to decline by 2 to 5 percent for the year as a whole. In several countries, the contraction in absorption, especially consumption, was expected to be somewhat less severe because adjustment would be by way of cutting primarily investments. The expected terms-of-trade gain, chiefly within the context of CMEA trade because of the declining Soviet fuel prices, was in any case to be utilized to mitigate adverse impacts on consumption. Aggregate output as measured by indicators of gross national product (GNP) or gross domestic product (GDP) would probably not recede by as much as NMP, owing to the more resilient service sectors and the expectation that there would be in effect no sizable capital scrapping in the short run.

Much of this whittling owed to the parlous state of the Polish economy. The Polish stabilization plan was predicated on a contraction in 1990 of about 5 percent in industrial activity, perhaps slightly less in terms of GNP. In the GDR, policy makers in early 1990 were mooting a cutback of aggregate output of perhaps 4 percent, the first time ever since postwar stabilization, at least according to official statistics. Hungarian policy makers reckoned with a contraction of about 2 percent in overall output, after several years of a virtual stagnation. Czechoslovak forecasts aimed at about even-level development. The implications of the reform intentions then held by policy makers in the rest of Eastern Europe were less explicit. But they never left any doubt that economic performance in 1990 would trail by a significant margin the already bleak one of the preceding year. The Soviet Union, on the other hand, had worked out a very optimistic plan for 1990 and was looking for positive growth on the order of 4 percent. Although this target was deemed to be too ambitious by most observers, few had been counting on a sharp contraction, say beyond the range of 1 to 3 percent, in the pace of overall economic activity.

Judging by the economic situation in Eastern Europe in early 1991, all of these expectations proved to have been wide off the mark. Indeed, aggregate economic activity in Eastern Europe, as measured by NMP produced, shrank at least by 10 percent (see Table 1.1), regardless of whether the collapsing GDR economy is factored into the average. Matters were not as bad in the Soviet Union, of course, but the drop in aggregate output, after correctly deflating for inflation, was nonetheless on the order of 8 to 10 percent, in spite of very good performance in agriculture and advantageous developments in foreign trade. Seen in terms of aggregate domestic demand, the contraction in Eastern Europe was less, perhaps 3 to 5 percent for the group as a whole and 2 to 4 percent for Eastern Europe. This paradoxical result emanated from inability to sell earmarked exports, which in some countries made machinery for investment purposes more abundant than had been anticipated. Also, worsening external accounts in some countries propped up this absorption.

In many respects the adjustment efforts that these countries embarked upon in early 1990 or were intent on introducing have led to a marked economic re-

Table 1.1: Macroeconomic indicators, 1980-1990 (average annual and annual growth rates)

	NMP	Industry	Agriculture	Investment	Exports	Imports
Bulgaria						
1981-1988	3.9	4.4	0.4	5.1	4.5	4.7
1989	-0.4	2.2	0.4	-7.7	-3.4	-6.5
1990	-13.6	-14.1	-8.8	-13.5	-26.0	-20.0
Czechoslovakia						
1981-1988	2.0	2.6	1.7	0.5	3.9	1.5
1989	1.0	0.8	1.8	1.6	-2.0	2.7
1990	-3.0	-3.7	-3.7	3.0	-13.0	0.0
GDR						
1981-1988	4.1	3.8	1.1	1.9	3.4	3.0
1989	2.1	2.3	1.6	0.9	0.5	2.4
1990	-19.5	-28.1	-30.0	-9.0	0.0	15.0
Hungary						
1981-1988	1.4	1.9	1.0	-1.3	3.9	1.1
1989	-1.1	-2.5	-1.3	0.5	0.0	1.0
1990	-5.5	-5.0	-7.0	-9.0	-4.3	-3.4
Poland						
1981-1988	1.0	1.9	1.8	0.2	3.3	0.7
1989	-0.2	-0.5	1.5	-2.4	0.2	1.5
1990	-13.0	-23.3	-1.4	-8.0	14.9	-15.6
Rumania						
1981-1988	2.0	4.0	1.3	-0.4	3.0	-1.8
1989	-7.9	-2.1	-5.1	-1.6	-10.8	3.7
1990	-10.5	-19.8	-3.0	-35.0	-46.0	4.0
Soviet Union						
1981-1988	3.0	3.8	2.1	4.7	3.2	3.1
1989	2.4	1.7	0.8	4.7	0.0	9.3
1990	-4.0	-1.2	-2.3	-4.3	-14.0	-5.0

Source: official statistical releases and own estimates.

cession. Negative output growth has been typical for the group. In some countries this has been accompanied by rapidly rising unemployment levels, rampant inflation, and a marked rise in capacity underutilization. Not a single one could claim positive growth in 1990. This observation holds even for Czechoslovakia, the country that has so far shown the greatest degree of economic stability and resilience, but only by postponing virtually all aspects of meaningful reform until 1991 and beyond.

There are a number of reasons for this discrepancy between expectations and events that bear on the short- to medium-term economic outlook of the area. Perhaps foremost is the considerable optimism displayed regarding the time and effort required to shape reform policies into feasible blueprints and implement them swiftly. Even more important has been the sluggishness in the response of policy makers to evident shortcomings in the pace of the reform drift. Particularly the delays incurred in adjusting supply to measurable shifts in product and factor prices have perplexed some observers. Most of this behavior could have been anticipated, however. Certainly, sudden external developments, both in CMEA and east-west relations, did not facilitate matters. Although these external events doubtlessly aggravated current socioeconomic performances in the region, their impact should not be exaggerated. Whatever the causes may have been, Eastern Europe as a group is in serious economic recession. Progress with genuine market-oriented reforms has been far more sluggish than expected under force of circumstance; in some countries, in fact, no noticeable progress at all could be registered.

The average contraction of aggregate output for Eastern Europe cited above masks a wide dispersion. In Czechoslovakia, for example, the downturn in 1990 was rather mild (perhaps 3 percent). But in Bulgaria, Poland, and Rumania the recession has been on the order of 10 to 15 percent. Particularly heavily affected has been industry. It was even worse in the former GDR. In Eastern Europe, it contracted on average by about 20 percent, again masking a wide variety of country performances. The industrial slump in Czechoslovakia was only about 4 percent, whereas it reached 20 percent or more in the GDR, Poland, and Rumania. True, some of these official measures do not accurately reflect the emerging private sector, but by the end of 1990 the increase in such economic activity as a share of total output cannot have been more than a few percentage points.

Certainly, economic activity in agriculture was less gloomy throughout the group. In fact, the Soviet Union attained a bumper grain crop but then ran into severe problems of securing the harvest at no more than average losses. Other crops did rather poorly, so that gross agricultural output contracted by perhaps 3 percent. In Eastern Europe, this was slightly higher. Looking at other sectors, particularly construction, investment activity more generally, as well as foreign trade have all shown more anemic performances than in the corresponding period of 1989. Thus, investment declined by from 4 percent in the Soviet Union to 14 percent on average in Eastern Europe, in spite of positive growth in Czechoslovakia; the contraction in Rumania was even 35 percent. Moreover, excepting Hungary and Poland (abstracting from the rising arrears in the latter's debt service), the current account in convertible-currency transactions for all countries sharply worsened. This was especially true for the Soviet Union, whose trade imbalance alone deteriorated by some $17 billion at the official exchange rate.

Part of the drop in output and the recession in economic activity more generally can be attributed to strikes, social disorganization, and, especially in Eastern Europe, unexpected external shocks. But much of the retrogression must be imputed to indecisiveness on the part of policy makers. This has been particularly noticeable in Poland, where the authorities waited with efforts to encourage supply responses to the very stringent stabilization policy adopted earlier in the year until the drop in output reached unprecedented levels - at least 20 percent by mid-year. Elsewhere, political indecisiveness compounded the already distressing disarray in production and economic policy making, reforms essentially being eschewed for fear of a sociopolitical backlash.

How wrong the expectations of policy makers turned out to be can be illustrated with reference to Poland, where, as noted, the most drastic deterioration in economic fortunes occurred; the GDR's calamity (with 28 percent drop in industry) is a special case (Protzman 1991). Industrial output in the socialist sector slumped by perhaps one fourth. Although the recession elsewhere was by no means as steep and export was booming, the contraction in purchasing power and imports, which was very steep during the first half of 1990, signal sluggish economic activity throughout the economy. Reflecting the rapid increase in private activities, possibly by as much as 25 to 30 percent in industry, albeit from a very low base, overall output in the economy may have been down by some 13 percent. The Polish stabilization program has brought some measure of price stability, though the pace was still over 50 percent, and growing, on an annual basis by late 1990; it was, of course, much higher for the year as a whole, owing to the sizable adjustments that were induced at the start of the stabilization program. It has also generated a significant export response and fewer frustrations in markets of consumer goods, basically because absorption was slashed.

Although consumers have gained in terms of sovereignty and disposal of time, on balance, the socioeconomic and political costs incurred thus far have been very high indeed. One might even question whether the benefits that have thus far been reaped justify the adjustment burden sustained through stabilization. The absence of clear-cut rules on property; the inordinate delay in getting the privatization law through the *Sejm*; the ability of the state monopolies to delay restructuring by calling upon their reserves and exploiting their monopolistic position; and the severe problems faced by private individuals trying to obtain access to bank loans, domestic supplies, and space from where they could commence operations on their own account explain part of the tepid supply response. It is an indicator of how *not* to proceed in other economies about to embark on incisive reforms. At the least, the Polish reform convulsions suggest that there is a need for erstwhile CPEs plagued by pervasive hyperinflationary pressures to design supplementary measures. For economies that are still roughly in balance, the Polish experience suggests that less radical policies might be preferable to the all-at-once stabilization. That does not call for abandoning speed, comprehensiveness, and order in the transition; it simply mandates tailoring priorities according to prevailing circumstances and the societal consensus of which policy makers can avail themselves implicitly or explicitly, as argued in Chapter 8.

In addition to comprehensive stabilization, which itself may have to be tailored slightly differently, genuine reform efforts on the supply side should be put in place as rapidly as circumstances permit. One exceedingly contentious issue in the measures pursued in the PETs is the role of democratic decision making. One may well ask whether at the outset of democracy, the political leadership should go out of its way to seek approval for each and every element of the institutional renewal from parliament. I am not simply arguing for or against the virtues of "benevolent dictatorship." The basic rule of thumb regarding the separation of powers should be that parliamentary organs legislate while government executes within some broad constitutional provisions (Dahrendorf 1990). Thus, I consider it not very wise to debate in parliament pricing policies once budgetary priorities are set or to agonize over exchange-rate policies, for example, once the new trade and foreign-exchange regimes are legislated.

Also in the GDR in early 1990 the situation began to unravel much faster than anyone had reckoned with. Industry contracted by 28 percent. Real exports stagnated, but real imports soared, owing to the sudden availability of *Deutschmark* spending power. At a time of deteriorating terms of trade, this could not but be indicative of problems with external payments. Furthermore, budgetary deficits continued to climb far beyond earlier appropriations. Even with economic and monetary union, the disarray in policy making and sheer clumsiness of those elected into public office took an appalling toll. Assistance from the FRG in all forms was most welcome. But even the FRG was unprepared for the chaos it was suddenly confronted with. It certainly had no patent recipe for what had to be rectified as quickly as circumstances permitted. With hindsight, economic, social, and monetary union with the FRG did not work out well. In response, the FRG set in motion the political, economic, and diplomatic machinery to achieve its long-cherished goal of German unification. This may even have been the root motivation of the FRG's policies from the very start.

In the two other ostensibly radically reforming economies, Czechoslovakia and Hungary, no noticeable progress with economic, in contrast to political, reform was made. Czechoslovakia managed to contain the damage in terms of lost output, unemployment, inflation, and current-account imbalances, as indicated by the nearly 4 percent contraction of industrial output in spite of considerable buoyancy in investment activity, owing to lost export markets; but a sharp drop in export and stagnant imports worsened the current account.

Also here, payments difficulties emerged. By mid-year the divisions within the government about basic reform strategy and tactics appeared to have been overcome. But new acrimony erupted toward the end of the year. Whether the partly coherent reform package emplaced in early 1991 can take hold and its adverse impacts on income differentiation, employment, and inflation mitigated so as to secure further societal support remains to be seen.

Hungary has been much less fortunate. The economic situation there is most discouraging, to say the least. Aggregate output declined by 6 percent, after a decade of virtually no growth. Industrial activity contracted by 5 percent and agriculture by slightly more, due to adverse weather conditions. Both export an import volumes declined, but the former by more than the latter. Nonetheless, the overall terms-of-trade gain led to an improved current account; but this did not stem from increased efficiency in resource intensity. The weak coalition voted into office in May would seem to have garnered support only for very gradual reform. In the meantime, the overall economic situation has further deteriorated with continued upward movement of prices. Although Hungary had already earlier put in place a number of basic laws on enterprise, privatization, joint ventures, property, banks, and many other matters, implementing these prescriptions in a climate of near political stalemate has proved to be exceedingly cumbersome.

In Bulgaria, Rumania, and, to a lesser extent, the Soviet Union, matters are much worse. In the two Balkan countries, economic activity has been quickly unraveling, as indicated by a loss in aggregate output of over 10 percent, in industry of over 15 percent, and investment of between 13 and 35 percent. Furthermore, there was a sharp deterioration in trade performance, with export quantum contracting by over a fourth in Bulgaria and nearly half in Rumania. In the latter, import volume even increased, which worsened the current account. In Bulgaria, however, import volume contracted by about one fifth.

Although economic performance in some countries has not yet deteriorated to the dramatic proportions observed in Bulgaria, the ex-GDR, Poland, and Rumania, the near-term outlook is very grim indeed. Even in the Soviet Union, overall growth as officially measured contracted by about 4 percent of NMP (perhaps 2 percent in GDP) and industry by about 1 percent, with a dramatically deteriorating external-payment situation. In fact, export volume contracted sharply (14 percent) while import volume at first soared but then declined for a contraction of 5 percent for the year as a whole. The only bright sign of tentative change was in investment activity, which contracted by 4 percent, but this may be seriously understated. However, the reported 2 percent drop in aggregate output, as measured by GNP, is almost certainly a vast understatement. It definitely does not reflect the growing imbalances between money incomes and what people can spend in official retail outlets. The burgeoning cooperative and underground outlets do, of course, provide alternative goods and services but at vastly inflated prices when compared to those in official retail outlets. By more conventional measurements, however, aggregate domestic output indicators worsened much more sharply - perhaps 7 percent for GNP and 9-10 percent for NMP; much worse is expected for 1991, given the continuing, and worsening, disarray in the societal makeup of the USSR.

Yugoslavia has not formed a proper part of "Eastern Europe" for many decades. It abandoned administrative central planning in the early 1950s, sought market-oriented reforms in several phases over nearly four decades, never was an integral part of Eastern Europe or the CMEA for that matter, since 1948 has never been as dependent on trade with Eastern Europe as the CMEA members, and its trade with Eastern Europe has in any case been settled chiefly in convertible currency for nearly two decades. For all those and other reasons, I usually omit Yugoslavia from analyses of Eastern Europe. I should like to divert occasionally from that position in this volume for two reasons. One is that Yugoslavia embraced a "big bang" path to convertibility at about the same time as Poland. It has gone through a wrenching stabilization effort with external support and has been looking for full and fast integration into the world economy, including the EC. Also, it has recently been experiencing adverse developments much like those of the Soviet Union, albeit on a smaller but no less ferocious scale. The internecine bickering, which on occasion resembles an undeclared civil war, may yet undermine the stabilization effort and hence lead to a reversal of internal convertibility. If that were to take place, and even more if accompanied by a *de facto* breaking up of the federation, it might be prescient to make room in any union arrangements, such as advocated in this volume, also for Yugoslavia. I shall therefore allude to the situation in Yugoslavia whenever justified for the particular purposes at hand.

Yugoslav economic performance in 1990 was full of contrasts. Consumption rose moderately for the first time since 1986, but investment contracted; exports hardly changed whereas imports soared; aggregate output receded sharply, owing to a substantial cutback in industry and tourism, but the recession was fairly widespread. The domestic convertibility of the dinar was held at a fixed exchange rate (at par with the Austrian Schilling) for most of the year in spite of inflation of nearly 600 percent as measured by the cost-of-living index. The resulting loss in export competitiveness brought pressure to bear on the current account (which was $2.6 billion in the red, a reversal by nearly $5 billion), and in December Yugoslavia was forced to devalue the dinar by nearly a third and to reimpose some exchange controls. The gross social product receded by about 8 percent and unemployment levels increased sharply, while real wages contracted by about one fifth. The ongoing near-civil war, with Slovenia and Croatia actively militating for secession from the federation, does not augur well for economic stability.

This brief review of the results obtained during the first year of transition underlines some of the obstacles encountered. There should never have been any doubt that reforming the administratively planned economies into viable MEs could not have proceeded without exacting a sharp toll on society. This would manifest itself not only in the form of adverse economic developments, such as apprehensible income inequalities by the precepts of these societies, inflation, and unemployment. More important would be the costs incurred in changing the behavior of economic agents, including households, firms, local and central governments, and foreign participants in the PETs. Such a transformation could not but evolve over time. Under certain conditions, then, a sharp contraction in economic activity, rising unemployment, and shifts in relative prices that impart an upward inflationary bias as subsidies on essentials are dismantled would be indicative of successful adjustment. Quite so, provided the "certain conditions" refer mainly to declining sectors and bankrupt firms that had earlier incurred losses and could not be rendered competitive in world markets in any case. Part of the ongoing shrinkage in economic activity can undoubtedly be attributed to precisely such mutations in production and consumption profiles. However, the overall situation throughout the group appears to be such that the contraction is much less discriminate than the pundits of "less is better" would like the unwary to believe.

From my reading of recent events in Eastern Europe and what can be anticipated in the near term, the current economic situation throughout the group is ominous, but more so for some countries than for others. The depressing economic data for 1990 and those held out for 1991 do reflect a much deeper-rooted sociopolitical malaise and inability to bring about structural change in a brief period of time. Certainly, the situation in the countries with clear-cut political gains, such as Czechoslovakia and Poland, is for the moment still supportive of ongoing reforms. The core question at this stage, however, is how long this tolerance for worsening suffering will last. As John K. Galbraith (1990, p. 51) noted, "The casual acceptance of - even commitment to - human deprivation, to unemployment, inflation, and disastrously reduced living standards" is currently even seen as therapy for incisive structural change.

Gloomy as the economic situation in 1990 was, conditions were comparatively rosy when placed against the backdrop of the problems that loom on the horizon of the early 1990s, except perhaps for Poland. As regards the external situation, the immediate problems ahead consist of a sharp shift in intragroup terms of trade as countries switch from TRPs to near-WMPs. At the same time, the global economic situation is not promising. Although the runup in fuel prices of 1990 is probably over for now, the fallout of the Gulf crisis continues. For one thing, several reforming countries had long-standing contracts with those most directly involved in the conflict, notably Iraq, that regulated repayment of loans or payment for shipments of arms in terms of oil. Not only did the embargo prevent delivery of these contracted volumes, it is doubtful that the underlying debts will now be repaid. Related to this is the fact that several countries, including Bulgaria, Hungary, Poland, and Rumania, had arrangements with notably Iran, Iraq, and Syria to obtain crude oil on barter terms. Considerable volumes of these earmarked shipments were diverted to world markets in late 1990. These countries have also lost sizable exports markets, given that Iraq had been the most important partners among the DEs for many

Eastern European countries. For some, worker remittances from Iraq were a significant source of foreign exchange. On top of that, a fairly pronounced economic recession in DMEs may be in the making. This would almost certainly cut into the export prospects of Eastern Europe. It might also cool the enthusiasm for helping the PETs.

Three features of the events in the course of 1990 stand out and have a bearing on what can be anticipated as regards the buoyancy of economic activity over the next year or two. One is the rapidly deteriorating socioeconomic and, in some cases also, political situation in a number of countries, particularly Bulgaria, the former GDR, Rumania, and the Soviet Union; Albania and Yugoslavia have joined that circle more recently but no less poignantly. The outlook for stabilization throughout the group is rather gloomy, even in countries where basic agreement on economic reform appears to be holding well. Second, though greater stability has prevailed in the three other countries, progress with reform has recently been slowing down for various reasons. Structural changes in Poland are being inhibited mainly for lack of various institutional actions. The reform in Czechoslovakia was started in early 1991, but with much less dash than had earlier been held out notably by Minister Klaus. In Hungary, matters appear to be stalled at this juncture. Rumania resorted to its version of shock therapy on 1 November 1990 and Bulgaria around 1 February 1991. The price reforms in these countries have not (yet) been accompanied by other essential changes, including foreign-trade liberalization and hardening of the budget constraint for state-owned enterprises (SOEs). In the other countries, little if any headway is being made with genuine economic and, in some cases, sociopolitical reforms. Finally, the pervasive sense of helplessness in the context of a rapidly deteriorating foreign-payment situation in all Eastern European countries may paralyze decision makers until economic crisis becomes so pervasive that only radical measures offer a glimmer of hope for changing course.

The exchange constraint has multiple origins. Perhaps the most outstanding is the switchover in TR trade and payment regimes. In addition, the collapse of the CMEA as a framework for economic collaboration, without having come to some alternative arrangements, simply compounds the disarray in policy making. The resort to disaggregated bilateral trade and payments agreements (BTPAs) does not augur well. Especially alarming is the degree of rigidity embedded in these arrangements. Also important have been the sudden renunciation of trade contracts (including by the GDR and its successor decision makers, Poland, and the Soviet Union) and sharp deterioration in terms of trade because of the situation in the Persian Gulf.

As regards prospects, the inability of balancing external payments at levels that support buoyant domestic activity particularly in Eastern Europe suggests a protracted period of austerity, with an incisive downward adjustment in absorption levels. Few policy makers in the area appear to be willing even to entertain the merits of introducing a payments union for the radically reforming countries. Instead, most hope that western assistance will be forthcoming not only to offset the deterioration in the terms of trade but also to finance the expected marked deficit in the current account with the Soviet Union. The latter assistance is unlikely to materialize in the magnitudes required to maintain trade volumes, if only because earmarked official development assistance (ODA) cannot be massively redeployed and raising total aid levels is a non-starter for now. As a result, the sharp cutback in aggregate demand in the group may have debilitating consequences for the reform movement and socio-economic stability in the area. Particularly worrisome is the near-chaotic situation in the Soviet Union which at times resembles sheer anarchy. Whether the country will be able to capitalize on its improved terms of trade depends critically on it finding a solution for the federation and the introduction of meaningful economic reforms. Current forecasts of Soviet oil exports in general and trade with Eastern Europe in particular set levels that would imply very pronounced reductions in output while domestic demand rises. 1991 oil exports are expected to be about half the levels of 1990 - no more than 61 million tons (see *International Herald Tribune*, 5 November 1990, p. 5 and *Izvestiya*, 4 November 1990, p. 2). From interviews with well-placed Soviet trade negotiators, I learnt that in late 1990 Soviet authorities were forecasting a reduction in trade with Eastern Europe (evaluated at new prices anticipated for 1991 but at old exchange rates) of some 35 to 45 percent an average.

Some extraordinary international action appears required to stave off the worst expectations of a deep recession in Eastern Europe. If nothing is done about the serious current-account position of especially the fuel importers, a pronounced recession throughout the group is all but unavoidable. Of course, absorption levels could be cut to generate export revenues, but that theoretical possibility is just that. A deep depression in Eastern Europe would work against reform, for societal support would evaporate quickly. This would not be in the interest of Western Europe. Furthermore, the prospects of massive recycling of funds to the east is unlikely to materialize, given the experiences of western commercial banks in the 1970s and 1980s and the substantial debt levels of Bulgaria, Hungary, and Poland in particular. Perhaps a solution might be found by recycling funds through the official institutions. But there is no confirmation as yet that this will materialize soon. In other words, the choice between a sharp cut in absorption levels and postponing it through borrowing is not a real one at this stage. The first could not but undermine the fledgling democracies in the area and might set off an unprecedented movement of people from east to west. Certainly in scale, if perhaps not in emulating the pressures in the GDR to emigrate in late 1989 and early 1990 (and now still within the all German context), it would be a calamity of major proportions. Western Europe is not prepared for such an emigration wave just like Eastern Europe cannot accommodate potential emigration from the USSR.

One critical ingredient of what is required to enable the area to weather the storms ahead is to find a way to overcome payments obstacles that inhibit the exploitation of profitable trade in support of marketization. Although all countries are bent on redirecting the bulk of their trade to Western Europe in particular, the sheer preponderance of intragroup trade, especially with the Soviet Union, will remain for the foreseeable future. If that commerce cannot be realized, a substantial contraction in activity levels is bound to occur in the short to medium run.

The problem can be looked at from another angle too. Severe payments problems can be worked off only by slashing absorption levels, borrowing in financial markets, or a cooperative strategy that dovetails judicious adjustment with external finance and advice. The first option would doom the reform movement and might even weaken the newly installed democratic regimes. The second, if feasible, cannot but lead to rising debt levels, which are already excessive for several countries, and perhaps a repetition of the debt crises of the 1980s. Such an outcome would only aggravate subsequent adjustment problems. Without hammering out a cooperative strategy to enable the fuel importers to run deficits while they at the same time radically restructure their economies, an anticipated sharp recession may turn into a protracted depression.

The similarity between Eastern Europe at this juncture and Western Europe after World War II is too great to dismiss out of hand the potential usefulness of innovating a payments union for the PETs with western financial and advisory support. A payments union could not, of course, meet the financial needs arising from structural payments problems. But it could facilitate the marketization of the reforming economies by allowing autonomous agents to engage in trade on their own account, even if shifts in the level, composition, and direction of trade were to lead to temporary imbalances. It might also help to finance wider intragroup deficits, provided the Soviet Union could be found able as exporter and willing as net creditor to rechannel part of its potential surplus to finance Eastern Europe's trade deficits in the immediate future.

3. The drift of the reform debate

Cooperative solutions for the shared problems of Eastern Europe have not been very popular since the *de facto* collapse of the CMEA in early 1990. Efforts to resuscitate the latter by placing SEI on a completely new last, without the socialist context and with completely new policy instruments and institutions, foundered. This state of affairs has not yet been formally acknowledged. For all practical purposes, however, this is the case and no alternative for the TR trade and payment regimes to help clear economically warranted commerce is at hand. None is actively desired by the new leaders, at least for now.

Since the political remolding of Eastern Europe, very little attention has been paid by anyone to the possibilities of pursuing genuine external reforms to permit the reforming partners to exploit their true comparative advantages. By then, the entire debate of the 1980s on reforming the institutions, instruments, and policies of SEI had reached an unbridgeable impasse (Brabant 1989a; 1990b; 1991e, h, k). In the aftermath of the momentous 45th Council Session (Sofia, 9-10 January 1990), the European members have been seeking dual relief. One has been the replacement of the entire TR trade and payment regimes with market-clearing prices - WMPs, if you will - and settlement in convertible currency. At the same time, another reform commission for most of the first half of 1990 worked at reshaping the CMEA in several directions. Serious stumbling blocks arose with the consistent pursuit of both reform directions. The result is a nonsystem at this stage.

Especially Central Europe at some points of the evolving debate exhibited considerable enthusiasm for replacing the TR regimes. But there was also marked apprehension about the clearing aspects of the alternative proposed by Nikolay I. Ryzhkov in Sofia and the fact that the Soviet Union as well as other CMEA partners would not have genuine firms to conduct businesslike negotiations for which they could assume full financial responsibility. This is particularly important for trade in manufactured goods - the heartland of what could be intragroup trade in Central Europe. By mid-1990, roughly around the time of the runup in oil prices, Soviet policy stances switched from clearing to actual payments in convertible currency, something that they reinforced by severely limiting at once exports of key items for TRs.

By then, of course, the magnitude of the reversal in imbalances with the Soviet Union had become the stuff of political controversy throughout Eastern Europe. Backtracking on the demand for immediate settlement in convertible currency, and to some degree also on switching right away to WMPs, started to pervade negotiations. Efforts to resolve this situation have been leading Eastern Europe back to strict bilateralism, in some cases pure barter at the interfirm level, which by definition cripples market-oriented reforms. It is most distressing to find Eastern European policy makers wholeheartedly endorse the rebilateralization of commerce in Eastern Europe as a desirable format for hammering out whatever can be agreed upon; it is even more painful to find this stance supported by the international organizations closely involved in delivering assistance to the PETs. The reasons for this attitude are those invoked against Western Europe's bilateralism after World War II (Vries 1969a, b), and then some. In many ways, this is a setback in economic thinking and policy making, if not necessarily in past-CMEA practices. Surely, if the radically reforming PETs were bent on catching up with world markets as quickly as possible and gaining full entry there, the avid pursuit of bilateral solutions to their foreign-exchange problems is the last option they should be counseled to explore, provided some credible alternative were available beyond simply cutting out that trade. This is especially pertinent when one of the bilateral partners is bound to be the Soviet Union, where market-clearing behavior is unlikely to be forthcoming soon.

As regards the debates in the new reform commission, matters came to a head in late 1990 and led to the tacit dissolution of the CMEA and much of what it has stood for, at least for now. But all along there was sufficient evidence that the room for genuine reform in the CMEA as a whole remained exceedingly narrow. The successor organization - the Organization for International Economic Cooperation (OIEC) - that has been proposed cannot be more than a weak regional secretariat like the Organisation for Economic Co-operation and Development (OECD) in Paris. As such, it can at most be entrusted with preparing briefs for consideration at the political level. But it will have no muscle to enhance economic integration. Further, virtually all vestiges of multilateral economic cooperation in Eastern Europe have been removed. All substantive aspects of foreign economic relations among these countries as a group or in various subgroups, say, according to their proclivity for market-oriented reform are henceforth to be dealt with bilaterally. Any suggestion to seek reciprocal support for the reform movement has been peremptorily rejected for reasons examined in Chapter 2. Yet, there would seem to be room to ease the external-balancing problems through a collaborative strategy that could measurably alleviate apprehensions about regional economic cooperation and indeed strengthen the reform process.

4. The nature of the payments problem

For the past two decades or so, most countries of Eastern Europe have been fighting external constraints of one kind or another. This may seem surprising, given that central planning should, in principle, have rectified the external-payments situation through mandatory allocation policies. There are many fascinating reasons why this has not been so. Most pertain to macroeconomic management of the CPE (Brabant 1987a, 1989a), hence they should not detain us here. The paramount question at this juncture in countries that have all but completed their political transition revolves around the level at which external payments can be balanced and why. To the extent that the PETs cannot avail themselves of some external flexibility, the factors that inhibit the transition to the ME cannot but exacerbate the cost of structural adaptation.

The current and near-term problems emanating from external accounts stem essentially from four sources. Some would have occurred in any case, regardless of reforms in PETs. Especially important would have been the need to work off inherited (in the form of debt levels) and current payments imbalances stemming mostly from faulty policy making in the past or inability to control economic events through administrative channels. Others could not have been foreseen because of shocks in the global economy. But there is also a group of issues that could have been managed in a cooperative fashion. This has thus far been absent for reasons to be invoked later in this volume.

Throughout most of the 1980s, many CMEA members suffered from the constraints emanating from the inherited convertible-currency debt. This had been incurred largely in the 1970s but, for some, the second half of the 1980s proved ominous. Among the first group Poland and Rumania stand out. Rumania succeeded in whittling its convertible-currency debt virtually to zero by 1989. But this salutary solution was achieved at an appalling cost in terms of enforced austerity. Not only was it very substantial, it was also imposed through Draconian policy measures that could only have been inflicted through the singlemindedness of Nicolae Ceauşescu and the repressive dictatorship of which he availed himself to the hilt. In Poland, the debt crisis continued to be stalemated throughout the period. Hungary succeeded in rectifying part of its external balances in the mid-1980s, but drift in policy making, especially in 1986-1988, simply resulted, once again, in a recrudescence of the external ills. Bulgaria had a similar experience. It had virtually wiped out its debt in the late 1970s and early 1980s mainly by reexporting Soviet fuels procured at TRs. In the late 1980s, it once again incurred serious convertible-currency deficits. In March 1990, it was forced to declare a moratorium on debt servicing. By the mid-1980s, the GDR found itself in much the same situation. But its privileged relationship with the FRG enabled it to avoid rescheduling and indeed to ease the external constraints. Through prudent management and some benefits of "normalization," Czechoslovakia controlled its external accounts.

The Soviet Union is a case apart. Unlike Eastern Europe, it gained from substantial shifts in terms-of-trade and fuel export revenues. In spite of rapid import growth, it kept its convertible-currency debt comparatively low. True, economic mismanagement in the first five years of *perestroyka* led to a sharp rise in current-account deficits with DMEs. Also, the development crisis rendered its earlier surpluses with DEs essentially unrecoverable. In an extraordinary disclosure to parliament in late 1989 (*Izvestiya*, 2 March 1990, p. 2), total outstanding ruble (Rb) claims as of 1 November 1989 were estimated to be Rb85.8 billion, more than half on account of socialist partners and the rest owed by favored developing countries. Most is unrecoverable.

It was only with the generalization of economic crisis in consumer markets in 1988-1990 that massive deficits on current account, hence a combination of borrowing and gold sales, had to be resorted to. Not only did the Soviet Union find itself in rising deficit with DMEs, it also was unable to weather the implications of the reverse second oil shock in CMEA relations in 1987-1990. In spite of balancing rules associated with BTPAs, the USSR was unable to avoid running substantial TR deficits. Its partners, given their payments problems, were hardly eager to tolerate such surpluses (see Chapter 2). On balance, several of them, while running large overall current-account deficits, were either in substantial debt (such as Poland) or already in sizable surplus (such as Bulgaria, Czechoslovakia, and the ex-GDR) with the Soviet Union. This stemmed from accumulated bilateral imbalances, some incurred because of so-called joint investment participations in Soviet fuel and raw-material projects.

Second, any effort to introduce greater rationality in the external commerce of the CMEA members individually or as a group would have entailed shifts in the level, commodity composition, and geographical distribution of trade. In the short to medium run, this would have lowered domestic absorption either because traditional imports could no longer be afforded or because exports had to be stepped up simply to manage external balances. Shifts in the commodity composition and geographical direction of trade would probably have given rise to terms-of-trade losses in the short run. Indeed, many exportables particularly from Eastern Europe can compete in western markets at best by slashing prices. Because transformations in the foreign-trade sectors would have required genuine structural change in the domestic economy, the capital cost of such a mutation would have negatively affected at least domestic welfare levels.

The third group of determinants of the external pressures arise from unforeseen developments in the global economy. Since I have earlier flagged most items on the direct and indirect effects of the crisis in the Persian Gulf, I can be brief here and refer essentially to two factors. One is the deterioration in the terms-of-trade for Eastern Europe. This would have called for extra expenses, even if accommodation within the TR regime could have continued. Declining volumes of Soviet oil exports would have forced Eastern Europe to procure incremental supplies from world markets at additional cost. There would also have been a medium-term effect with the rise in WMPs gradually being fed into the TRP formula. Of course, any adjustment to current WMPs could not but have hastened this process. The second aspect is the potential for gaining export revenues in convertible-currency markets, which have become less buoyant with the slowdown in key DMEs. It probably would also cool the enthusiasm of western partners for providing assistance to reforms in PETs. The question here is not only, certainly not mainly, earmarking financial flows. Rather, all efforts that seek to assist the reforms of the PETs have inevitable budgetary implications. In the event of a serious economic slump, such fiscal outlays will be reassessed on their merits as compared to their economic, political, and strategic opportunity costs.

Finally, the core of the external constraint prior to the eruption of the Gulf crisis stemmed from the decision of the CMEA members to change their intragroup trade and payment systems. In combination with the shift in global terms of trade and difficulties in marketing traditional exports, especially the Eastern European countries are bound to experience serious problems in managing their reserves. In the process, they may have to come to grips with a steep recession. If not attended to soon, it may eventually turn into a protracted economic depression, which could not but undermine the newly emerging, still markedly fragile, democracies.

In fact, the sharp recession has already been under way for over a year, as documented in Section 2. One cause has been intragroup economic relations being buffeted by several adverse crosswinds even before the formal abrogation of the TR rules. Indeed, these countries have been experiencing severe problems in clearing their reciprocal trade at least since 1988. Commitments made in BTPAs have been increasingly flouted. This has manifested itself in part because shifts in the terms of trade have made it difficult for potential surplus countries to maintain committed flows. The major cause in recent years has been the delayed transmission of the reverse oil shock of the mid-1980s into CMEA relations, owing to the TRP regime. As noted, this sought to set TRPs on the basis of a five-year average of WMPs and ruble-dollar exchange rates. Thus, weak oil prices in world markets in 1985-1986 and since then were funneled into the CMEA price formula only beginning in 1986. Of course, the full impact of the deep price slump of 1986 manifested itself only in more recent years. Also unanticipated output fluctuations and shifting export priorities, including of energy in the Soviet Union, have compounded intragroup commerce, thereby aggravating bilateral imbalances.

But growing incompatibilities in these relations must also be attributed to divergences in the national reform movements. Thus, countries that seek to devolve decision making, including in external commerce, to autonomous economic agents find it increasingly difficult, and in many ways counterproductive, to clear trade with unreformed partners. Of course, the eruption of rivalries among the ex-CMEA countries and the perceived need to "get even" for having been under the Soviet knout for so long have not helped matters at all. Efforts to have the Soviet Union compensate some Eastern European countries for their faltering economic performance, on flimsy grounds of wrongs perpetrated in the past, have predictably only exacerbated ties already strained by rancor. These metaeconomic arguments have not at all been conducive to smoothing already complex stances on commercial policy.

As a result, several CMEA partners have been reluctant to incur intragroup trade surpluses. To forestall their emergence, countries have inaugurated unprecedented domestic policy measures to stem exports to the TR area, because it continues to be very cumbersome to mobilize such surpluses. Furthermore, at least the GDR until mid-1990 and Hungary, Poland, and the Soviet Union even since then abruptly canceled orders for complex machinery placed before the political revolutions. Rather than being saddled with equipment that would be ill-suited to the envisaged new structures, they preferred instead to pay the then standard CMEA fines for breach of contract. The reaction of enterprises in the GDR to the introduction of the *Deutschmark* as monetary unit in July 1990 took the form of broad diversion of import demand to the west. This sudden cancellation of many export orders in partner countries had disruptive effects, particularly in Czechoslovakia and, to a lesser extent, Hungary and Poland, with the latter exacerbating matters through its own cancellation of previously placed orders.

The outcome for now of these incompatible policy stances has been a precipitous decline of intragroup commerce in the wake of severely limited import possibilities from convertible-currency partners. This trend cannot but gain further momentum in 1991 with the formal dissolution of the TR regimes. Eastern Europe's balance of payments will tighten rapidly in consequence of the sharp deterioration in terms of trade with east and west alike. This will be aggravated by export-revenue losses because these countries cannot offer each other the pivotal manufactures upon which radical structural reforms depend.

No decision maker in Eastern Europe is currently supporting any exploration at all of the potentials for bolstering intragroup trade through a cooperative strategy. Also, Soviet chaos is injecting profound uncertainty into the entire edifice. Policy making at this stage is primarily geared to short-term damage control set within the framework afforded by shortsighted policy stances. These prevent, or at least inhibit, economic agents from exploiting comparative advantages. Some nudging particularly by western donor countries may be required to point out to the new leaders of PETs that it is unproductive, to say the least, to ignore their intragroup trade potential.

5. Shocks of mutating trade and payment regimes

A natural question to ask in connection with the switchover in trade and payment regimes in Eastern Europe is the magnitude of the expected deterioration for some countries and of the benefits for others. Related to this is whether the interests of the two sides could perhaps be blended in some form, possibly with the participation of western countries. Although none of these issues is straightforward, it should be easiest to make an informed estimate of the impact of the switch in trade and payment regimes in Eastern Europe. Unfortunately, key parameters of this regime switch are not yet available. One can therefore only hint at what the replacement of the TR regime might entail.

Analytically, the exercise can logically be divided into quantum and price impacts both with respect to CMEA trade as such and the spillover that is bound to occur, in terms of prices and net incomes, in east-west relations. The first effect that could be documented is the cost that would have been incurred in a given year if trade had been invoiced at WMPs rather than TRPs at some realistic cross-rate between the ruble and the dollar. The accounting can start with export or import prices or both. Thus, WMPs for fuels could be taken at the official exchange rate and the divergence between TRPs and current WMPs derived. The key determinant of Eastern Europe's decline in terms of trade would then result from the realistic pricing especially of manufactures at official exchange rates. Alternatively, TRPs at realistic cross-rates, however estimated by the countries themselves, could be utilized as starting point. Although dollar prices of both Eastern Europe's exports and imports would be lower than those evaluated at official exchange rates, the key determinant of the decline in terms of trade would be the repricing of fuel imports.

Concrete data on the various factors involved in such a reversal are, unfortunately, not available (Rosati 1990). Estimates of the magnitudes of the shift in current-account positions range between \$1-2 billion for Bulgaria, \$1.5-2.5 billion for Czechoslovakia, \$0.5-2 billion for Hungary, and \$0.8-4 billion for Poland; the higher estimates indicate potentially sizable deficits with the Soviet

Union. Even if initially there would have been clearing, as Ryzhkov had held out in early 1990, at some point imbalances must be defrayed in scarce currency. The methodology that lies at the base of the above estimates leaves a lot to be desired, however. In most cases, it is not even clear what reference year these politically highly charged estimates of current-account reversals refer to. Without clarity on this issue, the sensitive political matters at stake, especially in relations with the Soviet Union, may well be utilized for utilitarian motives. This is an unhelpful stance from the point of view of formulating realistic economic options for decision makers.

The replacement of the TR regimes is eminently desirable to foster marketization. Nonetheless, there has never been any doubt that this is bound to lead to sizable terms-of-trade effects, however measured, mainly because of the sharp rise in the "real" dollar price of Soviet energy, oil in particular. Even if we limit our purview for now to the question of the additional cost of oil purchases, matters are not at all straightforward. For example, it bears to pause momentarily with the constatation that at the official exchange rate Eastern Europe's TRP for Soviet oil in 1989 (at TR15.42 pb) exceeded the corresponding price for exports to DMEs (at TR12.39 pb). That is, at the official exchange rate Eastern Europe would have saved $2.5 billion if it had paid the DME price rather than the TRP. But at any of the realistic dollar-ruble cross-rates adopted by the Central European countries for 1989 (sometimes, as for Czechoslovakia and the GDR, in retrospect), the price of Soviet oil in dollars (ranging from $5.3 to 10.5 pb) was but a fraction of the current WMP. Thus if 1989 Soviet oil had been priced at the average price obtained in trade with DMEs, Eastern Europe as a group would had to pay an additional $4.7 billion (at the Czechoslovak cross-rate) to $7.4 billion (at the Polish cross-rate). These amounts are, of course, only hypothetical as the ruble-dollar cross-rates of 1989 were palpably not market rates.

But the regime switch would have had effects well transcending the deterioration in Eastern Europe's terms of trade with the Soviet Union on account of the price of oil, even if no runup in WMPs had occurred. In addition to the effect of repricing oil at "real" WMPs, Soviet imports of below-standard Eastern European manufactures would probably be cut and the real price lowered, certainly over time. In this connection, it is very important to keep matters straight and compare like magnitudes. Commentators often confuse matters when assessing the "real" cost of the price adjustments. The extra cost of oil and raw material shipments is usually figured by taking the difference between actual dollar cost at some realistic exchange rate of the ruble to the dollar and presumed WMPs. For Eastern European exports of manufactures, however, the cost is usually seen as the difference between rubles earned and the "real" WMP that the Soviet Union, after conversion, is presumed to be willing to pay. This inevitably involves double counting, as the difference between the "real" dollar cost and the presumed WMP should be factored into both sides of the equation. If done this way, I conjecture that the "real" effect on prices of Eastern Europe's exports of manufactures depends very much on the time horizon one is willing to consider. Initially, the impact of the regime shift on Eastern Europe's exports is likely to be larger for quantities traded than for "real" prices. This proposition rests on the plausible assumption that the devolution from central to enterprise purchasing in the USSR entails a demand shift. Different economic agents will presumably gear their behavior to "own" demand preferences. Changes in relative prices, hence the terms-of-trade effect, are not so easy to extract. Indeed, in the short run many of Eastern Europe's traditional exports will continue to be required, for example, simply to maintain the Soviet machine park of Eastern European provenance. How large the effect in the end will be is something that has vexed many economists; it has been a natural bone to chew on and on for those bent on fanning controversy. Over time, however, the "real" price that the Soviet Union would be willing to pay for Eastern Europe's traditional manufactures is bound to decline substantially. Only a sharp transformation of Eastern Europe's supply during the transition process, so that part of the Soviet restructuring needs could be met, could avert this. The "real" price that Soviet firms will pay for such below-standard manufactures will probably decline the way the GDR's terms of trade with the FRG suffered in 1990; but the restructuring process in Eastern Europe and the Soviet Union, hence the effect on prices, will be much slower, of course.

In other words, price and income effects of the regime switch in Eastern Europe are bound to be sizable over the medium run, unless substantial structural change takes hold quickly in Eastern Europe's offer. The calculus may become more complicated by large trade diversion for two reasons. One is sentimental and cannot quickly be accommodated in an economic framework. It refers to the innate proclivity of reformers to divert trade to western markets, almost regardless of its underlying opportunity cost. The other is that lack of availability of some goods, possibly because of inelastic supply, will induce economic agents to explore third markets. This logical response to devolution is bound to assume growing importance over time as economic agents become more fully acquainted with the new rules of decision making. Such trade diversion may entail significant income effects for Eastern Europe and is bound to have that consequence for partners that cannot quickly modify their offer.

Regardless of how sizable the reversal in TR regime might be, deficits with the Soviet Union will be very large provided they can be financed and Soviet supply can be maintained - two assumptions of doubtful validity at this stage. Otherwise, these goods would have to be procured elsewhere, perhaps at higher cost, thus aggravating external balances with MEs. Without there being in place some mechanism to accommodate either or both of those deficits, Eastern Europe will have to implement a sizable austerity program that will cut out most of the buoyancy from the structural-reform programs.

6. Western assistance to combat liquidity shortage

The astoundingly swift, mostly peaceful revolutions of late 1989 and early 1990 in Eastern Europe were greeted with glee, approval, and understanding in many MEs. But they also gave rise to grave concerns, which have intensified since then. Especially Western Europe has been apprehensive about the shaky foundations upon which these anti-communist, rather than pro-democracy, sociopolitical mutations were predicated. Whereas the brunt of the assistance effort has been conceived primarily within the European context, other countries have pledged help too, as detailed elsewhere (Brabant 1990c, pp. 84-102). Some DEs too have shown more than casual interest in assisting the installation of MEs in Eastern Europe, including through trade and finance.

Especially Western Europe's assistance to the east revolves around two buzzwords: democratization and marketization. Western leaders feel it proper to see to it that the processes of moving toward more pluralistic decision making in PETs take firm root in the consciousness of the electorate of these countries. Related to this, but reaching far beyond the mechanisms and politics of democracy, is the attention being allotted to the physical, legal, and commercial institutionalization of market-oriented economies in Eastern Europe. Both features are as yet fragile. Western assistance could be critical in ensuring that the ongoing transformations are not prematurely derailed. Other countries have on the whole been sympathetic to the transitions in Eastern Europe.

In trying to ensure that the seminal changes in Eastern Europe do indeed contribute maximally to remaking Europe, a wide range of assistance efforts have thus far come to the fore. Some take the form of outright grants of financial aid and emergency food and medical help chiefly committed by governments or intergovernmental organizations. Aside from these direct supports targeted at alleviating critical short-run problems arising from the abruptness of the political and social mobility in Eastern Europe, western governments have sought to provide also more indirect inducements. These include formal and other guarantees, as well as various supports, for private and official capital mobility toward the east; facilitating access to western markets for the east's exports; and even entertaining some form of association of the PETs with the emerging unified market in Europe, whether limited to the EC's Single Market or the Europe of the Eighteen - the EES.

Western approaches to the *problématique* of transition in Eastern Europe have been of the *divide et impera* type, the objectives remaining rather conflated, if defined at all. They are certainly not yet integrated with the aspirations of the PETs, the real needs to make the transition work at a tolerable cost, and the kinds and volumes of assistance that the west may eventually be willing to disburse. Nevertheless, the key issues at stake revolve around a vast array of concerns that determine the engagement of the DMEs in favor of ambitious societal reforms in Eastern Europe. These certainly include political, cultural, nationalistic, economic, historical, social, and demographic factors. Some may set off palpable shocks on the European continent with wide-ranging repercussions for social and political stability, economic buoyancy, and international security. Critical has been strengthening the forces that may soon lead most of these countries to assume the key features of PETs (including full-fledged markets, private property, and quick integration into the world economy and merger into its institutions). This has on the whole been viewed within the context of the traditional approach of loosening Eastern Europe from the Soviet grips.

Of course, there are vast economic interests at stake as well. The presence of substantially underdeveloped markets of some size (about 289 million individuals in the Soviet Union and roughly 95 million in Eastern Europe (without the ex-GDR), with Poland alone accounting for 38 million; Yugoslavia would add another 24 million) holds the promise, at least in the medium to long run, of a marked expansion of effective European demand as well as supply, provided the eastern markets can be fully integrated and relative scarcities in the west can be replicated in the east. Eastern Europe offers a geographical area, where western countries in time hope to conquer sizable markets. Through the intermediation of commercial and financial agents, especially the transnational corporations (TNCs), they can expect to gain from a substantial presence. Inexpensive and relatively skilled labor together with capital, technology, marketing acumen, and managerial skills from DMEs may prospectively provide western markets with fairly cheap goods, yield substantial profits especially to the TNCs with embodied comparative advantages, and enable these firms to "capture" eastern markets.

Western assistance has by necessity taken on a variety of forms, including balance-of-payments support for countries that embrace far-reaching liberalization of trade and measurable progress toward currency convertiblity. The support provided by national governments, regional organizations, and the multilateral financial institutions to sustain the current account in the PETs has been very sizable, particularly in the case of Hungary and Poland; Czechoslovakia is beginning to gain access to similarly large facilities, although without the humanitarian and food components that were important for Poland, for example. Thus far the key precept has been to facilitate each country's immediate integration into the global concert as the most promising buttress for the reform movement. This would work rather well provided the supply elasticities in PETs were more positive than demonstrated so far. Also very critical is the buoyancy of western markets in which the radically reforming countries can hope to find support for key components of their cherished ambitions.

Otherwise, it might prove useful to set up a mechanism to bridge the possibly formidable chasm between where the PETs now stand and the world to which they will have to conform, including the obstacles to multilateral trade and payments embedded in western markets. It is true that there are few guidelines available that together add up to a custom-made model of how to transform administratively planned economies into MEs. Nonetheless, there should be little doubt about what precisely it is that needs to be done from a purely technical point of view once a consensus exists on what it is that the PET hopes to accomplish. There may be disagreement about the precise sequencing and the speed at which changes are introduced. But certainly a desirable sequencing and its pace can be arrived at, and modified if need be, through some societal consensus, as discussed in Chapter 8. Alternative options with their possible consequences should be submitted to the political leaderships, which must subsequently accommodate their choice with specific popular or social mandates as to what is tolerable and feasible.

The first consideration in mooting the subject is to ascertain what precisely it is that the beneficiary country is hoping to accomplish, perhaps in its regional context. Once the objectives are clearly delineated potential donors should decide for themselves whether or not it is in their political, ideological, humanitarian, or ideological interest to support that effort. Of course, potential donors may wish to influence the decision-making process and indeed the reform intentions of recipients. Assistance may be made conditional on these ideological or other foreign-policy precepts. But that is a subject for foreign policy rather than economics. By affirming this I do not wish to endorse the case for providing unconditional assistance. On the contrary: Donor countries should aim, at least in part, at solidifying the process of reform as formulated through consensus building that they can support after the purposes of the assistance have been clarified.

The second phase revolves around technical advice. Under no circumstance can foreign assistance be considered a substitute for sound macroeconomic management through appropriate institutions and policy instruments, given the set of policy objectives embraced. Aside from production possibilities and the normative elements embedded in the objective function of the economy as a whole, administrative structures are required to ensure that economic agents act in harmony with society's objectives, however derived (Campbell 1966).

The third phase of an assistance program, in my view, involves the determination of the amount of the assistance donor countries are willing to muster for the PETs and in which forms they are disposed to transfer it. A substantial amount of the assistance currently envisaged is conditional. The reasoning is that in such a way donors can target the groups most in need of help. Also, this procedure allows donors to transfer surplus goods (such as from stocks held through massive state subsidies) at a relatively modest incremental cost. However useful such targeting may be, both to reach the envisaged recipient quickly and to make the commitment politically, fiscally, and psychologically acceptable at home, this mode should primarily be limited to emergencies for which customary economic accounting and efficiency criteria do not apply.

Finally, there is the problem of how best to arrange for the efficient transfer of resources and to ensure that the recipient seeks to maximize the return on disbursed assistance. For that, a coherent approach to delivery of assistance under at least some coordinating and supervisory authority would seem useful.

One of the more constructive mechanisms for earmarking assistance without distorting the very fragile decision-making environment in PETs is buttressing the desire to move to currency convertibility and to pursue economic restructuring in spite of sizable obstacles encountered, including those arising from problems related to the management of external payments. In that respect, the problems with external payments of Western Europe after World War II and the cooperative measures devised to alleviate them should be very instructive. Just as the main trading markets of Western Europe were devastated by bilateralism during the 1930s, the ensuing World War, and the apprehensions about restoring stability while moving to a civilian economic setting, the disintegration of the CMEA poses intricate problems for Eastern Europe, the PETs in the first place. To these issues I now turn.

2

The collapse and dissolution of the CMEA

This chapter assesses the state of affairs in the CMEA through early 1991. It is presently slated to be replaced by the OIEC in mid-April. However, this book is manifestly not meant as a review of the meager results and many failures that this organization experienced during its checkered forty-two years. I have had ample opportunity to elaborate on these matters elsewhere (see Brabant 1989a; 1990b; 1991e, h). But I deem it all but impossible to understand what can be done for the PETs at this juncture, and indeed what these countries can now undertake by and for themselves, without carefully weighing the opportunities that regional economic cooperation with or without the CMEA organization present. Traditionally, the CMEA embodied serious drawbacks to smoothly progressing toward any genuine economic reform, especially one anchored to the promotion of markets. Now that the CMEA will soon be dissolved, it may seem quaint to inquire about what could be done in that context. Nonetheless, I perceive several instances in which the foundations of economic cooperation in Eastern Europe could usefully be reslated. I advocate this, although I am fully aware of the allergic reaction of many commentators to even remotely pondering such an option, at least for now.

The core of this chapter is twofold: to summarize briefly the state of affairs with CMEA reform through 1990 and to analyze the prospects of trade and payment relations among the former CMEA members. Section 1 investigates whether there is any purpose at all in exploring the room remaining for intragroup cooperation in the framework of the CMEA's successor organization - the OIEC - given the accelerating erosion of intragroup cooperation since 1989. The apparent outcome of the recent debates on reforming the organization is summarized next. The salient obstacles to more buoyant economic relations in the CMEA and the opportunities for the mutual reinforcement of reform objectives form the subject of Section 3. Next, I detail the disintegration of the orthodox TR trade and payment regimes and what this implies for sustainable levels of economic activity in the area in the short to medium run. A distinction will be drawn among trade and payments for essential inputs (especially fuels and raw materials), manufactures (especially those in support of the existing transportation and capital infrastructure), and consumer goods on the basis of both existing and expected comparative advantages. The chapter concludes with a few pointers to desirable reforms that are feasible even now that the CMEA has been put to eternal rest.

1. The CMEA's demise

In early 1989, the precise founding date still remaining uncertain (Brabant 1989a, pp. 26ff.), the CMEA turned forty. It should have marked the inception of a year of celebrations, not only because of the anniversary. Indeed, beginning with the hard-core negotiations at the summit of late 1986 through the two following Council Sessions of 1987 and 1988 as well as a plethora of ancillary policy meetings, the members had finally agreed on an agenda for negotiating institutional and policy reforms of the organization and the SEI endeavors it sponsored directly or otherwise. This blueprint on far-reaching transformations was promised to be ready as a final policy document in 1989. Commitments were made to the effect that, finally, the CMEA would be revamped with a view to supporting the then ongoing reform efforts in a number of member countries, including most notably the Soviet Union. In some versions of the agenda of what would soon be forthcoming, it was agreed that the CMEA would in fact begin to foster a socialist common market. Whether this time around the deliberations about such an august objective had moved far beyond the declamatory stage remains unknown. There is indeed little evidence that the idea was ever discussed in detail against the backdrop of the real possibilities for cooperation in Eastern Europe. Nonetheless, at least some preliminary investigations were made so as to shape the purposes of such an effective economic union mainly in Eastern Europe. What precisely was held in store for the three developing-country members (Cuba, Mongolia, and Vietnam) will never be known in detail. According to some versions, the European partners had offered to establish a common development fund as a substitute for a wide range of transactions that had previously been subsidized through a bewildering variety of mechanisms. It was widely felt that such voluntaristic, yet erratic, assistance policies could no longer be supported because of their steep cost and also because it would in any case be contrary to the creation of markets (Brabant 1990e, 1991d).

In this connection it bears to recall that, although debates on far-reaching, genuine cooperation reforms were very intense between 1987 and late 1989, the organization had been under considerable scrutiny with a view to promoting various substantive reforms during most of its postwar evolution. In fact, efforts to achieve just that were initiated almost from its very inception in 1949. But they notably failed at that stage, as they would on every subsequent occasion. Yet, when at long last some substantive decisions on streamlining the regional organization and restructuring SEI seemed to be around the corner in the late 1980s, the entire effort was abruptly abandoned and reslated from square one, only to end in utter failure. It is not only the meager results of the aforementioned deliberations that made investigating the CMEA such a depressing occupation. The very painful road toward the reform debates of the late 1980s and the CMEA's evolution by default during the last decade or so have left at best an fortifying pinch for the few scholars and decision makers who may still be bent, if only intellectually, on fostering economic cooperation among some or all countries of Eastern Europe. The organization proved to be unable to transform itself into an effective buttress for even the most modest market-oriented economic reforms in its component economies. In fact, members blatantly failed to formulate viable proposals for altering the political and economic landscape of their complex interrelations, including in trade and payment regimes. All these factors plus the rancor that lingered from the earlier enforced cooperation experience have strengthened the contention that the peculiar international economic organization for all practical purposes died in early 1990, something to be formally acknowledged only toward mid-1991. But to size up the CMEA's *raison d'être* at this juncture solely against the recent political backdrop would be shortsighted. At any rate, it could possibly be a highly misleading way of assessing recent developments and their longer-term implications.

Because the notion "CMEA" has frequently been used in different contexts, it is instructive to clarify precisely what is meant here. Those who had been advocating the CMEA's demise, and presumably now welcome it, do not always make it clear which of its incarnations they were smugly applauding. That the CMEA in some meanings did not die by default at the 45th Council Session in January 1990 must be made absolutely clear. Elucidation of this very point is crucial in pondering the transition phase of even the most liberal PET, including the non-European members (Brabant 1990b, e; 1991d), but they do not form the object proper of this study. Of course, that clarification itself needs to be placed against the backdrop of the rapid political changes and the ambitious aspirations for genuine economic reform since mid-1989 in most of Eastern Europe. Because the structural components as well as the basic nuts and bolts of these contemplated alternatives are as yet to be designed and machined into fairly polished pieces that fit into a coherent, functioning whole, it seems all the more useful to scrutinize the key issues at stake. To do so, I shall examine five cloaks of CMEA economic relations. It will become clear that there is little reason to cheer on the CMEA's dissolution or to ignore the means for priming its remaining life-support system without carefully weighing the alternative options for the various actors in the process.

A first way of looking at the CMEA is its capacity as a regional economic organization entrusted with monitoring and recommending improvements in trade and payment regimes, especially of the European members. From its inception, the CMEA was the organ entrusted with the more general streamlining of the economic relations among its members with a view to fostering production specialization as distinct from market integration pursued in the context of MEs. In that respect, debates on how best to reform the CMEA, as noted, evolved at least from the late 1970s until early 1990. Those that were still on the policy agenda through 1990 stemmed from the obstacles encountered in the attempt of policy makers in all Eastern European countries, but less so in the Soviet Union, to maintain a satisfactory pace of economic growth well above population growth and buoyant intragroup trade expansion in the 1980s. But the accent of how best to tackle these complex facets had, of course, necessarily shifted by 1990.

After protracted debates, the CMEA economic summits of June 1984 and November 1986 (Brabant 1989a, pp. 110-17 and 132-4) identified five areas in which major changes would have to be fostered. These were: (1) rebuilding the institutional features of the regional organization in its own right; (2) revamping relations with the three developing-country members, especially in terms of rendering development assistance, with a view to economizing on limited resources; (3) the most desirable strategy of SEI; (4) the economic mechanism, which envelops macroeconomic policies, institutions, and policy instruments, to take full advantage of the possibilities offered by SEI so as to ensure profitable economic interaction among the component economies; and (5) the desirability of aiming prospectively at the creation of a unified or common market in Eastern Europe and how this could best be fostered.

It is useless to deny that the CMEA as a regional organization had been in considerable disarray well before the mid-1980s. Dysfunctional incompatibilities among the European members in particular had come to the fore at least since the late 1970s. In some respects, one may even trace (see Brabant 1989a, pp. 82-91) the *problématique* all the way back to the failure to act upon the more promising positions taken at the time *Integration Program* (whose full title is *Comprehensive program for the further extension and improvement of cooperation and the development of economic integration by the CMEA member countries*) was launched in the late 1960s and endorsed at the 25th Council Session, Bucharest, 25-29 July 1971 (see Tokareva 1972, pp. 29-103 for an authoritative reproduction). Hopes for its painful recovery have repeatedly been dashed under impulse of weak commitment toward reforming the organization; by now, they have altogether faded.

Excepting the first two reform items, nothing much had been achieved by the time the sociopolitical revolutions of late 1989 in Eastern Europe radically reshaped the landscape and framework for economic interaction within the CMEA. If only because of the inability to reprofile itself as far as the strategy and mechanism of SEI are concerned, the CMEA was by late 1989 all but beyond salvation. Certainly, all vestiges of socialism and "integration" with the Soviet economy by early 1990 were beyond negotiation. These political attitudes are bound to linger at least until thorough democratic political and market-oriented economic reforms in the Soviet Union will be well under way - neither of which is likely to jell any time soon.

With the seesaw changes in political regimes since mid-1989, one may well question whether the reform aspects debated and negotiated in some detail during 1987-1989 are still pertinent to the subsequent policy agenda. Whereas some aspects of the "old" deliberations have undoubtedly been overhauled by the societal mutations in key members, others still confront policy makers with difficult choices. Indeed, the original economic motivations of the debate and their various technical angles are very much germane to the economic transition of especially the PETs. To be useful, however, recent economic and political changes, and indeed a good deal of positive economic realism, on all of these issues need to be factored into the debate.

In its second cloak, the CMEA has frequently been viewed as an alliance with strong political overtones, simply an extension of the Warsaw Treaty Organization (WTO) or Warsaw Pact into the security aspects of international economic dependence. In other words, the organization was seen as essentially providing the economic underpinnings for enhancing military strength and Soviet hegemony over much of the socialist world. There have undoubtedly been periods in postwar intragroup relations when Soviet hegemonic supremacy held sway even over elementary economic considerations. In that respect, many changes both in the Soviet role in Eastern Europe as well as in the merits of the Warsaw Pact. It was formally agreed in February March 1991 to dismantle the military structures by late April 1991, with other elements to follow later.

For now, however, the potential military role of the Soviet Union in Eastern Europe should not yet be downgraded to zero. Yet, I am fairly confident that in this second cloak, namely a direct economic prop of a military alliance, the CMEA or its successor is beyond salvation. This characterization is not meant to disregard the geography and politics of Eastern Europe's relations with the USSR. However, the seminal changes in security and defense "New Thinking" under Gorbachev's leadership since 1985 considerably weakened the usefulness of the CMEA as an instrument for reinforcing the military linkages in the WTO's context. Of course, the latter were also sharply eroded because of the marked reduction in east-west tensions in the period following the Cold War and the revendication for full sovereignty on the part of the PETs. In that respect, the CMEA certainly was not much alive in recent years. Likewise, there is hopefully no need to resurrect the Warsaw Pact any time soon.

A third possible meaning of the CMEA was as the simple collection of BTPAs. From its inception, the CMEA as a regional organization was kept separate from the way in which the members arranged their reciprocal trade and payments. The heartland of trading in the postwar period has been bilateralism. Not only that, this peculiar trade policy has been anchored to detailed trade contracts negotiated at the intergovernmental level or by institutions directly subordinated to the state monopoly of foreign trade and payments (MFT). The behavior of both was in critical respects geared by the price-equalization mechanism. Literally, that buttressed domestic price and policy autonomy by keeping foreign prices on the whole divorced from domestic prices through government subsidies and taxes. The latter's size depended on the nominal exchange rate chosen.

With the reforms under way, and in view of the inability during most of the 1980s to maintain buoyant economic intercourse and support economic reform through BTPAs, I firmly believe that the CMEA in that respect was dangling at the end of a tightening rope ever since the reform process got under way.

This was especially so for the members that have been engaged in or been envisaging the creation of greater market-orientation. Any effort to devolve financial autonomy to economic agents in a competitive environment is bound to founder under rigid bilateralism. As a result, a strong current has emerged that advocates not only genuine decentralization in economic affairs, but also the dismantling of the traditional bilateralism in favor of anchoring trade to WMPs and conducting settlements in convertible currency. Such seminal shifts in relations within Eastern Europe could not but elicit major changes in this particular character of the CMEA.

As a counterpart of the preceding meaning, the CMEA can also be seen as having been the custodian of its own intragroup arrangements for trade and payments. Though this particular notion of the CMEA is closely related to the former some nontrivial differences must be noted. For most of its existence, until late 1990, the CMEA had indeed its own distinct arrangements for smoothing intragroup trade and payments. These imparted a different meaning to the organization that diverged from it being simply the aggregate of BTPAs. Thus, bilateralism in Eastern Europe was anchored to detailed BTPAs negotiated at rather peculiar TRPs; clearing arranged through the TR at the IBEC, which was also the emittor of the TR; purely formalistic regional multilateralism; and some measure of intragroup capital flows (Brabant 1987a, 1989a). In addition, the field of operation of these instruments was interwoven with the mechanisms for coordinating national economic plans. Through this device some members hoped to foster integration on the basis of production specialization rather than market interactions.

Major transformations have materialized especially in this area. The events since early 1990 have underlined how archaic the traditional TR arrangements for intragroup transactions had become. In fact, in many respects they proved to be utterly dysfunctional in the context of efforts to promote market orientation. But these old ways of conducting business are not yet fully dead for practical reasons. Indeed, some may be sustained for several years into the 1990s as individual countries, even the most radical (see *Rynki Zagraniczne*, 16 March 1991, p. 2) grapple with their own possibilities to disengage from their dependence on intragroup relations. There is no doubt, however, that such arrangements are no longer satisfactory to the key reformers in Eastern Europe and even those that are by and large still overwhelmingly administratively steered.

Finally, the CMEA can be viewed against the backdrop of the regional dependence in trade and payments that crystallized over nearly half a century of economic collaboration. Although there have been serious obstacles to maintaining the trade volumes gradually built up over the years, in part through detailed agreements about intragroup production specialization, all countries continued to depend on each other for between 40 and 80 percent of their overall trade through 1989. Of course, because exchange rates in Eastern Europe until then remained rather meaningless, as explained in Chapter 4, and relative TRPs differed from relative WMPs in a number of respects, it was difficult to measure accurately the degree of relative trade dependence of the various countries in Eastern Europe (see UNECE 1991b, pp. 29-32). Because the ruble - hence the TR - was generally overvalued in terms of convertible currency, any realignment of exchange rates with underlying costs tended to devalue the ruble as well as the TR, and hence lowered the CMEA's share in trade. Note that the actual calculus of real versus nominal measures of dependence was, and remains, far more complex, as discussed later in this chapter. Nonetheless, the proportions given here indicate that these countries for many years relied primarily on each other's commercial capabilities. But such dependence stretched well beyond the simple exchange of goods and related services.

Indeed, substantial components of that trade are funneled through a unique transportation infrastructure. This consists, among others, of oil and gas pipelines, standardized river barges, roads, ocean-going vessels, a common pool of railroad cars, and a uniform electrical-power network. Furthermore, there continues to be a need to service a machine park that has been constituted overwhelmingly with equipment manufactured in Eastern Europe. Not only that, this equipment was designed to produce machinery and other manufactures for eastern demand. Moreover, many human skills, such as in engineering, have been built up with a view to servicing eastern markets.

If only for the aforementioned very pragmatic reasons, and others examined in Chapter 3, the CMEA context is certainly not yet a complete void. Forgoing such commercial ties would require diversion of trade to MEs and very incisive structural changes to be introduced abruptly and necessarily chaotically (Protzman 1991). The cost of the required adaptations to accommodate trade switching and related adjustments on a broad front in PETs would be so massive that one cannot but be concerned about the tensile strength of the sociopolitical fabric, which is already stretched taut, of these countries. But there is another factor to be reckoned with: Although a rational allocation of economic resources within the region would certainly lead to a very different level, geographical direction, and commodity composition of trade than prevailed over the past decades, such a reanchoring of commercial relations on the basis of economic computations would not altogether suppress intragroup trade. In other words, there are significant comparative advantages embodied in resource endowments in the region as a whole. With positive growth anticipated from economic reforms, after some transitory difficulties, also dynamic comparative advantages are bound to materialize. True, proper institutions, instruments, and policies are required to exploit these advantages and thus to enhance welfare in the region and elsewhere as well. These elements are explored in the next chapter.

2. CMEA reform discussions

Since the political watershed of 1989, either the PETs or those economies not yet in a position to enact swift changes paid little attention to the possibilities of pursuing genuine CMEA reform. Any such endeavor should, of course, essentially focus on the fifth meaning of the CMEA just discussed. But there would, naturally, be incidental consequences of establishing institutions, instruments, and policies to enable partners in Eastern Europe to exploit their real comparative advantages for some of the other cloaks too.

Many efforts were made in the 1980s to reform the CMEA from within. That exploration received a major impetus from the two summits of the 1980s (June 1984 and November 1986) and the debates around them (Brabant 1989a, pp. 102-26; 1990b; 1991e, h). A marked change in the drift of the reform deliberations occurred between the November 1986 "working summit" and the subsequent Council Session (the 43rd "Extraordinary" Session[1] in Moscow, 13-14 October 1987). Especially the understandings reached during the latter Session led in late 1987 to the appointment of a reform commission headed by Academician Oleg T. Bogomolov that was formally subordinated to the Executive Committee.[2] Its main mandate was to formulate a comprehensive proposal for incisive reforms to come to grips with the five areas discussed earlier.

The Bogomolov commission's tentative proposals were first mooted during the 44th Council Session (Prague, 5-7 July 1988), where they should have constituted the major contribution to the ongoing reform discussion. But the intensity and scope of the debates that erupted after the Moscow Session suggested that finalizing a blueprint for earnest CMEA reform would require more time. The realities of economic reform in Eastern Europe were evidently too complex to be dealt with expeditiously. In the end, the reformulated reform proposals were meant to be the key input into the seminal discussions of the third economic summit of the 1980s, which was intended to chart SEI into the 1990s and beyond. This summit had initially been slated for March 1989 in Prague (Brabant 1990b, 1991e). Its recommendations were then to have been confirmed during the subsequent 45th Council Session, originally scheduled for June 1989 in Sofia. The first meeting never materialized and the second was repeatedly postponed. In the end, it was not convened until January 1990, right after the extraordinary transitions in Eastern Europe's political landscape. This Session highlighted, if further need there was, that the efforts of the preceding two years had unquestionably reached an all but unbridgeable impasse (Brabant 1989a, pp. 394-418; 1990b; 1991e).

The 45th Council Session (Sofia, 9-10 January 1990) had originally been programmed as the crowning achievement of a three-year intensive search for

[1] An "Extraordinary Session" was one usually convened out of the sequence of "Regular Sessions." This should statutorily have been held during the second quarter of the year, but that rhythm was rarely observed in recent years. For an explanation of the special nature of the 1987 Council Session, see Brabant 1989a, pp. 140-2.

[2] This was the key CMEA organ in-between Council Sessions. The Council Session itself was officially the "supreme organ" of the CMEA. For details on the evolution of the organization's structure, see Brabant 1989a, pp. 127-205.

CMEA reform. After arduous negotiations, the Bogomolov reform commission tabled there its proposals for resuscitating the CMEA and all it could stand for, including SEI, and the policies, institutions, and policy instruments for effectively moving forward with the creation of a socialist common market. The new leaderships of Eastern Europe, however, simply rejected the recommendations out of hand for their "timidity," given the radical reform sentiment then sweeping the area.

The items that the Bogomolov commission tabled at the Session have, unfortunately, never been divulged. But they are unlikely to have diverged markedly from the mainstream themes contested during the debates of the preceding two years, as summarized earlier. Likewise, the concrete objections of the new ministers of economic and financial affairs are not known. However, from the campaigns around the Session, there is no doubt that the very essence of economic cooperation within the CMEA context, namely plan coordination and the TR trade and payment regimes, amounted to a huge thorn in the eyes of those bent on moving their economies quickly to ME status.

Encountering such stiff opposition to reform proposals that it had earlier blessed, the Soviet Union at the Session offered to move swiftly, beginning in January 1991, to commence trading at WMPs and settling reciprocal accounts through convertible-currency clearing or perhaps even actual payments. The proposal tabled by Soviet Prime Minister Nikolay I. Ryzhkov has, to my knowledge, never been spelled out in detail. My summary is based on what I have learnt from the published discussions at the Session as well as private conversations with a host of well-informed observers in Eastern Europe and elsewhere. Although probably not entirely plucked out of thin air, as so many recent Soviet "initiatives" in international affairs appear to have been, Ryzhkov's recommendation certainly had not been well thought-out, given the old and new realities of Eastern Europe. But it initially responded to Eastern European pressures to do away with all vestiges of the TR regime. The switchover would entail a major shift away from the traditional patterning of TRPs after average WMPs of the preceding five years and clearing within the TR settlements mechanism supervised by the IBEC (for details, see Brabant 1987b).

Though Eastern Europe exhibited some enthusiasm for such a shift, if only because it corresponded exactly to revendications made prior to the Session by the newfangled leaderships in Czechoslovakia and Poland in particular, there was also considerable apprehension about the clearing aspects and the fact that the Soviet Union and some other Eastern European partners, let alone the developing-country members, would not have genuine firms to conduct commercial negotiations for which their microeconomic agents could assume full financial responsibility. This feature would be especially critical in conducting trade in manufactured goods - the backbone of commercial growth among developed countries in the postwar period and the newly industrializing economies (NIEs) more recently. This would in all likelihood exert negative effects on the clearing of trade as market adjustments would at best be rather haphazard. To the degree that constraints on clearing remained, the determination of the level, commodity composition, and geographical distribution of trade would continue to be affected by them.

In roughly predictable CMEA fashion, the Session in the end resolved to appoint another commission and entrust it this time with the formulation of "radical" reform options. It was initially headed by Ernő Kemenes, chairman of the Planning Commission of Hungary, and since May 1990, following the transition in the Hungarian Government after the first free parliamentary elections, by Béla Kádár, Minister of Foreign Economic Relations of Hungary. This commission, assisted by at least three technical working groups on reform dealing with organizational, legal, and financial-economic matters, met on and off chiefly during the first half of 1990. Its deliberations focused mainly on the desirability of charting a new mission for the CMEA and, as far as economics *per se* is concerned, on what precisely that should entail in terms of regional organization, trade and payment regimes, and policy instruments. In this context, it was called upon to focus its proposals in particular on the requirements for reviving CMEA trade and payments and on how best to provide an impetus to integration "from the bottom up," even if at the risk of splitting up the CMEA edifice into several tiers. The technical experts assisting the reform commission were to have prepared their proposals by late April 1990. The commission was originally slated to consider them in May with a view to preparing its own recommendations to the "leading" CMEA organs around mid-year. Soon thereafter, probably in September according to the original timetable, another full-scale economic summit or a substantive Council Session was to have been convoked. These schedules seriously slipped as the deliberations proved to be far more rancorous and protracted than anyone had anticipated.

Some Eastern European observers maintain that the Kádár commission concluded an agreement at its third session in late June 1990 and that the understandings reached there were immediately transmitted to the Executive Committee; Minister Kádár intimated as much to me in an interview held in early September 1990. The Executive Committee was expected formally to consider these matters in late October or early November 1990. This would have been the prelude to either another full-scale economic summit or at least a Council Session. Other commentators claim that the third session of the commission in June was far from unanimous on what should be done with the CMEA and suggest that further deliberations in July and August and even more recently were required, as later confirmed by Mr. Vyacheslav V. Sychev (1990, p. 19) - the CMEA's Secretary. There would, however, now seem little doubt that, sometime in the third quarter of 1990 some agreement was transmitted to the Executive Committee for its consideration as soon as possible. But these were apparently far from rounded off, as in late November further negotiations on issues related to the new name and statutes of the successor organization were still being debated as reported in the daily and weekly press (see *Hospodářské Noviny*, 1990:116, p. 4 and *Népszabadság*, 23 November 1990,

p. 8). Its recommendations were expected subsequently to be transmitted to a full-scale economic summit or Council Session. But that could have come to pass only if the Executive Committee had unanimously approved the reform of the CMEA, rather than being asked to extinguish the organization without having forged a successor framework. The deadline of late 1990 slipped by without the meeting having been convened, allegedly at the "request" of the USSR. These recommendations were finally discussed by the Executive Committee on 4-5 January 1991. Its proposals were then transmitted to the Council Session - the 46th scheduled for Budapest - to put a formal end to the CMEA later that month and initiate the OIEC; it was subsequently rescheduled to 27-28 February 1991. Also those dates slipped by. The deathknell meeting is now "finally" scheduled to be convened 17-18 April 1991 in Moscow.

The proposals that may have been endorsed in mid- or late 1990 are not, of course, fully known. In spite of sweeping reforms and eastern-type *glasnost'*, the CMEA continued to be a curiosum as far as details about its actual and planned operations are concerned. Yet, there is sufficient evidence that the room for genuine regional economic cooperation during the deliberations was exceedingly narrow. The position of especially Czechoslovakia, Hungary, and Poland was twofold. On the one hand, they sought to downgrade the organization and what it symbolized into something like the OECD at best - a weak regional secretariat devoid of any muscle as regards integration tasks. The successor organization would essentially be a secretarial organ entrusted with preparing briefs for consideration at the political level, collecting and disseminating information, and perhaps initiating technical and macroeconomic research. But it would be without any muscle in terms of enhancing regional economic integration. To reanchor the organization and much of what it had stood for in terms of intragroup trade and payments, as well as change its name, two major documents were finalized. One deals with the conceptualization of a new system of economic cooperation among the former CMEA members. The other encompasses the statutes of the new organization and indeed the final rechristening of the CMEA.

The proposed reform was threefold. First, new statutes for the successor organization were drawn up. As a weak regional economic secretariat, it was to have been entrusted with preparing briefs for consideration by policy makers; collecting, organizing, processing, and disseminating statistical information; and drafting background reviews of the current economic situation of the members in their regional and global contexts for intragroup consultations, and possibly technical and macroeconomic research on demand. The project on the new concept of cooperation still left room for joint action in material production, science, technology, infrastructure, fuels and energy, the environment, and information, among other tasks. But these were to have been regulated through specific, mostly bilateral, agreements "in full harmony with global economic conditions," not through statutory obligations to collaborate, as this had previously been enshrined in CMEA documents. In fact, the drift of the arguments was strongly in favor of regulating henceforth all these other activities through *ad hoc* agreements between pairs of interested countries, thereby literally removing all vestiges of multilateral economic cooperation.

Second, the CMEA's name was to be altered together with its new organizational makeup. Basically three contenders were reportedly being considered: Council for Economic Cooperation, Organization for Economic Cooperation, and Council for Mutual Economic Interactions. Any designation preserving the Russian acronym for CMEA - SEV - was highly favored by the Soviet negotiators and, of course, keenly contested by most Eastern European participants in the debates. In this connection, it is worth reminding ourselves that much of the remnants of the CMEA throughout the reform debate, even on trivial matters, remained shrouded in mystery. Thus, after having bandied about with several potentially acceptable names *Hospodářské Noviny* (1990:116, p. 4) with date line 31 October 1990 reported that OIEC had been selected. This was confirmed by Zdenko Pírek (1990) in a report prepared at the latest in early November 1990. Reporting later from Moscow, however, in an interview in *Népszabadság* (23 November 1990, p. 8), specialists of the CMEA still characterized it as the "internal working title" of the new organization. The January Executive Committe meeting finally settled the matter and recommended *Organizatsiya mezhdunarodnogo ekonomicheskogo kooperatsiya* or OIEC - very much like the Organisation for European Economic Co-operation (OEEC), with the 'I' being substituted for the 'E,' in the postwar period. But the new organ's mandate, formal as well as informal, will be vastly more secretarial.

The revamped organization will reportedly be sharply slimmed down (Budzinski 1991), both in terms of structure and staffing. There will be only two key organs. A secretariat will be entrusted with economic research and related tasks of a technical nature such as those already cited. The CMEA's futuristic headquarters in the form of an "open book" near the Moskva river in Moscow will apparently be kept, although several commentators and participants in the reform debates favored moving the new organization's center to Central Europe - perhaps Prague. Staffing of the new organization will be only a fraction of the roughly 2,000 professionals mandated for the CMEA in late 1987 or the less than 1,400 that were to have been in place in 1988.[3] The Secretariat's activities will henceforth be charted under the aegis of a representative organ composed of national government delegations. Whether it will be patterned primarily after the former CMEA Executive Committee or rather the looser Council Session remains unclear at this juncture.

[3] The staff mandated in late 1987 had been slated for a reduction by some 31 percent as a result of the reform moves of 1987-1988. Most of this was to have been accomplished through attrition as international staff on secondment was rotated. However, I have not been able to ascertain that such a sharp compression did indeed take place before the CMEA's demise.

Finally, all substantive matters of intragroup trade and payments as well as attendant variants of economic, scientific, technical, and other forms of cooperation will henceforth be regulated bilaterally. The focal mechanism for smoothing commerce was envisaged to revolve around market operations conducted by financially independent agents acting on their own account, but within a coherent national macroeconomic framework, including for commercial and foreign-exchange policies. The main objective was to establish a businesslike environment to approximate as closely as possible the conditions prevailing elsewhere in the world. This genuine "normalization" of relations in Eastern Europe has been repeatedly stressed in the tortuous debates about the CMEA's future.

Parallel with the reform deliberations, a sequence of intensive bilateral negotiations was inaugurated. For most countries, these are still continuing in connection with the formulation and implementation of trade and payments agreements for 1991. Particularly vexing is that previously ironclad BTPAs now no longer guarantee execution, given the fundamental disarray in decision making in the Soviet Union. These talks have aimed at resolving many outstanding and prospective issues through purely bilateral relations, but they have not been confined, as during most of the postwar period, to what could be hammered out by government negotiators. Indeed, rather than search for multilateral solutions for the shared trade and payment problems, most members have actively been reinforcing bilateral relations through *ad hoc* arrangements that fall short, at least for now, of placing their reciprocal exchanges on a full-fledged market-clearing, convertible-currency footing. These arrangements, in some cases, aim at emplacing actual or imputed WMPs and eventually moving to full-scale convertible-currency trading among independent firms. Czechoslovakia, Hungary, Poland, and the Soviet Union signed enabling bilateral agreements[4] effective 1 January 1991 (but with exceptions as reported in *Rynki Zagraniczne*, 16 March 1991, p. 2).[5] But the evidence about how inevitable imbalances will be worked off has remained scant and opaque.

At least until the recently signed Czechoslovak-Soviet agreement (*Izvestiya*, 5 September 1990, p. 5 and *Rudé Právo*, 2 September 1990, pp. 1, 2), there was not a single hard sign that these countries had resolved what to do with bilateral imbalances that are bound to emerge unless the confines of bilateralism

[4] Also the former GDR had reached such an understanding with the Soviet Union. Since 3 October 1990, these relations have become an integral component of the "package unification deal" struck by the FRG with the Soviet Union, however. This means that, in fact, the GDR's commitments have been assumed by the FRG government. The latter is trying to facilitate execution of such contracts through subsidies, loans, loan guarantees, and similar supports.

[5] Poland and the Soviet Union already earlier resolved to transact up to 15 percent of their committed TR trade for 1990 in convertible currency. Because of the sharp divergence between Soviet commitments and what actually took place, the share of convertible-currency trade in total Polish-Soviet trade in 1990 was sharply higher than the envisaged 15 percent. Also, for 1991 TR transactions with the Soviet Union were continued to end-March.

explicitly suppress them. Hungary continues to posture that it will not engage in any agreement that deviates from regular convertible-currency trade and payments, thus settling the balancing issue, provided an agreement can be reached. But it has in the meantime allowed transactions negotiated in TR before the end of 1990 to be settled on clearing account at least during the first quarter of 1991. For some time in late 1989, Czechoslovakia took the same attitude and, after wavering during much of 1990, apparently struck such a deal in late August and finally on 16 November 1990; further outstanding issues were settled in late 1990 and indeed some still are on the negotiating table at the time of writing.

There are several features of the present arrangements, especially in relations with the Soviet Union, that should be borne in mind. This point can be illustrated on the basis of what is known about the Czechoslovak-Soviet trade agreement. Instead of full-fledged world-market conditions, trade will apparently be conducted at three levels. The essential or core arrangement is bartering most of Soviet exports of fuels and raw materials for Czechoslovak manufactured goods to be enshrined in "indicative lists," a notion that loomed large over Finnish-Soviet trade for many years. These transactions will be conducted on a clearing basis with settlements effected in commodities. Enterprises will still have to negotiate concrete agreements within the confines of the overall barter arrangement. These agreements can be hammered out at three levels, namely the union as a whole, individual Soviet republics, and lower-level organs, including regions. It is estimated that in the near term about two thirds of trade will be transacted in this manner or some combination of hard currency and barter, especially as concerns the periodic settlement of imbalances. The remainder of trade will be transacted at "world" terms and can be negotiated among enterprises acting on their own account. These arrangements may involve pure barter or settlement in any combination of barter and convertible currency. The agreement specifies that Czechoslovakia will initially be able to draw upon its accumulated trade surplus with the Soviet Union, but only after the endorsement of a "proper" exchange coefficient, something yet to be negotiated.[6] A Soviet spokesman held this agreement to be indicative of the type of trading relations that the Soviet Union was intent on negotiating with the rest of Eastern Europe.

[6] Minister Václav Klaus was in the Soviet Union in early November 1990 to negotiate this coefficient. Apparently he brought back some agreement whereby the transactions of Czechoslovakia with the Soviet Union would be kept "on special accounts" in Moscow and Prague, suggesting pure clearing. The coefficient was apparently negotiated when Deputy Prime Minister Valeš went to the Soviet Union in December 1990. It is reportedly one dollar for one ruble basis. According to reliable information, so far nothing has been settled on how this claim can be utilized to offset prospective Czechoslovak deficits with the Soviet Union. Also, nothing has been arranged on how present and future imbalances will be regularized.

As noted, ongoing discussions leave marginal scope for bringing order in Eastern Europe's intragroup trade and payments, regardless of the claims lodged on and off by various policy makers. Short of fully embracing WMPs and convertible currency as the principal means of settlement or of being able to divert trade without incurring sizable terms-of-trade and export-revenue losses, it might be useful to look at a successor regime that is manifestly not anchored to barter or bilateralism. With some political goodwill the CMEA in its fifth connotation could be revamped, as examined in Chapter 3.

3. Salient obstacles to buoyant intragroup interactions

Since mid-1989, economic relations among the CMEA members have been considerably buffeted by powerful crosswinds. Two technical aspects thereof deserve to be clarified. One is that these countries have been experiencing severe problems in clearing their reciprocal trade. Commitments made in trade agreements have been openly flouted more and more, as noted, in part because of recent shifts in the terms of trade due to the TRP formula. These made it difficult for oil-importing countries in potential surplus with oil exporters to maintain committed flows without incurring substantial net exports. Furthermore, unanticipated developments in output levels and shifting export priorities, particularly of Soviet energy, have further aggravated bilateral imbalances. Reluctant to incur TR surpluses, which are difficult to mobilize, several countries have inaugurated unprecedented domestic policy measures to stem exports especially to the Soviet Union. Particularly severe has been the abrupt change in cross-rates. For example, Poland devalued the ruble against the dollar on 1 January 1990 to 4.5. This compared to 2.2 in early 1989, 2.5 in mid-year, and 3.2 in December 1989. Because of its TR surplus, it further devalued the ruble for transactions conducted outside the trade protocol on 28 May 1990 to 9.5 and on 1 August 1990 to 19; for a few days it was even as high as 95! The cross-rate was reset again to 9.5 on 24 September 1990. Needless to say that this vacillation must have perplexed Polish exporters. A similar trade policy germinated in Hungary but not by manipulating the exchange rate. Rather, in early 1990 Hungary forcibly cut exports to the Soviet Union, even at the risk of forcing several key firms, such as the Ikarus bus works, into financial jeopardy. It succeeded in holding the surplus down, but with nominal trade value for the year as a whole remaining sharply below earlier transaction magnitudes.

These examples illustrate the grave problems that arise when countries conduct their trade in a currency that is not even transferable. Rather than extend nearly interest-free loans at a time of sizable pressure on the external payments with MEs, the potential surplus countries in Eastern Europe on the whole preferred not to live up to their obligations under the relevant trade agreements; mainly the Soviet Union retaliated by further cutting oil and gas deliveries, thereby setting off a new round of downward adjustments of realizable trade volumes. The result was a gradual contraction of intragroup trade in 1989 and a sharp drop in 1990. The cutbacks foreseen for 1991 are unprecedented and cannot but cause painful adjustments at a time of already severely limited import possibilities from MEs. This tendency is being sharply accentuated by the politically and bureaucratically motivated posturing around the trade protocols for 1991 and apparent disagreement about where to go from here with intragroup economic relations. This adverse circumstance will continue to hamper smooth trading even if the decision in principle to move toward convertible-currency settlement of transactions evaluated at WMPs were to be realized any time soon.

Relations have also been strained for practical reasons on account of diverging economic mechanisms. Reforming countries that seek to steer their economy rapidly according to market criteria encounter problems in dealing with partners that, by and large, still adhere to detailed administrative planning. Matters are becoming much worse in relations with the Soviet Union, given its administrative and political chaos. There are many angles of the latter situation that could be discussed. Perhaps most important for our purpose is the cloud that hangs over who possesses resources. There is as a result very pronounced uncertainty about the executability of any contract negotiated at any level. Inasmuch as the Eastern European economies are heavily interdependent, as noted earlier, gradually reserving ampler room for autonomous microeconomic decisions that are coordinated through proper macroeconomic policies can proceed only if intragroup relations too are placed on a solid economic footing.

Both developments have contributed to the sharp contraction in levels of economic activity throughout the group reported in Chapter 1. By this I do not mean to intimate that the current economic crisis of Eastern Europe stems solely or even fundamentally from obstacles encountered in clearing intragroup trade and payments. The roots of the economic malaise in the region unquestionably lie much deeper. Hindrances in trade and payments reflect only on the surface these more fundamental obstacles. But the peculiar TR trade and payments arrangements and the problems of streamlining them in line with comparative advantages as perceived by enterprises have not at all helped. The pervasive uncertainty about the reconceptualization of the intragroup economic mechanism in line with the common interests of participants has further complicated matters. In the meantime, regional trade is being needlessly compressed simply because payments imbalances cannot be accommodated. Furthermore, the unconventional ways in which intragroup trade and payments are still being conducted in Eastern Europe weigh heavily on the pace and direction of the more ambitious national economic reforms. For that reason, some of the PETs prefer to reduce their heavy dependence on intragroup commerce and to place the remainder on a convertible-currency footing. This gives rise to two vexing conundrums. One concerns how to accomplish this trade diversion. The other addresses the question of transforming the remainder into genuine convertible-currency transactions conducted primarily by autonomous firms acting on the strength of their own profit motive.

Because the Eastern European countries were tightly interlinked in their trade, at least until 1989, and remain dependent on each other's markets for many products, it would be very costly in the short run to indulge in substantial trade diversion for its own sake. Also, the economic structures in place, including the capital stock, can be redesigned for western markets and many of the skilled workers can be retrained in support of such a renovated production profile only at a high socioeconomic cost. Much of the available knowledge and embodied technology would need to be scrapped altogether if a significant diversion of trade were to be carried out quickly. Furthermore, as already noted, the transportation infrastructure in its broad sense is overwhelmingly inward oriented. The alternative is to amortize gradually those assets that still yield competitive goods for the Eastern European markets but for which there is little, if any, demand elsewhere, and to retrain employees over time.

There is, of course, a cost involved in maintaining the present inefficient production structure for now. When to switch one for the other depends essentially on the comparative cost of temporarily supporting inefficient production structures as opposed to scrapping them for new investments; this may not be forthcoming soon owing to the scarcity of capital and the rising need for social supports, starting from a much lower level of economic activity. Even if the PETs wanted to incur such a cost now because they thought it politically opportune to pursue this goal assiduously, for practical purposes the adjustment could only be absorbed over time. There would, therefore, remain a considerable demand, for example, for spare parts, components, maintenance, and service to keep the obsolete machine park running, at least to supply the residual Eastern European demand. Furthermore, unloading and processing facilities for critical fuels and raw materials other than those directly linked to intragroup, especially Soviet, supplies are simply inadequate to blot up a sudden trade diversion of any substantial magnitude.

Perhaps more fundamental than short-term dependence is the presence of static comparative advantages within Eastern Europe's ambit. Only some have thus far been exploited. With restructuring, a certain proportion of these exploited advantages will disappear together with the emergence of new products and the changeover of personnel and decision making in firms that are gradually gaining greater autonomy (see Chapter 3). But other opportunities should be taken into account. Trade throughout Eastern Europe has thus far, by and large, been determined not by scarcity indicators but by planning priorities that were on the whole radially linked to the Soviet economy rather than the exploitation of relative cost or price differences. Furthermore, they were heavily focused on exchanging Soviet fuels and raw materials for manufactured products, chiefly investment goods, from Eastern Europe. If markets are created, there will be room to exploit such actual cost differentials and improve allocative and productive efficiency. Furthermore, as a result of national reforms and structural change, also dynamic comparative advantages are bound to crystallize from shifts in demand and supply, productivity gains, as well as income effects expected to emanate therefrom (see Chapter 3). For that, proper institutions, trade policies, and commercial policy instruments are urgently required to guide the PETs into choosing trade lines in which they have or hope soon to have a true comparative advantage.

Even if a dramatic change in the geographical distribution of trade were to be an explicit policy objective in its own right, the paramount technical issue of how to accommodate intragroup relations in the interim, until the regional cooperation mechanism can be thoroughly overhauled or the PETs can redirect a substantial part of their trade to MEs, remains to be addressed. This invokes concerns about the transition. Regarding the transformation of the TR pricing and payment systems into WMPs and convertible-currency clearing or payments, matters are somewhat different from the issues pertaining to the desire to diversify trading markets.

It is important to distinguish transactions among PETs from those conducted with unreformed partners. Once domestic prices are aligned with those observed in east-west trade to avoid excessive arbitrage, firms in PETs can negotiate prices and quantities of transactions on the basis of their own profit motive. Only then can one properly speak of market-clearing prices - WMPs, if you wish - in intragroup trade. WMPs will by definition filter through into that process because of the resolve of PETs to link their trade with domestic prices. Microeconomic agents in such economies should not be concerned about the selection of exchange rates and the settlement of imbalances - both tasks for the macroeconomic management of trade and foreign-exchange policies. Placing such trade on a dollar-cash basis invokes two apprehensions in the short run. One stems from the need to raise the size of current transaction balances of scarce foreign exchange. The other arises from the distinct possibility that the country may exacerbate its deficit and thus have to raise its convertible-currency reserves. The severity of both policy concerns can be eased through a multilateral clearing scheme (see Chapter 5).

Transactions of economic agents of PETs with countries that do not even remotely strive for genuine markets, and thus the creation of a substantial number of autonomous agents able to compete with each other, cannot be conducted by firms only. Prices in such transactions must of necessity be negotiated, usually at a fairly high administrative rung, if only to ensure that the contract can be executed. There may be a desire to emulate WMPs. But the current debate on doing so revolves entirely around "constructed" or "imputed" WMPs that have little to do with underlying scarcities in either the PETs or the nonreforming eastern partners. Though it is not yet clear what precisely is meant, most likely the imputation process will involve documenting prices charged by "leading" western firms. For example, the price quoted for a tape recorder produced by Philips or Sony would be taken as the "indicative" WMP for a Soviet tape recorder, perhaps after some adjustments for the most overt styling and performance differentials. This rather arbitrary procedure has in the past given rise to numerous disputes that have needlessly aggravated CMEA relations (Brabant 1987b, pp. 113-30). Furthermore, to the extent that quota trade is involved it would be undesirable to let these distorted prices filter through into the reforming domestic economies, unless firms in the unreformed country could decide on prices and quantities - a rather unlikely eventuality. But authorities in the PET should, of course, be apprehensive about potential imbalances that may drain scarce foreign exchange. A proper exchange-rate policy may go some way toward eliciting more rational microeconomic behavior *vis-à-vis* the distorted partner market.

To reconcile the trade and payment regimes that prevailed until late 1990 with the aspirations of the reforming economies, gradual accommodation through economic discipline is required. On that basis, processes that cannot be justified on solid economic grounds must be phased out as quickly as circumstances permit. That is not to say that such activities should be suppressed forthwith. The reforming economy may find it cheaper to subsidize such production over some period of time than to provide welfare benefits in a situation where supply is rather inflexible in the short run and the threat of chronic unemployment, as a result, serious. Others that ought to be fostered on the strength of both static and dynamic comparative advantages are in need of more suitable accommodation than these countries have thus far been able to muster.

4. Reforming the trade and payment regimes

The core components of the CMEA trade regime through 1990 were market segmentation through the MFT, price equalization, and BTPAs. These elements and their ramifications run counter to the very essence of the reform's intentions and must, therefore, be removed soonest. For east-west relations, it is essentially up to each individual country to come to grips with realities. As regards eastern trade, however, matters cannot be satisfactorily resolved unilaterally. All that countries individually can do is to filter through into trade negotiations as much as possible the emerging rationality in the domestic economy and to take advantage of opportunities for intragroup reform (see Brabant 1990f).

A three-phased approach could usefully be considered. At the center stands the question of how best to ensure that domestic economic decisions, especially in the microeconomic sphere, will not be overburdened by the irrational prices and administrative commercial regulations so prevalent in intragroup relations for more than forty years. In the short run, central authorities that have signed away or inherit commitments in formal BTPAs may feel impelled to honor these obligations for now. To do so, *ex post* subsidies and taxes need to be instituted for all such trade flows. This is necessary to safeguard against the likely eventuality that the transition toward effective competition based on WMP signals would otherwise be obstructed or hollowed out from below. This mechanism would function in much the same vein as the erstwhile price-equalization account (Brabant 1989a, pp. 201-3). Of course, if trade with world markets is very small the anchor to subsidies and taxes will have to be constructed on the basis of the *desirable* relative price pattern in the reforming economy, given domestic economic scarcities.

The second step should ensure that the PET leaders negotiate the next sequence of BTPAs chiefly on the basis of the microeconomic efficiency guidelines prevailing domestically. Practical reasons may necessitate that also these agreements be negotiated - or validated - bilaterally, as under the traditional TR regimes, at a fairly high administrative level rather than by individual firms. Even so, these deliberations need to be guided as much as possible by the emerging indicators of a more rational allocation pattern so that government negotiators engage firms for what they can economically support. Trade obligations entered into that are not economically warranted, hence for which firms cannot normally make a profit, should be subsidized from or taxed by the general budget. Because this may be cumbersome, bilateral trade flows may have to be curtailed, including to preserve approximate current-account balance.

The final step consists in working toward reforming intragroup economic relations from within the trade regimes in place. This can take several forms. One would be outright replacement of the administrative integration mechanism with a decision-making environment anchored closely to economic efficiency indicators in the emerging market-oriented countries. Another would be to seek groupwide reform with the promotion of direct enterprise relations as core. If firms from a reforming economy can take advantage of the nonscarcity pricing incentives maintained through administrative regulations in partner countries, there is no reason why they should be discouraged from exploiting this temporary niche for profit making through legitimate arbitrage, provided settlement problems are addressed adequately at the macroeconomic level. Would engaging in such trade retard structural adjustment, defer gaining a more competitive position in world markets, or freeze an inefficient production structure, as argued by many observers (Inotai 1990)? That is a fallacious argument, as argued in Chapter 7. Suffice it for now to note that if firms operating on a competitive basis are satisfied with earning the gains from arbitrage and no other agent is *willing* to contest those profits so that the former would be encouraged to seek higher profits elsewhere, there is nothing wrong with producing goods that are not at world level, whatever the latter claim may mean!

In this connection, it needs to be recognized that there are now several countries of Eastern Europe wedded to pursuing radical economic reform. Relations among them could increasingly be based on simple market relations conducted by firms whose behavior is guided by the profit motive, provided a solution can be found for the imbalances that are likely to emerge as countries move toward full-fledged marketization. I appreciate that this cannot be done right away as the reforming countries are still overwhelmingly steered through administrative methods. It would, therefore, seem advisable to look for ways to facilitate payments and thus to forestall the further erosion of trade.

Arguably the most critical payments problem among the CMEA members is twofold. One is the chronic shortage of convertible currency. Likewise, external pressures are such that these countries are extremely reluctant to earmark this limited foreign exchange for defraying payments that used to be denominated in TRs and cleared in some fashion through the TR settlements mechanism. If the Soviet federation were to disintegrate into several *de facto* external trade and payment regions, the problems faced by the PETs would multiply, yet be easier to resolve provided an accommodating mechanism is put in place. There are several ways in which the issue could be tackled. One would entail opening up Eastern European markets to competition. Another would be creating a convertible-currency fund for the reforming countries. Also, an effort could be made to tie such a fund to reforms anchored to moving directly toward current-account convertibility. For reasons explained in Chapter 4, this should for now enable all holders of national currency to obtain foreign exchange in payment for current merchandise and invisible obligations other than those stemming from the need to service outstanding debts. In my view, the first option - the "big bang" approach - is too costly, even if it were feasible for sociopolitical reasons. The second solution may simply throw good money at maintaining a bad situation. The third alternative strikes me as not only being in line with what the reforming countries and their western donors appear to be aiming at. It would also hold the reforming countries to an agreed-upon schedule of reforms and enable the donor countries to influence that process through tight macroeconomic surveillance.

In deliberating about instituting an payment facility, it might be useful to rethink the experiences with the European Payments Union (EPU) after World War II. Whether the course then adopted was wise, in retrospect, is not really the issue here (see Brabant 1990c, pp. 103-19). What matters is how the EPU contributed to Western Europe's return to convertibily and envigorated intragroup economic cooperation. But the principal arguments in this debate need to be briefly recalled. Revisionist economic historians argue that Europe was already well on its way to recovery before aid under the Marshall Plan became available, that the latter aid accrued in particular in support of current-account deficits rather than of imports to buttress private investment, and that countries with endemic balance-of-payments problems were thereby dissuaded from swiftly overhauling with determination their pervasive administrative controls and interferences in economic affairs, including in foreign trade. Some of the latter were remnants of the economic nationalism that prevailed in the 1930s or were imposed during World War II; but restraints were also adopted for balance-of-payments reasons after the war. In spite of the at times acrimonious debates among economic historians on the specific contribution of the Marshall Plan to European recovery after World War II (Diebold 1988; Hogan 1987; Knapp

1981; Milward 1987, 1988, 1990; Rees 1963; Wexler 1983; Wood 1986), there has been little dispute about the EPU's role in these countries regaining current-account convertibility. Certainly, from the very beginning some observers (Dittrich 1954, Hieronymi 1973) decried the administrative complexity and weak supervisory authority. But the balance in the end tilt against these justifiable objections. Was that a fortuitous outcome?

Policy makers in Western Europe at the time had committed themselves to pursuing economic stability and gradually reintroducing full-fledged market relations, but only after regaining domestic stability. Realization of this ambition was being markedly hampered, and occasionally explicitly thwarted, by the severe dollar shortage, given the importance of foreign trade to the reconstruction of the war-damaged economies. Whether this constraint on flexibility with external payments could have been removed by other means than adherence to rather inflexible domestic policies, an overvalued exchange rate, and a wide spectrum of exchange and trade controls is a matter of counterfactual history that can never be satisfactorily revolved. The point is that to manage such trade, that is to avoid chronic external problems, Western Europe found it necessary to resort to a wide spectrum of exchange and trade controls, including through formal bilateralism. This confined the mutually reinforcing benefits from buoyant intragroup commerce for economic recovery and growth. The EPU was created precisely to bolster opportunities for such intragroup trade by eliminating bilateralism and encouraging countries, even those facing severe payments problems, to opt for multilateral settlements and trade promotion. Furthermore, the EPU provided a carrot for countries to liberalize their trade regime as debtors were not immediately held fully responsible in convertible currency. Neither could creditors right away fully benefit from their surplus. But the asymmetry in settlements tended to encourage exports. A capital fund in dollars contributed by the United States in the context of the European Recovery Program (ERP) ensured that the asymmetry could be covered. When countries became chronic debtors or creditors, the Managing Board recommended remedial action, usually prodding chronic creditors to institute more expansionary policies, especially by liberalizing trade, and debtors to pursue contractionary policies through the reduction in domestic absorption. By requiring that intragroup payments be increasingly effected in fungible assets managed through the EPU (Kaplan and Schleiminger 1989; Rees 1963; Tew 1967, pp. 109-23; Triffin 1957, pp. 168ff.), by 1958 Western Europe essentially regained convertibility in the sense of article VIII of the Articles of Agreement of the International Monetary Fund (IMF or Fund).

Judging from the recently published history of EPU's operations (Kaplan and Schleiminger 1989), for which there is considerable support in an earlier roundup (Rees 1963), the impression of weak supervision stemmed more from the quiet commercial diplomacy conducted than actual application of the EPU's rules. Alan Milward (1990) has attacked that interpretation as being self-congratulatory, rather than a reflection worth of economic history. Brian Tew

(1990) has on the whole supported the version prepared by Kaplan and Schleiminger. More on this feature, including my own conversations with J. Kaplan, is analyzed in Chapter 6.

The central task of alleviating the constraints on current trade among Eastern European countries is slightly different from the EPU's root motivation, which was bolstering the opportunities for trade through multilateral arrangements. In Eastern Europe, the core short-run objective is obtaining support for revamping within-group economic relations (level and commodity composition as well as direction of trade) and supporting more buoyant economic interchanges on the basis of rational economic decisions chiefly taken by autonomous and financially responsible firms acting in their own profit-making interests. One obstacle in bringing about such a transition is precisely the shortage of foreign exchange. Efficient market relations to buttress domestic and foreign economic reforms cannot be secured without moving decisively toward establishing currency convertibility in virtually all trade relations. This can be achieved either through the "big bang" approach to convertibility, as currently aimed at by Czechoslovakia and Poland. It can also be put in place more gradually. Inasmuch as several Eastern European countries have expressed an unambiguous preference for the latter, there is a need to ensure that this commitment to gradualism does not get dissipated under force of circumstance. The alternative paths to currency convertibility and what they entail for economic cooperation in Eastern Europe are discussed in Chapter 4.

A clearing institution with some supervisory muscle would seem to offer the preferred route. I base this preference on three arguments. One is that there are benefits in pursuing some form of free trading within Eastern Europe, as detailed in Chapter 3. But these gains cannot be realized without there being some transferable currency for reasons discussed in Chapters 4 and 5. Second, countries are reluctant to conduct their trade immediately in convertible currency or, at the least, are bent on avoiding imbalances to be financed from scarce foreign exchange. Finally, trade diversion engenders sizable negative terms-of-trade and export-revenue effects.

I refer to this institution as the CEPU because membership would in all likelihood initially be reserved for the countries of Central Europe bent on seeking radical market reforms as soon as practicable. But the facility need not remain so exclusive as other countries in the region seek to adopt similar changes in economic policy in an effort to enhance their integration into the world economy. Indeed, the key architecture of the CEPU should envisage the erection of a scaffold that can eventually serve the reconstruction needs of all of Eastern Europe, once decisive steps toward marketization will have been set. The latter proviso would be particularly pertinent if the Soviet Union were wholeheartedly to embrace marketization, regardless of the future shape of the Soviet federation; a weak confederacy would offer all the more reason to make the mechanism accessible for the republics seeking to create effective markets.

Without going into the details here, two factors would seem critical. One is that participants in the clearing scheme must be committed to moving toward market orientation. It needs to be reemphasized in this connection that any clearing scheme that does not allow for the rapid emergence of more rational trade and domestic prices will undermine any kind of multilateral clearing, regardless of how sophisticated the technical accommodations laid down may be. The validity of this proposition has been amply demonstrated by previous attempts at multilateralizing CMEA trade and payments (Brabant 1987a, pp. 273-8), progress with which invariably faltered on the bumpy pricing bedrock. Continuing bilateralism, even if revolving around imputed WMPs, is bound to entail disparate prices, which will inhibit multilateral settlements.

For that reason, I still have technical reservations about including the Soviet Union *ab initio* in the clearing arrangement. But it might be politically wise and economically farsighted to conceive the payments union with the Soviet Union counted in, particularly in the event of a *de facto* disintegration of the federation, when settlements problems among republics resemble international payments problems. Of course, as with the CEEU (see Chapter 3) there is a solid dose of politics involved in seeing to it that reforming countries are brought under the auspices of the clearing scheme. Inasmuch as the CEPU in my scheme of things is partly under the control of the outside sponsor, it would be easier to accommodate some flows than would and could be allowed. The room for policy flexibility in this respect depends to a large extent on having at least a transferable currency to nurse along cooperation in the CEEU, regardless of whether it will be based on a customs or a more ambitious economic union.

While the main tasks of the EPU and CEPU are, therefore, slightly different, the ways of reaching the disparate goals exhibit considerable commonality. The central purpose would be to accommodate bilateral imbalances by transforming them into multilateral ones, fostering economically warranted trade without being overly concerned about imbalances, and ensuring that the net surpluses or deficits *vis-à-vis* the group as a whole remain manageable. These features are detailed in Chapters 3 and 5.

5. Balance-of-payments constraints and a payments union

Quite apart from the PETs reconfiguring their intragroup economic cooperation, arguably the most critical problem of these relations, and serious obstacle on the way to market orientation with current-account convertibility, presently confronting the PETs is the foreign-exchange constraint. This has multiple origins that deserve to be recalled here. In some countries, the core problem stems from inability to raise sufficient export revenue to satisfy import demand at the level of economic activity and welfare that these countries desire to support. In others, the constraint is being compounded by the need to service substantial external debts. This tight situation is being aggravated by untoward developments, both in intragroup relations as well as trade with other partners.

In addition to all the factors influencing the foreign-exchange constraint, another aspect of the demise of the TR regime needs to be touched upon. The TR regime was intricately bound up with the immediate-payments system by which exporters were paid and importers invoiced in domestic currency on presentation of the proper shipping documents. That is now being jettisoned for the more normal trading regulations by which, especially in trade of manufactures, substantial grace periods (for 90 to 120 days) are as rule granted by the exporter. There may also be a need to provide long-term financing for exports of investment goods. If desired, the exporter should be in a position to discount the proper documents or promissory notes through the financial system at home or abroad. The latter is not yet in place in Eastern Europe and suppliers hardly possess adequate currency reserves to finance their own exports for some time to come. This regime switching cannot but further raise the demand for convertible currency for transaction purposes but also as a precaution against running imbalances that need to be financed (Bond 1991).

What will happen with so-called noncommercial payments of the now defunct TRP regime is a question yet to be resolved. One solution would be to permit all economic agents to conduct their transactions simply in convertible currency. But doing just that is problematic in view of the prevailing foreign-exchange constraints. On the other hand, jettisoning such transactions altogether would not only inhibit the flow of people and ideas in Eastern Europe so soon after having won this mobility the hard way, it would also pose serious problems in coming to grips with essential noncommercial transactions (such as the transfer of pensions, grants, scholarships, royalties, and alimony). An alternative option would be through the organization of auctions for local currency or letting the parallel market, as in Poland, set the rates. At least at some point in 1989-1990, the Polish parallel market was an important funnel for the legitimate conversion of local currencies of the Eastern European countries - as well as convertible currency, of course. Whether it still does is hard to say. This market for local currencies may well have fallen apart under impulse of the great concerns about safeguarding national balances, hence proclivity to inhibit the transfer of local currencies across national frontiers. But exchange rates are still quoted in the daily Polish press (such as *Rynki Zagraniczne* and *Rzeczpospolita*), but I have no evidence of the transaction volumes involved. Given the problems of preventing local markets from being creamed off by "shortage economies," I hazard the guess that the volumes conducted are largely for legitimate tourism as well as trading through the underground economy.

Given the prevailing state of affairs, there is some urgency to devising a solution for the problems the reforming countries face in managing their external payments, particularly with former TR partners. As argued in Chapter 5, invisible transactions other than for merchandise purposes should not be quickly merged with the provisions now being made for the clearing of merchandise and related transactions. But once swift movement in realigning domestic retail prices occurs, there is no reason why such transactions could not be settled in the same way as commercial payments. In the interim, the parallel market could cater to that demand. There will certainly be very gainful arbitrage. But its dimension is unlikely to be such as to induce policy makers, on legitimate grounds of preserving economic stability, to innovate all kinds of ingenious stopgaps to undercut that arbitrage. The best way for an economy bent on erecting effective markets and moving steadfastly toward convertibility is to encourage doing just that; in other words, to facilitate conditions for autonomous economic agents to engage in market relations and to let arbitrage play its constructive role in the interim, evidently within an acceptably managed transitory macroeconomic framework.

Under the circumstances, the process of moving toward genuine markets with broad competition may get nipped in the bud because the populations of these countries are unlikely to support voluntarily the sociopolitical cost of economic adjustment in the short run. They would certainly not be prepared to support a "big bang" approach. Once these societies implode and domestic economic activity slides into chaos with runaway inflation, stalemated policy making, unserviceable foreign debts, inability to progress with reform, and other factors that made the Polish experiment initially acceptable by society at large, one may well be able to engineer a big bang with considerable success and move on expeditiously to structural transformations. There are simply too many risks for too few rewards in this approach for most PETs at this stage, however. Surely, concerned economists and dedicated policy makers should be able to do better than simply letting the economy deteriorate beyond recognition before remedies for recovery and convalescence are put in place.

3

Economic union in Eastern Europe

For many years it has been a matter of subtle debate whether the CMEA was ever conceived as an organization designed to bring about genuine economic union among its members. Genuine in this context means that the principal motivations for bundling forces within the region found their justification in the gains that can be reaped from narrowing relative scarcities across a larger market than the national one. In other words, regardless of the concern about safeguarding socialism, the conceptualization and implementation of reciprocal adjustments within the union (whether planned or induced by market forces) in response to differences in relative prices would have been basically linked through the umbilical cord of the economic calculus. Prices in this context refer to all terms at which alternatives are or could be traded. As such they include product and service prices (in retail as well as wholesale relations) and factor prices (wages, rents, and interest rates), all possibly directly codetermined by price relatives in world markets for traded goods.

By referring to the economic core of integration policies, I neither wish to invoke economic determinism nor willfully to disregard the politics of forming an economic union. In the case of the CMEA, however, one has had to look far and wide to identify isolated grains of an economic rationale in the regional organization and the kinds of specialization, labor and capital movements, and trade and payments arrangements it stood for tacitly or overtly from early 1949 until late 1990. The same holds for the attitude of the Eastern European countries toward regional economic cooperation since the inception of the recent political renaissance.

This chapter addresses the core economic arguments in favor of economic union among some or all countries of Eastern Europe. Section 1 sets forth the major issues at this juncture. Next I look at the arguments that could be invoked in pleading the case for the formation of some kind of economic union among the PETs. The points that can be mustered in its support can be divided among four groups: ordinary customs-union theory, trade theory, transitory comparative advantages, and the underdeveloped and distorted nature of trade in these countries. The following two sections briefly discuss the theoretical and more practical considerations, respectively, that favor economic union in parts of Eastern Europe. There are, of course, also drawbacks other than those embedded in the second-best framework of discourse adopted here for the sake of argument. How such economic cooperation could be promoted from within the group of countries as well as from without, most notably through the formation of a payments union, concludes this chapter.

1. The outlook for economic union at this juncture

At the outset of the economic revolutions in Eastern Europe it was stressed as an act of faith as well as a renewed commitment to the democratic spirit that the CMEA was *passé* - hence its subsequent collapse. Regional economic cooperation could at best be entertained as a strictly transitory necessity to be abolished and replaced by global conditions as soon as circumstances permit. The longer-term goals should indeed revolve around the conditions to be met in order for these countries to integrate themselves as quickly as possible fully into the (western) European concert of nations and indeed into the global economy. How best to capitalize on reciprocal trading opportunities for two or more reforming countries has hardly ever been considered. There are many reasons for this state of affairs. But surely one important factor has been that the economic arguments to be invoked under the circumstances have invariably been commingled with various nontechnical analyses. Add to these weighty political and ideological precepts, and it will become clear that the pros and cons of regional integration, whether in the past or prospectively, in Eastern Europe can be discussed only in a highly convoluted setting.

Yet, effectively exploring the opportunities for trade and cooperation among the reforming countries themselves on the basis of economic motives is - at any rate, it certainly could be - pivotal in charting the longer-term development strategy of Eastern Europe. Rather than actively exploring this room for mutually beneficial opportunities, since early 1990 at the latest various policy measures have been embraced that, in effect, actively discourage mutual trade and broader economic cooperation. In some cases, the negative implications for intragroup intercourse emanated as a byproduct from the incipient market-orientation of the PETs. But some measures were specifically imposed to compress the room for intragroup trade and cooperation. As noted earlier, these include the enactment of customs duties, the forceful cutting of potential exports to the TR area through administrative measures, the conversion of imbalances at *ad hoc* exchange rates of dubious economic merit, and the ruthless, in some cases capricious, revaluation of the domestic currency in terms of the TR. None of these measures is apt to stimulate harmonious economic relations. Some are highly dysfunctional in the sense that they debilitate exports of firms that under more normal conditions - namely, those that will prevail once the market-oriented reform is well under way - would be economically justified. How some kind of economic union could assist the reforming countries in capitalizing on their static and dynamic comparative advantages in support of far-reaching domestic structural reforms and the ambition to fully integrate into world markets forms the core argument here.

It bears to remember that the politically motivated attitude that militates strongly against forming any type of trading bloc has some solid rationale, albeit a flawed and myopic one. As noted in Chapter 2, the alpha-and-omega of the TR trade and payment regimes has been written around market separation through the MFT, price equalization, and BTPAs. All three have to be excised to safeguard the very essence of the coveted economic reforms. Unlike in east-west economic relations, where it is essentially up to each individual PET to come to grips with realities, intragroup exchanges and possibilities can be smoothed only in two ways. One is to abandon all hope of capitalizing on the opportunities offered by regional economic cooperation, if not as a buttress, at least as an important support for the envisaged economic reforms. The other is to seek a cooperative solution at least among the reforming countries themselves and preferably also with the nonreforming countries so that orderly and economically justified trade relations can be maintained. This would be desirable at least to prop up feasible levels of economic activity in reforming countries. Individual countries can seek to funnel the rationality that is emerging in their domestic economy into trade negotiations as much as possible and to take advantage of opportunities for reform among them (see Brabant 1990f). This is not an ideal solution. The embedded constraint is important because western and eastern markets are not simple substitutes as sources or destinations of traded goods and services, at least for now. It is also crucial because the discussions about reforming intragroup trade and payment provisions are now fully bogged down on issues that, even if they were soon to be resolved, are unlikely to provide a buttress to reviving buoyant intragroup commerce or related forms of regional cooperation (Brabant 1991a, e, h, k).

The argument pleading for the rapid increase in economic cooperation among the reforming countries in Central Europe is almost self-evident, though many observers are not easily persuaded thereof. To the degree that these PETs do indeed succeed in fostering economic decentralization, the behavior of their economic agents should increasingly be guided by the profit motive. Until full participation in the multilateral trading world can be ensured, that is, current-account convertibility can be sustained, a solution for the prevailing imbalances and those likely to emerge when moving toward full-fledged markets needs to be found soonest. The argument in favor of greater regional economic cooperation in Eastern Europe could markedly be strengthened if the Soviet Union were to be fully committed to market-oriented reform. There is now a distinct possibility of this being in the offing. But it is unlikely to occur tomorrow because of radical reform of the union or *de facto* fragmentation of the federation into multiple republics, each with its own trade and payment problems. Under certain scenarios (see Chapter 1), the same argument could be invoked for Yugoslavia, although its deeply rooted problems are evidently of a different order of scope and magnitude than Eastern Europe's.

Seen against the above backdrop, the international community is now being offered a unique opportunity to reflect upon the possibilities of formulating and implementing a nearly groupwide solution that will eventually prepare those, perhaps including newly created, countries for regular participation in multilateral trade and payments in the global economy. Of course, the metaeconomic factors that have thus far exerted such a powerfully negative influence on the examination of the opportunities for self-help will have to be overcome. Concerted international action with some guarantees, rather than outright financial assistance without conditionality, may well be the only way left to persuade the PETs that exploitation of the opportunities available to themselves should be pushed as far as possible. In this connection, it bears to stress that fostering warranted economic cooperation in Eastern Europe is being considerably burdened also by the very sharp deterioration in the external-payments position of these countries due to events in world markets. The resulting constraints can be resolved only through fairly rapid changes in the economic structures and levels of domestic absorption of those countries.

2. The desirability of economic union

Throughout the recent deliberations about regional cooperation (particularly within the context of the CMEA and the Central European, Adria-Alps, and *Pentagonale* meetings), little thought appears to have been given to the possibility of introducing tiered integration in Eastern Europe. True, leaders from Czechoslovakia, Hungary, and Poland on several occasions since early 1990 debated whether it might be possible and desirable to do so. Thus far, the answer has been a clear rejection. The option of facilitating intragroup economic cooperation has not been deemed feasible at this stage essentially for political obstacles emanating from the long-held grievances about the CMEA framework. Also unrealistic promises by western policy makers, or perceptions and interpretations thereof by leaders of the east, have deterred the germination of some bold move toward placing Eastern Europe as a viable economic region on a different last. But at least the intrinsic economic merits of proceeding in this way at some future point in time have been acknowledged in principle.

As observed in the introduction, most observers reject any kind of intragroup economic cooperation in the post-CMEA world, even if limited to the reforming countries, on the ground that it would deflect attention from what is required to integrate quickly into the global trade and payment framework (see Brabant 1991k, UNECE 1991a). But that position is often based on a questionable reading of what the CMEA was and, even more, what Eastern European economic collaboration could have been and could prospectively be all about. Yet, given the multiple problems of transition in the PETs and pretransition economic crises elsewhere in Eastern Europe, including most notably in the Soviet Union, the fluid environment appears to be congenial to setting in motion serious discussions on revamping intragroup economic cooperation. This may sound paradoxical. But it is not in view of the realistic policy options available at this stage. Such a reconstruction of intragroup economic cooperation could best be undertaken within a full-fledged constitutional framework, as noted in Chapter 2. This might be enshrined in the statutes of the OIEC. It could be conceived along the lines of the core of, for example, the Treaty of Rome, which has been so important in charting the EC's evolution. By separating juridical, legislative, and executive aspects of Eastern European economic integration through a well-defined constitutional framework, the boundaries within which individual members and their agents can advance their own cause would become clearly demarcated. A fairly flexible arrangement would then enable some countries ready to move forward with integration more rapidly than others to do so without harming the latter's fundamental interests (Brabant 1989b) and without jeopardizing the benefits that they can expect to reap from maintaining fairly strong intragroup ties. Of course, the CMEA's dissolution offers such an option by default. But it is a degenerative one, inasmuch as the facilities in place in the TR regimes are not now being replaced, even though the newly envisaged reform options would warrant such a fundamental reconceptualization.

The existence of comparative advantages among these countries themselves should not be ignored. These have not been fully exploited in the past because of inadequate institutions, faulty policy instruments, or policies that sought to shape trade according to criteria that the market would simply not have validated. Some of these advantages are strictly temporary. A few derive from existing goodwill, such as knowledge of markets and linguistic abilities. Others arise from demands that are bound to shrink over time. Among the latter, servicing the existing machine park and taking advantage of the existing transportation infrastructure stand out.

Any cooperative solution, whether at the level of the CMEA or of the radically reforming countries, unfortunately, is not at all seriously entertained at this stage. The countries of Eastern Europe as well as the Soviet Union are instead reinforcing bilateral relations through *ad hoc* solutions that fall well short, at least for now, of placing the economic exchanges involved on a convertible-currency footing and conducting those transactions at market-clearing prices, as earlier coveted by several countries. This wholehearted encouragement of bilateral solutions to regional economic problems is in many ways a throwback in economic thinking and policy making, if not necessarily in actual intragroup trade and payment practices of the past forty years or so. Surely, if the radically reforming countries were bent on catching up with world markets as quickly as possible and gaining full entry there, the last thing to be recommended would be the avid pursuit of bilateral solutions for these countries themselves, as remarked in Chapter 1.

Especially the Central European countries among themselves stand to gain considerably from actively pursuing regional integration, perhaps through a customs union. Finding the proper ways and means of exploiting their comparative advantages seems to constitute one key ambition of domestic reform. But this goal presently appears to motivate chiefly trade with the west. The points to be made in favor of reviving regional economic cooperation can certainly be developed on the grounds of: (1) ordinary customs-union theory, (2) trade theory, (3) transitory static comparative advantages, given the legacies of planning and CMEA collaboration, (4) the underdeveloped nature of trade in these countries, (5) the dynamic comparative advantages that should jell as the reform progresses, and others. Not all of these points can be examined in detail here. But the essence of each argument should be summarized as it provides a key input into the propositions favoring the formation of a payments union for Eastern Europe.

I find it very difficult to grasp the rationale behind the peremptory rejection of Eastern Europe as a viable trade horizon. Even on the simple grounds of the well-known second-best arguments regarding regional union-formation among competitive economies, it would be worth considering at least the feasibility of regional integration from a technical point of view. The potential participants may on the whole all be rather poor economies competing with each other (Lipton and Sachs 1990a, Portes 1990, Sachs 1990). As such, Eastern Europe's potential as a viable ME comes nowhere near that of the most vibrant global markets. Yet, these countries must possess static comparative advantages, only some of which have been exploited during postwar economic cooperation in the CMEA context. Under proper conditions, they could not but reap sizable trade gains.

From the experience in the postwar period, the examples of fruitful cooperation by Belgium and Luxemburg in the context of the BLEU and the broader efforts of these two countries in conjunction with the Netherlands in the context of Benelux immediately spring to mind (Szabó-Pelszőczi 1990, 1991). With the shifts in economic fortunes of the PETs, no one knows where precisely they stand in terms of levels of development. Nonetheless, the Benelux countries in the late 1940s were hardly more advanced than Central Europe at this juncture. More important, the size of the market of the BLEU (under 10 million) and the Benelux (less than 22 million) was considerably smaller than any viable regional unit in Central Europe. Czechoslovakia, Hungary, and Poland together encompass about 63 million people; with the former GDR added into the effective market, although it could not now, of course, be a constituent part of a customs union, such a grouping could cater to a population of just under 80 million strong. If Yugoslavia's problems with maintaining convertibility and joining the EC at least on a *de facto* basis were to entice it into an economic alliance with the three Central European countries, the union's strength would be just under 88 million. Although income levels in these countries for now are rather low, the potential for fairly rapid economic growth once market-orientation takes hold, especially if international markets were to remain open, would effectively enlarge the "economic size" of the region rather markedly.

There is one other major difference between the Benelux in the late 1940s and Central Europe at this stage. The former at the time had only limited options among more advanced trading partners. This is clearly not so for Eastern Europe (Ecu Banking 1990, Romainville 1990). However, the PETs cannot compete in these advanced markets for now without incurring substantial welfare losses and, hence, economically warranted intragroup cooperation could provide an "integration workshop" (Jozzo 1990).

The case for union formation can be made even more compelling by reaching beyond the stylized customs-union model. Whether there will remain an open worldwide competitive framework in which Eastern Europe could integrate itself quickly is a question that is usually not addressed. Even if there were an open trading system, it is not yet accessible to the PETs without magnifying their adjustment problems certainly in the short run. Furthermore, these countries cannot quickly transform themselves into full components of an open multilateral world that could partake coherently in such a globally transparent competitive market, if it did exist. There are simply too many adjustments to be made within the group *before* the full burden of restructuring in tune with global conditions could be quickly imposed. In other words, the choice for now is between trade with the former partners or cutting domestic absorption levels for lack of sufficient export demand.

Certainly, Eastern Europe's trading and specialization potential in the near term comes nowhere near that of the most vibrant global markets. Yet, these countries must possess static comparative advantages, only some of which have been exploited in the course of postwar economic cooperation within the old CMEA context. A revamping of the trade and payment regimes on economic grounds would doubtlessly lead to a different level, commodity composition, and geographical orientation of commerce. One unambiguous impetus comes from economic restructuring. This cannot but eliminate trade based on administratively assessed comparative advantages devoid of economic justification. But such economic transformation should not altogether cut out that trade. It might in fact lead to a significant rise in commerce among the smaller CMEA members, given that in the past their trade was primarily radially linked by administrative criteria to the needs and potentials of the Soviet economy. Moreover, it favored the exchange of primary goods and fuels from the Soviet Union for chiefly investment goods from Eastern Europe. Likewise, economic reforms that succeed in generating positive growth in factor productivity should soon yield reciprocal dynamic comparative advantages. I certainly see no reason to ignore these potentials. They are discussed in greater detail in the next section.

Especially the countries of Central Europe among themselves stand to gain from actively pursuing regional integration, perhaps through a customs or a more ambitious economic union, once trading relations are fully entrusted to autonomous enterprises. Finding the proper ways and means of exploiting their dynamic comparative advantages would seem to constitute one key ambition of domestic reform. But this goal presently motivates chiefly trade with the west. A customs or broader economic union can technically function well only if the participants adhere to market-based relations, including in payment matters for which at least a transferable currency is a *sine qua non*. For that reason, membership in the union must initially be restricted to economies committed to pursuing market orientation and willing to move rapidly toward that status.

Whether eventually a reforming economy such as the Soviet Union could be admitted into such a union is an eminently political question. Such a union might be particularly useful in case the Soviet economy were to disintegrate and Central Europe would no longer be able to procure substantial volumes of primary goods from it in exchange for tailored manufactures. In the short run, however, without massive western credits Central Europe could only drastically cut its domestic absorption, hence levels of economic activity. This cannot be a desirable option for anyone interested in seeing the seminal transformations in Eastern Europe in general and in the PETs in particular succeed. From an economic point of view, it would be useful to conceive such a union with potential participation of the Soviet Union or its successor republics. But actual accession should be made contingent on the USSR (or its republics) setting decisive steps forward with marketization.

3. Theoretical merits of a customs union

The economic case for establishing a CEEU, as distinct from current foreign-policy considerations about such a union, are fairly indisputable. It was made on several occasions after World War II (see Wandycz 1970), most recently after the reversal of the decentralization attempts of the 1960s (see Brabant 1976, 1989a; Machowski 1973). The economic merits derive from the comparative advantages built up over the years, opportunities for profitable trade that were ignored in the postwar period, and other advantages that are bound to emerge if the reforms take hold. Conceptually these comparative advantages for Eastern Europe could be separated into static and dynamic ones, and the former could be disaggregated into four subgroups.

Considering static advantages, one could distinguish between those that will vanish under the weight of reforming economic structures and those that will remain and indeed be strengthened through economic reforms. Among the genuine static comparative advantages, some have been exploited in a rather haphazard way, given the peculiar trade and payment regimes adopted by these countries in the postwar period. The smaller countries of Eastern Europe trade among themselves essentially manufactured goods, which were previously "exempt" from the obligations (Brabant 1991g) assumed by the countries (Czechoslovakia, Hungary, Poland, and Rumania) that became contracting parties of the General Agreement on Tariffs and Trade (GATT). Furthermore, zero tariffs were resorted to because these countries did not steer their trade through conventional instruments of commercial policy. Moreover, there was an element of self-satisfaction and propaganda in pointing fingers at the discriminatory arrangements maintained by MEs in comparison to their "open" regime.

Certainly as newly applied by Hungary and Poland[1] in 1990, MFN tariffs on this trade are fairly high (on average some 20 to 25 percent). In fact, the size of the tariff was providing such a degree of protection to domestic monopolies in Poland that the managers of the transition decided to reduce virtually all tariffs and suspend a whole range of them beginning with 1 July 1990.[2] Czechoslovakia was contemplating the introduction of a fairly high tariff during the transition phase and effectively began to apply its GATT-bound tariff, which previously was just nominal, to nonsocialist countries beginning with 1990 and socialist partners in 1991. An import surcharge of 20 percent has already been levied on existing tariffs, which are rather high[3] for a wide range of products, especially consumer goods. Residual relations with the former GDR are, of course, subject to the EC's external tariff. While admittedly rather low on average (5 to 6 percent *ad valorem*), that tariff is rather high for many manufactured exports of direct interest to Central Europe. Of course, the EC's nontariff barriers, including the notorious common agricultural policy, now apply to the former GDR's trade with Eastern Europe as well. All in all, the effective rise in landed import price on account of all of the above and related factors is adding to the incremental restrictions on some of the traditional commercial interactions among these countries, whether reforming or not.

As noted, because of the biased focus on radial links with the Soviet Union and on concentrating trade on primary goods and investment products, a number of scale effects could at best only inadequately be explored under central planning, whether traditional or modified. These and other, in many ways simpler static comparative advantages have thus far not been exploited. There are many reasons for this state of affairs. Paramount is that trade among these countries was traditionally managed according to administratively set plan priorities. Because the economic structures of these countries are fairly similar, there should be plenty of room for reaping scale economies, albeit in products that for now are difficult to market in the west, but not only because of inferior quality. These would in the first instance emerge in consumer goods, food, and

[1] Traditionally, most CMEA countries had a three-column tariff, the zero column being applicable primarily to "socialist" partners. The lower of the two remaining tariff columns applied only to imports from nonsocialist countries that had granted the CPE most-favored nation (MFN) treatment (see Brabant 1991g).

[2] This measure was to have been terminated by late 1990, when a new tariff structure was to have been put in place. For various reasons, including the convoluted political situation in Poland in late 1990 and the ongoing renegotiation of Poland's accession as a Contracting Party to the GATT, the lowering of the tariffs with suspension of many items continues into 1991, without there being any deadline at this stage.

[3] Czechoslovakia is renegotiating its status in the GATT, which has been rather peculiar (Brabant 1991g) for historical reasons. If and when a new tariff will be "bound," a more definitive conclusion can be drawn as to the effect thereof on the country's traditional trade ties with Eastern Europe.

even more in light manufactures, as well as components and parts, given the previous biases in trade patterns toward finished goods and machinery products. Such effective regional specialization would enable these countries to maintain fairly buoyant trade volumes during the process of forcefully restructuring their economies. Indeed, an integral component of this changeover is adapting economic operations to reflect intragroup needs but also to cater to world demand. There might be room to consider how best to provide the financial support to help along this switchover. In intragroup trade, at least a transferable currency will be required to enable the reforming countries to separate macroeconomic issues (such as those revolving around the exchange rate and foreign-exchange management) from microeconomic preoccupations (such as the profitability of firms deciding for themselves on traded quantities and prices). Unless trade can immediately be placed on a convertible-currency footing, there will be a need for an external financial facility and supervisory discipline to guide this process, which is precisely one core aim of the CEPU.

In addition, there are bound to be evaporating comparative advantages. One category comprises goods that hopefully will soon vanish from Eastern Europe. Perhaps the most critical at this stage derives from the overconcentration of trade in finished manufactures, investment goods in particular, most of which are below "world standard." To the extent that this machine park has to be maintained because it cannot be replaced all at once, regardless of embedded inefficiencies, there exists for now a dependence on each other's parts and components. The same applies to their maintenance and servicing. Much of the infrastructure for foreign commerce has indeed overwhelmingly been geared by intragroup needs, some catered to through specific agreements on production specialization, rather than east-west economic relations. To the extent that countries succeed in covering variable costs or are willing to subsidize production for sociopolitical reasons, the residual demand for spare parts, components, service, maintenance, and so on should not be ignored. Also, for the time being the nature and structure of demand may be such that the less sophisticated, perhaps even outmoded, products offered from within the region are "preferred" to the sleeker, far more expensive western analogs. Especially the latter advantages will disappear over time as the economic reconstruction leads to the replacement of inefficient capital goods with more modern plant and equipment that is also more economical in the specific use of energy and raw materials. But there is no reason to ignore altogether these advantages from the very outset of the reform process.

Moreover, these countries have traded with each other for over forty years. In the process, they must have built up "knowledge" of each other in the broad sense that, on the margin and in the short to medium run, should give Eastern European exporters an edge over western or southern competition. Related to this past cooperation is the accumulation of goodwill and other intangibles, such as knowledge of partner markets, acquaintance with some producers and institutions, linguistic skills, and others. Also these comparative advantages are bound to disappear as decentralization and marketization take hold in partner countries, especially under impact of the successful promotion of structural, managerial, and institutional changes.

Finally, the very destruction of some static comparative advantages cannot but lead to newly emerging - dynamic - comparative advantages. With proper reform policies, these are bound to be very incisive indeed. Market-oriented reform with steady gains in factor productivity, deriving in part from marked shifts in the underlying economic structures of the PETs, cannot but usher in new, dynamic comparative advantages. This should be self-evident for it constitutes the essence of market-oriented reform in a pluralistic environment.

Taking all of the aforementioned conditions into account, customs-union theory suggests that the proposed CEEU would primarily be trade creating rather than trade diverting; at the very least, it would avert - or attenuate in the very short run - the willful destruction of intragroup trade that is economically warranted. Paramount in arguing this case is that the underlying economic structures of potential participants in such a regional economic union are mostly competitive, rather than complementary. Competition has not so far been fully exploited. Furthermore, past patterns of trade with each other and outside markets have been constrained for systemic reasons. These countries would hence stand to reap substantial scale economies. Trade creation will in the first instance benefit cooperating partners. But after initial adjustment, sizable spillovers should emerge for other countries as well.

Apart from the suggested trade gains, a customs or economic union in Central Europe would strengthen the market orientation of these economies. It should also enable them to enact structural adjustments in a more orderly fashion than is possible when traditional output and export lines are being expressly inhibited. Furthermore, the short-term sociopolitical cost entailed by this adaptation process should be inferior to what would have to be absorbed if adjustment were to be forced upon the PETs as a result of direct competition in world markets. This would be even more so if the transformation process were to be accompanied - indeed actively fostered - by outside financial support and supervisory discipline (see Chapter 5).

Perhaps even more important, greater subregional cooperation would in all likelihood elicit considerable Western European support. Among the several reasons, three deserve some amplification. First, the successful implementation of such a cooperative venture would postpone the diversion of substantial volumes of trade to western markets. Substantial is, of course, a relative concept. However, any diversion that elicits trade-restrictive measures on the part of western partners or that entails short-term terms-of-trade losses of, say, more than 5 percent per year on average would qualify. Second, with Eastern Europe in deep recession and the Soviet economy and society in utter chaos, the threat of sizable numbers of people moving into Western Europe in uncontrolled, indeed uncontrollable, waves is rising. Western assistance to stabilize the east to some degree would therefore be in the west's self-interest. Western

Europe is likely to find it difficult in the short run to accommodate rapid trade diversion and massive demographic movements, especially in view of the EC's other priorities and reluctance to compound its already sizable adjustment burdens. These derive from the still incomplete integration of the southern European countries (Greece, Portugal, and Spain) into the EC, the formation of the Single Market by 1992, the need to come to grips with the *de facto* accession of the ex-GDR, coping with the pending applications (Austria, Cyprus, Malta, and Turkey), further applications that may soon be lodged (such as by Iceland, Norway, and Sweden and perhaps the remaining EFTA countries as well), reviewing the existing preferential arrangements with DEs (including the Mediterranean and Lomé agreements), and the requirements of the EES. Finally, in this way it might be "easier," measured in terms of speed, distribution, and magnitude of the adjustment burden, to change Eastern Europe's economic structures so that the reforming countries can eventually be fully integrated as MEs into the EC. Because of the time gained, orderly accession deliberations could be scheduled for later into the decade.

I should like to stress most emphatically at this juncture (more on this topic in Chapters 7 and 8) that I do not cast the CEEU as a CMEA successor regime or an alternative to joining "Europe." Quite the contrary: I see it essentially as a temporary stage to facilitate the transition phase, both in terms of the time required and the costs incurred in the process, toward most Eastern European countries eventually becoming fully integrated members of a united Europe - perhaps around the turn of the century. However desirable that all-European process of cooperation might be, there is no way in which it can meaningfully be enacted soon.

4. Practical problems and economic union

As suggested earlier, any proposal aiming at institutionalizing economic cooperation in Eastern Europe now that the CMEA no longer exists will quickly get entangled in noneconomic objections to such a proposal. I do not wish to enter into the polemical, political, historical, psychological, or sociological obstacles to fostering regional economic cooperation within that area. All these factors are real and should not be belittled since they constitute very important hindrances to businesslike cooperation most of the time. A solution for most of them will have to be found somehow if regional cooperation is to be successfully advanced at all. But even if that kind of goodwill could be generated in the near term, regional cooperation cannot but get bogged down in technical matters. Among the many factors that could be considered, I shall look at three.

First of all, in reinvigorating regional cooperation among the countries of Eastern Europe decision makers in east and west alike will have to come to grips with the fact that the restructuring plans of the various countries differ and that, for all practical purposes, some are only at the stage of "talking."

Furthermore, even those that already have operational reform blueprints exhibit considerable differences in objectives and envisaged ways of getting there - reform strategies, if you wish. This lack of synchronization is unlikely to disappear in the near term. In fact, it is intrinsically hard to dovetail the reform ambitions if only because the existing defects that reforms are to correct vary considerably from country to country.

Under the circumstances, would it be desirable at all to conceptualize and negotiate a new infrastructure in support of enhancing regional economic cooperation among Eastern Europe and the Soviet Union, or at least some of these countries? If a positive answer can be found, the requirements for clearing markets in Eastern Europe must be pondered. The most critical objective would be the removal of the impediments embedded in the dysfunctional features of traditional intragroup relations. Only in this way could the pace of implementation of domestic economic reforms in the countries that are committed to establishing full-fledged MEs be steadied in due course and carried forward as quickly as the sociopolitical fabric of these societies allows.

It would seem, then, that the root problems of intragroup collaboration could be divided into three groups: (1) political impediments to any scheme that seeks to enhance regional cooperation, (2) institutional-organizational obstacles to regional economic cooperation, and (3) how to invoke the economic calculus into the decision making as quickly as possible. Among the political obstacles certainly the perceived recriminations about more than four decades of enforced cooperation and Soviet-type centralized economic planning figure prominently. Also, the bald naïveté displayed in approaching the question of how to merge into the global economy in general and the integration framework of the EC or EFTA in particular is not very helpful. In addition, the lingering divisions, rivalries, and recriminations between some pairs of eastern countries, such as Hungary and Rumania, are inhibiting economic cooperation. Finally, serious domestic disagreements about objectives and even more about the means of reform, let alone nationalistic sentiments that are rending the cohesiveness of some countries, complicate the process of coming to grips with technical economic matters forthrightly.

Among the institutional-organizational obstacles, two major sets need to be distinguished. On the one hand, the present vacuum in intragroup trade and payment regimes and the inability of most of the countries to make a quick transition to multilateral trading conditions figure prominently. There is little doubt that all reforming countries, and even those that are still only talking about formalizing an approach to incisive economic transformation, refer rather platitudinously to the desire to fully integrate themselves in the global economy as soon as circumstances permit. Against this background, all support the complete replacement of the traditional cooperation mechanisms anchored to the TR. But how quickly this should be implemented in fact and to what degree the overhauling should be pursued with determination are questions yet to be fully addressed in a coherent technical framework. Most would probably wish to maintain some vestiges of the former TR trade and payment regimes for now (for a review, see Brabant 1991k). But this state should be prolonged only to the degree that it cannot be done without during the transition phase. The latter's goal with respect to regional trade is eventually to all but sever their regional ties in favor of full integration within the EES, if full membership (at least on a *de facto* basis) in the EC were for the near future to be precluded for one reason or another (UNECE 1991a).

On the domestic economic front, the legacies of forty years of central planning for the institutions, legal infrastructure, managerial culture, and human attitudes toward entrepreneurship, asset accumulation, work, and risk taking, to name only a few, weigh heavily on feasible renewal policies. Most critical are the complex issues arising in attempting to shift the kind of administrative decision making so typical for such a long time for most of these countries. The very absence of the most elementary features of, what might be called, the nuts-and-bolts of the ME must be rectified as quickly as possible. To take but one example, there is simply nothing in place in the PETs, not even on the blackboard, regarding how to come to grips with the two most serious external shocks that they face in early 1991, namely the transition in TR trade and payment regimes and the aftermath of the Gulf crisis for global economic stability. It would be useless to try to formulate any comprehensive inventory of what is required. In Chapter 8 I present a brief overview of what is at stake, particularly as regards adjustment policies to galvanize the complex payments situation of the PETs and other former CMEA members.

5. Linking a payments facility with an economic union

For as much as I can fathom the ongoing reform debates, eastern policy makers appear to have given little attention, if any, to the possibility of negotiating some constitutional framework for regional economic collaboration (Brabant 1989b) in lieu of the orthodox mechanisms embraced in the postwar period. This could have permitted the more radically reforming members to move ahead in forming their own, more ambitious, economic union without severing beneficial "old" relations. Others could have wedded themselves to these more ambitious schemes once their own reform would meaningfully justify - indeed make desirable - such a move on economic grounds. Unfortunately, to date this option does not appear to have been seriously explored at all. Certainly, the more romantic reformers of Eastern Europe in early 1990 sought to tackle shared and similar problems of Central Europe through trilateral cooperation. But this effort foundered. It did so not because the economic rationale was missing, but because such opportunities for galvanizing the emerging markets of Central Europe were deliberately curtailed for metaeconomic reasons.

This ignoring of the possibility of reanchoring Eastern European economic cooperation is all the more incomprehensible given that many economists and decision makers deem it useful to maintain, at least in the short run, some vestiges of the former trade and payments arrangements (see Brabant 1991k, Budzinski 1991, Daianu 1991, Kazandzhieva 1991, Luft 1991, Válek 1991). Most observers refer in one way or another to the need for the creative destruction of the old trade and payment ties, in other words the desirability of some gradualism in embracing full convertible-currency settlements and free-market negotiations among enterprises on the basis of market-clearing prices. Incidentally, the latter category is rarely considered for what it may mean in terms of influencing demand and supply and funneling information among various economic actors.

The legacies of forty years of ill-directed economic cooperation within Eastern Europe may have sufficiently deterred the newly installed leaderships from trying to reconceive their regional organization or innovating a replacement. As a result, the more substantive aspects of what regional economic union, mainly anchored to economic rationality, might be all about have fundamentally not yet been broached. The almost complete disregarding of the potential for intragroup economic collaboration, even if at a lower, more pragmatic scale, has been baffling. Certainly, prevailing foreign-policy options argue in its favor. These *exclude* being integrated with Western Europe in the short run on a preferential basis. It would, therefore, stand to reason to inquire into an interim solution that can ease some aspects of the adjustment tasks common to these reforming countries.

In this connection I wonder whether it would not have been desirable - and possible - in the context of the ongoing reform debates to reexamine the bases for regional preferences in Eastern Europe. Certainly, some observers stress most emphatically that there is no need any more for maintaining strong, discriminatory regional preferences - reaching for a socialist common market, if you wish. But there are transitional needs that argue for maintaining some of the "old" arrangements. Would it not then have been desirable to construct some mechanism to ease the widely shared economic problems of Eastern Europe (UNECE 1991a)? If some group of countries can agree on preferential arrangements, even if only to cater to a rump post-CMEA world, why would they be so averse to anchoring it to a more formal arrangement?

Arguably the most distressing facet of the current debates on finding a framework for intragroup trade and payments is the wholehearted encouragement of bilateral solutions for regional problems, as argued earlier. This observation is particularly pertinent when one of the partners thereof is bound to be the Soviet Union, whose marketization as a policy aim is not even conceptualized at this stage. It is even less palatable that with the drift toward marketization serious observers could justify bilateralism as a desirable format for hammering out whatever can be agreed upon. In the same vein, it is hard to endorse the prescription of some policy makers that the only way to improve Soviet terms of trade, and thus infuse greater economic rationality into post-CMEA economic relations, would be by switching to convertible-currency settlements (Bogomolov 1991, p. 164), especially if these were to remain for now on a clearing basis. This commingles two distinct phenomena, namely prices are seen together with exchange rate and settlements matters. The first is a microeconomic issue that should be resolved by independent firms acting in their own interest. The second are tasks for macroeconomic management. The two sets of concerns are not, of course, entirely disjoint. But insisting, as many reform-minded policy makers do, on the primacy of attaining greater efficiency soon, while at the same time advocating bilateral clearing rather than actual payments or at least finding the proper ways to accommodate imbalances, strikes me as reflecting mutually incompatible recommendations.

Rather than obliterate all forms of cooperation in the post-CMEA framework, what is required first and foremost is putting in train policies, institutions, and policy instruments to enable these countries to exploit their comparative advantages through ordinary means of economic decision making. This they have not been able, or have deliberately not wanted, to do for quite some time, owing to the peculiar planning, trading, and payment systems that they wedded themselves to with the transition to detailed administrative planning in the late 1940s. Also the ideology underneath the perceived need to provide fraternal economic assistance confounding politics, economics, and issues pertaining to development assistance. As such, it simply made it impossible to sort out what was intrinsically profitable from relations justified on metaeconomic grounds. In addition, the domestic allocation process could be considerably streamlined in support of a more buoyant pace of economic growth. This cannot but give rise to dynamic comparative advantages as well.

There is no doubt that the replacement of the TR mechanism with conditions that approximate those prevailing elsewhere in the world economy is highly germane to the success of the economic transformation. There is equally no doubt that this switchover cannot but have painful consequences for most countries. One is the rise in the demand for convertible currency at least for transaction and precautionary purposes. This is a vital concern that can be solved in the end only by having the PETs adopt current-account convertibility at least for merchandise and related transactions. This is critical for transforming the CMEA members into open MEs and permitting them to "regulate" economic decisions through the orthodox instruments of economic policy, rather than through administrative means of intervention. A major impetus to marketization will materialize for these economies once the switch to convertible currency and current market-clearing prices will be accomplished. But how long will that take? I very much doubt that it will exert a beneficial impact right away.

Before the reforming economies can fully fuse themselves into the world economy major changes in economic structures must be enacted. Also, policy makers must gradually create room for independent operators to explore prevailing and emerging comparative advantages. These will eventually also be identified in intragroup relations. This rationalization of intragroup economic relations can emerge only if the proper policies, institutions, and policy instruments are put in place. Doing so through the transition to competitive markets is being considerably hampered by prevailing constraints on maintaining buoyant intragroup trade and payments.

Market clearing is one of those key categories that receive short shrift in most reform discussions. At least in my understanding of how economies operate, market-clearing signals include by definition the ability of supply and demand to adjust to each other through changes in prices and quantities, the respective effects depending on the elasticities of supply and demand. Unless bilateralism is redundant, by definition it precludes such an option. Many reformers hope to have autonomous and financially independent firms that can negotiate market-based trading. But these cannot be expected to emerge overnight, especially for as long as property rights are ill-defined and changes in monitoring management, and indeed in replacing the old-style management, are not under way. In any case, even the most radically reforming PET does not yet have fully autonomous microeconomic agents whose behavior is, or will soon be, motivated chiefly by profit considerations. Would it then not stand to reason that for some time to come SOEs will continue to operate according to precepts that differ in some vital respects from those that should be enforced in a market environment, albeit only for reasons of transition such as mitigating unemployment and gradually ushering in creative destruction?

Given the obstacles to incisive economic transformation arising from the present inability of the PETs to maintain buoyant trade and payments, there is ample room to explore the desirability of erecting a mechanism through which these countries could come to grips with their shared external-financial problems without being forced to back down on their commitment to instituting market-oriented reforms with multiparty decision makers. There are several ways in which this could be undertaken. Whereas loans on favorable terms, fostering foreign direct investment (FDI), promoting technology transfer, and related issues are useful in themselves, depending upon the concrete conditions, the external-payments problems of Eastern Europe differ from the obstacles to marketization of the Soviet economy. For the latter, technical assistance in the widest sense is urgently required (UNECE 1990, pp. 13ff.), provided the political will to move toward the creation of a viable ME were present there - not something that can be taken for granted at this stage. For Eastern Europe, however, one critical bottleneck in the short to medium run is bound to arise from constraints on external payments.

One way in which such problem can be mitigated, solid gains made toward sustaining currency convertibility, and steady progress in transforming domestic macroeconomic policies "recorded," perhaps with the assistance of outside donors, is through a payments facility. This could take on various forms that fall broadly into two categories. One in essence amounts to bribing the PETs into moving toward a convertible currency (at least for merchandise and related transactions) and price and trade liberalization as quickly as feasible in exchange for obtaining a convertible-currency stabilization fund and perhaps some extra financing to take care of the increased demand for convertible currency.

Declaring precisely that is the starting position of the proposal worked out by the group of economists around Jeffrey Sachs.[4] It seeks to link a payment facility with the adoption of domestic convertibility in the three Central European countries. In addition, it aims at providing financing for the Soviet Union in exchange for acting on a credible reform program (such as the one worked out by the group around Stanislav Shatalin). The financing facility would call for the transfer of some $15-20 billion in 1991 (and similar amounts in the following several years), provided certain conditions are met, and an acceptable and adequate surveillance program for the countries willing to engage in the effort can be put in place. The money would presumably be raised chiefly by the EC and the official multilateral financial institutions. Sachs and his colleagues feel that the financing would not pose any problem.

If the preset conditions can be met, such an approach would be highly constructive. Unfortunately, I have reservations about that leaping assumption on four counts. One revolves essentially around the willingness of the PETs to adopt convertibility and to start appropriating scarce foreign exchange to finance their *intra*group trade. If that were to be the case, a virtual collapse of intragroup trade in 1991 and beyond could hardly be forestalled. Also, if supervision over such a facility were to be entrusted either to the Fund (but how could the Soviet Union be dealt with for as long as it is not a member?) or the European Bank for Reconstruction and Development (EBRD), the question of the adequacy of demand-management, on which more in Chapter 6, must be addressed. Furthermore, such a major new injection of funds into Eastern Europe is likely to lead to friction with a number of DEs. Finally, I am skeptical that such a sizable financial package could be mounted at all at the present juncture. If it could be constituted, it would certainly need to be very carefully orchestrated to ensure that it is fully in tune with rapidly moving toward convertibility and undertaking incisive adjustment in the recipient countries, including first and foremost the Soviet Union.

The other extreme solution for a payment facility takes the form of a payments union. This should preferably be anchored to ways and means of encouraging trade and cooperation at least among the countries that are bent on creating markets as rapidly as circumstances permit. The latter's advocacy depends in good measure on the proposition that whatever can be put together by way of easing payments relations is more than casually contingent on the residual room for cooperation within Eastern Europe or subgroups thereof. In other words, to the degree that these countries can effectively pool resources, they should in principle be in a position to ease the problems they would

[4] I am not aware that this proposal has been written up thus far. It was presented and debated at some length at a two-day meeting in Helsinki, 1-2 October 1990. The following is based on my notes of that discussion.

otherwise fully face by acting individually and attempting to deflect trade mainly to Western Europe.

My proposal on the desirability of setting up a payments union was motivated by several objectives: guiding the reforming countries to current account convertibility, inducing them to develop their intragroup ties as rapidly as warranted on economic grounds and averting a collapse of present trade relations, fostering the process of economic decentralization, preparing these countries in a cooperative approach for greater marketization, and entrusting enterprises with full financial autonomy as rapidly as possible. The union would consist of a payment facility as well as a surveillance mechanism to ensure that the transition to marketization and convertibility is completed as quickly as feasible and that reforms do not get prematurely derailed. The basic assumption is that several of the reforming countries feel that it would be too costly in the short run to introduce a convertible currency.

Western economic assistance in support of the transition in the countries that are committed to democratization and marketization is critical in either of the proposals. Whereas the brunt of the adjustment burden will have to be borne by the PETs themselves, the depth of the economic and social hardships to be weathered in the process can be contained and its magnitude spread over time with properly targeted western assistance. Because the latter's volume is necessarily limited, the question of how best to proceed with the transition arises. Currency convertibility for current-account transactions would be an extremely useful instrument in promoting rapid marketization. This provides a very constructive target for western assistance.

There are several ways in which convertibility could be brought about. In my view, barring untoward circumstances, a gradual approach with preset commitments on the part of national and international policy makers provides the least costly way for most countries. Those that are emerging from utter chaos, exhibit hyperinflationary tendencies, and experience economic contraction may wish to proceed differently from the path available to countries that still enjoy some economic buoyancy with moderate inflationary pressures. This could formally be enacted by setting up a payments union for the countries that are committed to market-oriented reform and pluralistic decision making. Such a mechanism would provide a critical avenue for these countries to be able eventually to compete effectively in world markets and hence to integrate themselves organically into the global economy.

6. Key features of a payments union

The proposed CEPU has two main features. One revolves around providing external financial assistance to help clear intragroup trade without raising the absolute degree of discrimination among trade partners; but trade liberalization could be pursued asymmetrically, thus raising the degree of relative discrimination. The other is that financial assistance is predicated on participants heeding macroeconomic policy advice. This plays an essential role in keeping the union manageable. The core purpose is to accommodate bilateral imbalances by transforming them into multilateral ones, fostering economically warranted trade without having to worry too strictly about imbalances, and ensuring that the net surpluses or deficits within the group remain manageable.

Manageability is intimately linked to the above two purposes. One concerns the adequacy of financial resources to operate the clearing mechanism and finance imbalances. It also presupposes sufficient supervisory clout to "guide" partners into mutually reinforcing trade behavior to ensure that imbalances do not get out of hand. There probably would have to be asymmetry in defraying the multilateral imbalances through specific combinations of payments and claims on the union for debtors and creditors. This calls for a common fund from which the clearing union can finance residual currency claims. At the same time, it should be conceived in such a way that, on balance, the demand for resources from the central fund required for the orderly conduct of flexible trade decreases over time as a steadily rising proportion of cumulative imbalances is paid in convertible currency.

If intragroup trade were to expand quickly, though relative imbalances decline as desired, the absolute imbalances may initially increase. It would not be wise to suppress this. Sponsors of the scheme might well provide extraordinary additional funding, perhaps in conjunction with exercising greater supervisory authority. Similarly, imbalances existing prior to the inception of the union would probably have to be worked off outside the union or be revalued at more realistic prices.

Of course, many grave questions in connection with the CEPU proposal remain: How long will it take to reach convertibility? What conditions need to be met to ensure that the clearing agency can operate in a stable environment? Who will exercise surveillance? How will this macroeconomic discipline be administered? What interest rates are to be applied and how best to induce surplus countries not to withdraw suddenly their excess earnings for settling imbalances outside the union? What is to be done with the inherited imbalances, including those incurred on account of voluntary and other loans? What could be done with the capital resources available when the clearing fund's very rationale evaporates? Many other technical and existential questions immediately spring to mind. Some aspects are of a highly technical nature and can be settled only through negotiations. Others result from specifying the CEPU's most desirable features. These issues can best be discussed in detail once the problems of economic union and currency convertibility have been dealt with (see Chapters 5 and 6). But a few critical topics can be flagged from the outset.

First of all, it has to be clearly realized that a payments union by its very nature necessarily leads to self-destruction, namely when currency convertibility is reached; participants may choose to continue with some type of clearing thereafter, but that would essentially call for technical accounting to manage liquidity balances. Regarding the duration of the payments union, everything depends on how quickly these countries can move to convertible-currency trade. This may be more difficult to achieve than was the case for Western Europe. Indeed, the eastern countries not only need to introduce market-oriented reforms from first principles. They must also restructure their external trade and payments almost literally from the ground up. The task of maintaining trade volumes, while effecting radical changes in the commodity composition thereof in line with comparative-advantage indicators and enacting the concomitant structural shifts, is a daunting one. The assignment becomes even more complex when it is realized that the restructuring of the domestic economy along rational economic criteria can proceed only by revising the traditional pricing structures, particularly in intragroup relations, and ensuring that the necessary structural changes materialize by knitting meaningful linkages among domestic and trade sectors. This is a tall order indeed even under favorable domestic and external economic and political circumstances.

Second, the scheme should be kept administratively as simple as possible. If the rules governing settlements are unambiguous and not overly complicated, the cost of operating the scheme, given modern communication technology, should be minimal. Every effort should be made to entrust the technical aspects of running the facility to an existing financial institution that can ensure that the marginal costs of operating the payments union are kept low. For reasons argued in Chapter 5, I suggest as agent the Bank for International Settlements (BIS), of which most Eastern European countries are members, as the institution to be entrusted with the technical operations of the payments union.

Third, any clearing scheme suffers from a fundamental theoretical weakness. To require in principle that all countries balance their current account within the clearing system is tantamount to assuming that they balance their accounts with countries outside the system. Without this, participants are tempted to utilize their surplus to offset deficits with outside trade partners but deficit countries have no incentive to repatriate their surpluses with outside partners.

In the case of the EPU, this temptation was on the whole not very significant for several reasons. One was the size of intragroup trade. Most participants conducted the bulk of their external commerce among themselves, once the currency devaluations of 1949 took hold and the process of moving toward solid economic recovery was well on its way. These countries accounted in any case for a substantial volume of world trade, thus the asymmetry in trading relations for EPU participants and others, including the EPU's main sponsor, was relatively low. Furthermore, these countries had gained a great degree of political trust and confidence in each other, and were, therefore, on the whole bent on nearly scrupulously observing the agreed rules. But even that required at times some cajoling on the part of the guarantor, especially through the Economic Cooperation Administration (ECA), and indeed considerable financial diplomacy on the part of the EPU's Managing Board (Kaplan and Schleiminger 1989, Milward 1990, Rees 1963). As a result, each was willing to pay some price for making the EPU and the transition toward convertibility work. This helped to reach consensual solutions for otherwise intractable technical problems. Also, trade and payment flows with outsiders were overwhelmingly with the United States, hence in a convertible currency. This country had been one of the main sponsors of the EPU to begin with and had little interest in draining its own currency from the fund.

Critical in this respect was that the United States, which was not, of course, an EPU member as is sometimes alleged, explicitly allowed EPU participants to discriminate against dollar trade through the payments mechanism rather than through more orthodox commercial-policy instruments, such as tariffs, quotas, and other nontariff barriers, let alone even less desirable discriminatory instruments of commercial policy. Certainly, *de facto* discrimination was maintained through a multipronged approach to trade liberalization. Nonetheless, the ECA was very much concerned about ushering Europe into the envisaged postwar trading world. Furthermore, the Managing Board persuaded EPU members to pursue rapid trade liberalization on a broad front for as long as it was compatible with payments positions. A similar support for the CEPU, this time extended on behalf of the EC, could be very useful indeed. Some positive discrimination in currency matters, rather than through tariffs or quotas, would unquestionably also help to solidify the foundations of the CEEU and persuade potential members that it would be in their own interest, including in their endeavor eventually to link up with the EC, to first transit through the CEEU.

The severe problems of managing external payments of some eastern countries, including most notably Hungary and Poland, however, may undermine the CEPU scheme from the very beginning. It would, therefore, be useful to find a way to permit these countries, at least for now, to focus on current trade (and perhaps services other than on account of the foreign debt), while the apparently intractable problems caused by their inherited external debts are addressed differently. I have no ready suggestion on what could be done. However, the ongoing east-west assistance efforts coming to fruition at this juncture may well embody a greater degree of political capital and potential commercial interest in a pragmatic solution. This should ensure the separability of the stock of debt from current payments for trade and services other than debt service. That such constructive solutions can be conceived was underlined in early 1990 in the context of the rescheduling of a considerable portion of Poland's official debt to the Paris Club, and on 15 March 1991 by the enactment of about 50 percent debt relief.

The potential financial cost of a CEPU is bound to be a major factor in determining whether setting it up would be worth the effort. In my estimate, as detailed in Chapter 5, the cost is likely to remain rather small, perhaps a fund of $2.5 billion. This is very little particularly when placed against the backdrop of the east-west assistance efforts that have been coming to fruition since mid-1990 particularly in the context of the Group of Twenty-four. It might be useful to explore the possibilities of earmarking some of these commitments for setting up a capital base from which the PETs could find support for moving in a relatively short period of time toward convertibility, at least for current-account transactions. The benefits promise to be very sizable indeed for east and west.

Perhaps most important, a CEPU would reinforce the commercial relations among the PETs, especially if those were to be buttressed through a CEEU, and assist them with the industrial restructuring that needs to be enacted in any case. Not only would it support the reform trends from within and strengthen intragroup relations. It would also transfer assistance in a form that interferes least with the emerging economic incentives for microeconomic agents and the macroeconomic framework being elaborated. Finally, it would stave off the pressure on Western European markets to accommodate significant trade diversion from Eastern Europe and soften the contraction in levels of domestic activity in the reforming countries during the restructuring process. Prevailing supply rigidities would render the latter option rather expensive.

The question remains, of course, what reforming countries should do about their relations with unreconstructed CPEs, the USSR in the first instance. Moving over to convertible-currency payments and invoicing trade at imputed WMPs has been one proposal. Even if a major reversal in imbalances could be averted, the mooted option is not very attractive on two grounds. Utilizing prices that have little to do with underlying economic scarcities is a half-way solution, if that. These prices are likely to be set in the course of laborious bilateral negotiations with the kind of "advanced haggling" that has been the hallmark of the intransparency of trading relations based on the TR regimes for so long (Brabant 1987b). Perhaps more important is the issue of what precisely the Soviets may have meant by "clearing," "indicative lists," and "barter."

Clearing is a weaselword of major dimensions that gets abused for partisan politics. A distinction should be made at least between simple bookkeeping of transactions with the proper "standard" payment conditions (cash payments for most raw materials and supplier credit of perhaps 90-120 days for most manufactures), actually effecting payments according to these standard conditions, and operating accounts that will periodically (perhaps monthly) be settled, whose balance must be kept very close to zero, or that will be settled according to *ad hoc* arrangements. All of these and variants thereof have been proposed, as discussed earlier. To the extent that the question of what to do with eventual imbalances has not yet been unambiguously resolved, current arrangements are far too vague to be practicable especially for PETs. Clearly, imbalances reached in trade conducted at relative prices that have little to do with actual east-west prices will be offset in dollar payments only with the greatest reluctance by the deficit country. It would simply defer the core problem of the TR pricing and payment regimes to another currency unit and the bilateral level. This would, on the whole, constitute a serious regression in thinking, if perhaps not in trade practices among the countries of Eastern Europe.

Under the circumstances, particularly for as long as it remains impossible to settle imbalances in a convertible currency, it might be more productive especially in trading with the Soviet Union to manage imbalances through quantitative export or import controls, as suggested in Chapter 2. This would naturally complicate the room for independent maneuver on the part of firms. Also efforts should be initiated to relax the stringency of this regime whenever some segments of the Soviet economy will be placed on a genuine economic footing. Only then will it make sense to let Soviet firms negotiate with firms from PETs on the microeconomic merits of the transactions or to eliminate the quantitative restrictions that are now being enforced.

4

Paths to convertibility

The postwar world economic order conceived during and right after World War II (Brabant 1991g, pp. 22-39) was to rest on multilateralism, nondiscrimination, reciprocity, currency convertibility, and free trade. The existence of MEs with largely privately owned firms as members of that global order was simply taken for granted. Among the initial key precepts was substantially, if not fully, liberalized markets for goods and services. Later on capital markets too were to be freed up, though perhaps not all the way. Many advocates of this arrangement held on to the notion that freedom to access each other's markets with minimal state regulation and interference would be the *nec plus ultra* to attaining the other, more practical objectives.

In the wake of war conditions, it turned out to be far more difficult than anticipated by the architects of the liberal world order to attain those objectives. These obstacles applied not only to DEs and the emerging liberalization movements of the former colonies. They were also endemic to most DMEs, in view of the array of knotty postwar adjustment problems they were then facing. In fact, only the United States and to a lesser degree Sweden and Switzerland among the DMEs were ready to abide by the key prescriptions on foreign payments hammered out at Bretton Woods; even so, the trading environment of the latter two European countries was by no means free of interferences that, strictly speaking, were contrary to the spirit, if perhaps not the letter, of the world envisaged at Bretton Woods. Although the United States as the *primus inter pares* sought to enforce the rules it had successfully promoted at Bretton Woods, albeit with some reluctance notably on the part of the United Kingdom, in practice it proved much more cumbersome to carry them out. As a result, the concomitant free-trade edifice would essentially have to be negotiated brick by brick rather than simply inhabited by those willing to abide by the rules of the game.

This chapter first briefly summarizes the key objectives of the global order negotiated at Bretton Woods and the attendant conferences held throughout the 1940s and why it proved so difficult for most countries through most of the 1950s to adhere to agreements reached only months before war's end. The concept of currency convertibility and the possible paths to convertibility that could be followed are recounted in the next two sections. How Western Europe chose to tackle its rebuilding tasks, or rather how postwar European reconstruction was organized under benign U.S. tutelage, is the subject of Section 4. Why convertibility is an essential, and under some conditions also an urgent, goal of economic policy in PETs and how this could be realized through a payment facility, possibly a payments union, forms the subject of the final two sections.

1. The global economy at Bretton Woods

The postwar economic order emerged with several paradoxes. One of the core problems that are critical to this inquiry would soon occupy the center of the Cold War. It revolved around the interest shown by key negotiators about the postwar world economy in establishing a free liberal economic order. This view was diametrically opposed to the position advocated chiefly by the Soviet Union. The latter promoted instead the need for shared power relations of tightly controlled components of the world economy, otherwise known as "spheres of influence."

Although there were divisions of opinion even within the western alliance, the majority embraced this postulated liberal environment as a core aim of the postwar institutional arrangements. This target was chosen in spite of the adverse experiences during the interwar period, especially the 1930s; the appalling disarray caused by the war, especially in Europe; and the adjustment problems that were anticipated to emerge, once hostilities ceased, upon the launching of efforts to restore buoyant economic activity without firm government guidance. Why it was felt necessary to reestablish free trade at the same time that leaders recognized the inevitability of an ascending role of the state in national and international economic management deserves an explanation.

Particularly the U.S. planners for the postwar economic order never presumed that the individual parts of the total solution of the world's pivotal economic problems should be dealt with in isolation. They viewed relief, reconstruction, and development lending; balance-of-payments adjustment problems, especially those relating to "current" transactions, on which more below; monetary and trading matters; countercyclial income policies; and national and international economic policies as highly interrelated tasks to be mastered through carefully steered international economic management. The major objective of trying to come to grips with these issues by separating trading, monetary, and financial regimes was to provide for a world in which competitive market forces could operate with minimal state interference. The latter would by and large be restricted to occasions when the market fails to live up to a modicum of policy makers' expectations regarding stability and near-full employment. This core U.S. philosophy was propagated in the belief that in the longer run, in most circumstances, market forces yield optimum results for all. Exceptions, therefore, could be dealt with through limited interference by the state. The latter would restrict itself to precisely defined deviations from the mainstream market-adjustment mechanisms. Although not every U.S. policy maker shared that conviction, the outcome of the discussions in Washington and other capitals by the mid-1940s was essentially the determined pursuit of the most liberal solution at the earliest possible opportunity.

Yet the eventual role of the state in domestic and international economic management figured prominently in the deliberations about the specific tasks of trading, financial, and monetary institutions to be created. Certainly, there were wide differences of opinion among chiefly the U.K. and U.S. negotiators. The U.S. commitments to multilateralism and free trade, among others, were part of a broader concern among policy makers about how best to ensure steady growth and full employment through national and international state regulation. A major source of inspiration was provided by the currency depreciations after World War I and the cycle of devaluations in the 1930s. The first were believed to have interfered with economic recovery and contributed to internal inflation. The latter and its associated deflationary policies distorted international trade in a number of respects. Moreover, though concern about the international trading, monetary, and financial regimes was widespread, the prime motivation for regulating these three respective spheres of operations was maintaining a high level of domestic economic activity and indeed restoring economic equilibrium in the war-torn countries. At the time, excepting the United States, and to some degree perhaps also Sweden and Switzerland, countries had little inclination to abandon exchange and licensing controls all at once or even in the medium term. There was, in fact, a widely expressed doubt that such an aim would be a constructive, hence desirable, objective of government policy at the national level. There was even less of a consensus on fostering such policies through firm international commitments.

Rationalizations of the debates during and after World War II tend to suggest that the major participants were bent on working out a master plan for postwar international economic collaboration (Condliffe 1950, p. 644). This would form one cornerstone of foreign policy. Accordingly, the program for postwar collaboration was intended to permit as substantial a degree of free multilateral trade as possible without stripping countries with strained balance of payments of their safeguards against cyclical pressures on their payments situation. The greatest obstacles to freer trade emanated from exchange controls and import quotas. These were the main safeguards to which countries with a weak balance of payments had resorted in the 1930s. They were bound to adhere to them in the postwar period, if only on account of the inflationary pressures built up during the war.

Aside from efforts to prepare for the postwar economic order as a matter of foreign policy, the chief participants in the U.K.-U.S. debates had more limited, practical as well as pragmatic, objectives. Resource mobilization in support of the war effort had distorted the production and price structures of many countries. Because modern war cannot be waged after the taxes to finance its machinery are collected, the affected countries had issued more currency than what would be available for purchases, and so inflationary pressures were bound to erupt. They would potentially create havoc upon the lifting of price and exchange controls. Such an undesirable outcome could be curtailed through severe deflationary policies. However, recent memory of the protracted and painful stabilization efforts after World War I made this option none too attractive. There was, therefore, eagerness to devise plans to foster full employment, if necessary by letting countries avail themselves of exchange controls for balance-of-payments purposes. In this, wariness about the U.S. business cycle and the anticipated deflation in the postwar period there played an important role particularly in the thinking of key U.K. advisers to postwar planners (Bernstein 1984, p. 15).

2. On currency convertibility

Convertibility can be a very powerful tool in the swift formulation and expeditious implementation of a cohesive economic policy under proper conditions. Because most Eastern European commentators on the subject generally fail to specify all key parameters when they endorse such a policy stance,[1] their advocacy gives rise to multiple interpretations, all legitimate but none authoritative. Unwary western enthusiasts spuriously infuse their own hopes for change in these countries into the interpretation of these vague statements. Such a muddled approach, a lack of clarity in policy perceptions and their rationalizations, should be avoided whenever possible.

This uncertainty is especially pronounced when, such as at present, the objectives of ongoing policy discussions, feasible long-term policy goals, or emerging institutions are being comprehensively reassessed or when they are already in considerable flux. To avoid erroneous evaluations, observers should not entertain unrealistic policy options for changing the model and development strategy of the former CPEs. It is as meaningful to affirm that convertibility for the ruble, forint, leu, or any other Eastern European currency is impossible as it is to assert the converse. Rhetoric aside (Colombatto 1983, p. 488), there has never been any structural or systemic impossibility of establishing some highly circumscribed form of convertibility by legal means even in a very orthodox CPE (see Altman 1962, p. 367). But it is very hard to transform these regimes into a coherent economic framework within which convertibility can be meaningfully applied and, even more, supported over time. To see this, some perspective on the legacies of central planning and the traditional trade and payment framework of the CMEA may be useful.

Before doing so and looking at the requirements for sustaining currency convertibility, I should like to emphasize that efficient market relations in

[1] For a summary of Eastern European attitudes, see Brabant 1987a, pp. 357-71; 1989c; 1990a; 1991m. For some useful Eastern European views, see Dubrowsky 1989; Kazandzhieva 1983; Konstantinov 1989; Nikolov 1988, 1990; Rybalko 1989; Shelkov 1989; Spacek 1987, Zhivkova and Petkova 1990a, b.

support as well as in emanation of domestic and foreign economic reforms cannot be secured without moving decisively toward the establishment of currency convertibility. To deal meaningfully with this issue, an operational definition of the particular type of convertibility envisaged by policy makers may be useful. This is by no means obvious (Brabant 1987a, pp. 365-9; 1989c; 1990a). For practical purposes, I shall use as guideline the definition embodied in section 4 of article VIII of the IMF's Articles of Agreement. This limits the meaning of currency convertibility essentially to nonresident current-account transactions. That is to say, convertibility of some currency simply connotes the ability of some class of holders of that currency to exchange it for another or into goods on demand. I have specified on purpose "some class" among the holders of currency to remain realistic, but I am not imposing any restriction on the ability of that class to convert its money holdings. Let me explain these qualifiers.

For most countries since World War II convertiblity essentially means what is stated in article VIII, section 2 of the Fund's statutes: "no member shall, without the approval of the Fund, impose restrictions on the making of payments and transfers for current international transactions" (IMF 1978, p. 29). Prior to the Second Amendment of the Articles of Agreement, the Fund considered a currency to be totally convertible if: (1) it can be used without restriction of a currency character for any reason whatsoever; (2) it can be exchanged for any other currency without restriction of a currency character; and (3) it can be used or exchanged at its par value, or at a rate of exchange based on the par value, or at some legal rate of exchange defined in any other way considered desirable (Gold 1971, pp. 1-2). This still holds, except for references to par values (Gianviti 1990).[2]

When economists invoke the notion of convertibility they chiefly refer to the one embodied in the above-cited quotation. The excerpt of the Fund's prescription has three operative qualifiers (namely "international transactions," "restrictions on transactions," and "current transactions") that need to be interpreted (Gianviti 1989, p. 270). International transactions are those among residents of different countries. Restrictions on payments are present when a country by administrative decision denies or curtails the request for foreign exchange for a proper international transaction (Edwards 1985, pp. 390-1). Such restrictions may, however, be imposed with the Fund's concurrence, in which case the currency is as a rule still classified as "convertible" in the Fund's sense. Finally, "current" refers to payments for foreign trade, other current business, and normal short-term banking and credit facilities; for interest on loans and as net income from other investments; of moderate amounts for amortization of loans or for depreciation of direct investments; and moderate remittances for family

[2] I am most grateful to Jacques J. Polak for his efforts to extract for my benefit a contemporary interpretation of the IMF's rules as earlier done by J. Gold (1971) through the good offices of Mr. François Gianviti (1989, 1990), legal counsel at the IMF.

living expenses (Gianviti 1989, p. 271). But what precisely "moderate" means in this context is left unspecified.

In practice, especially with reference to section 4 of article VIII, convertibility has been understood to apply mainly to current-account transactions by nonresidents in consequence of the regulation of relations between member banks of the Fund (IMF 1978, p. 30). Restrictions on current-account transactions of residents are condoned provided the banking system does not unduly inhibit commercial payments (Edwards 1985, pp. 390-1). But what precisely is a current transaction, especially as to the acceptable magnitude of some current payments, is not clearly spelled out, not even legally.

By a recent count, there are 67 members of the IMF (out of 152 at the end of 1989) that fall under article VIII's regime, although some are using a *de facto* multiple exchange-rate system (IMF 1990, pp. 568ff.). Many countries apply convertibility to residents too. Of the total Fund membership subscribing to article VIII, only 51 are listed as not having current-account and 28 as not having capital-account restrictions (for resident-owned funds) as defined by the Fund. In addition, there are three countries coming under article XIV that impose neither capital nor current-account restrictions, and 18 out of the 85 coming under that regime do not maintain current-account restrictions. In other words, there are comparatively few countries that allow their currency to be converted on demand for whatever purpose a holder may entertain; there are a few more, but still a minority, that maintain current-account convertibility without restrictions. Against this backdrop, one could term the złoty (Poland's currency) convertible since 1990, even though that distinction applies only to resident merchandise and related transactions by duly registered businesses other than those conducted in TR or other clearing accounts. Private individuals as well as foreign-owned entities can resort to a parallel market. The latter is linked to the official one. However, the intermediation is neither instantaneous nor complete.[3] In principle, the central bank intervenes when the discrepancy between the parallel and commercial rates exceeds ten percent. The actual link, however, is discretionary.

3. Possible roads to convertibility

To grasp the dimensions of the key problems faced by the PETs, it is useful to recall briefly how resources used to be allocated in these countries, and hence the legacies emanating therefrom. In orthodox CPEs, economic resources are *de rigueur* distributed with the explicit approval of the relevant planning authori-

[3] A similar regime, but with more restrictions on accessing foreign currency, was introduced in Czechoslovakia on 1 January 1991. As of now, Czechoslovakia does not, however, have a parallel markets and citizens have the right to obtain at most 5,000 korunych (circa $180) per year.

ties. Because the plan rather than the availability of financial assets is the motive force of the movement of resources, money cannot command goods and services within the enterprise sector. As a result, money balances in that sphere are extremely inconvertible, both in the financial and in the commodity sense. Goods inconvertibility prevails because the holder of a currency balance must generally pass through the planning hierarchy and obtain clearance prior to being granted title to mobilize the balance. That is, any producer with net bank balances can only acquire inputs with the explicit approval of the relevant planning authorities. The associated money flows are merely an automatic response to prior decisions about the movement of resources. Just as it cannot purchase local goods, an enterprise with a money balance cannot normally acquire other currencies without first obtaining approval of the banking, trading, or planning administration.

The degree of commodity convertibility will remain highly confined for as long as the planner preempts the decision-making process by allocating goods directly rather than through some market mechanism. Internal commodity convertibility is being avidly sought by reformers by scrapping major components of the material-technical supply system in favor of wholesale trade. Those that have set a meaningful step in the direction of the devolution of decision making have by necessity created some limited range for real markets.

Convertibility is a convoluted concept. There are first of all many meanings of convertibility. As indicated, here I refer exclusively to its economic sense and chiefly to goods convertibility. This requires the anonymous and automatic conversion of currency balances held by some class of economic agents into goods or another currency on demand. As such, convertibility provides a mechanism through which information about relative scarcities from foreign markets is funneled into the domestic economy. Not only that, it also offers economic agents the chance to compete with minimal interference in whatever market offers the best opportunities for profit making. That is to say, to create a flexible home market PETs must liberalize foreign trade and exchange with determination as rapidly as feasible.

Convertibility is a complex, certainly a confusing, concept also because there are multiple paths from among which policy makers can choose to enhance the competitive basis of the newly emerging ME. To clarify the key issues involved in the relevant Eastern European discussions, four basic variants may suffice for our purposes here because they are being tried or are being considered by one PET or another. Most spectacular has been the big-bang approach as implemented in Poland since early 1990 and Czechoslovakia since early 1991; Yugoslavia did likewise in December 1989. The measures taken were primarily meant to stabilize the economy. As such, they were directed at stifling hyperinflation through Draconian monetary control and budget slashing. As far as convertibility is concerned, the Polish approach simply unleashed most market forces at once. This included rapid liberalization of the trade regime, in the first instance in relations with MEs. It also freed up most domestic prices and removed the vast bulk of price-subsidy transfers from the government budget. True, not all of these controls and subsidies were abolished in January 1990. But the vast bulk of them were introduced in the first months of the stabilization program.

In some of its interpretations, the big bang is associated with the expectation that both demand and supply will be sufficiently elastic to respond appropriately to the newly created market incentives. This assumption tends to be validated, and expectations are consequently rather quickly met, inasmuch as demand is concerned. But swift responses on the supply side simply do not come to the fore for a variety of reasons. Most important has been that big-bang stabilization programs ignore the primordial need for structural and institutional change to induce the desired supply response. Certainly, Poland has sought this route. It was able to do so because of the unique circumstances prevailing in early 1990. Unlike Yugoslavia, which was forced to devalue the dinar in December 1990 and has had to reimpose some exchange controls since then, Poland has succeeded in maintaining convertibility at a stable exchange rate, possibly owing to specific conditions.

For one thing, Poland in January 1990 and Yugoslavia in December 1989 found themselves in a highly unusual conjuncture. Key were the runaway inflation of 1989, the crisis of confidence in the political leadership, and the all but completely destabilized economies and societies. Furthermore, this action was taken after decades of tinkering with various reforms and some liberalization of prices, foreign-exchange allocation, and competition. Also, the move was made with substantial external support for convertibility and domestic agents holding sizable foreign-exchange reserves. The costs in terms of unemployment, idled capacity, inflation, a sharp recession, destruction of liquid wealth held in local currency, inelastic supply response, and other indicators have been very substantial. Furthermore, the pace of inflation picked up during the second half of 1990 and early 1991. It is important to contrast these features with the initial conditions in a country like Czechoslovakia. Its environment in early 1991 was by and large still that of strict central planning. Furthermore, most of its trade had been conducted primarily in TRs for so long. The short-term costs of adjustment in relative terms are likely to exceed those of either Poland or Yugoslavia.

As regards the success with convertibility, it is undoubtedly true that Poland has thus far succeeded in propping up its variant of convertibility at a stable exchange rate without making use of the convertible-currency fund provided by the west, in spite of over 80 percent erosion of the domestic value of the dollar in 1990. It is doubtful whether the authorities would have been able to sustain the desired exchange rate without the sharp recession that ensued from stabilization, mainly owing to the very considerable supply inelasticity and absence of especially the financial wherewithal to foster marketization. Also important have been the determination of policy makers to control nominal wages and the ability of economic agents, households as well as SOEs, to mobilize their foreign-currency holdings to meet internal liquidity needs. Furthermore, the substitution of dollars for złoty balances, in part because of the pervasive destruction of liquid wealth in late 1989 and early 1990, and the confidence inspired by the convertibity loans notably from the IMF and some DMEs also helped to prop up the exchange regime.

I have spelled out all these caveats, not to belittle the courage of Polish policy makers or the experience, but simply to portray the "unique" Polish policy decisions in a more realistic perspective. This is absolutely necessary because, as I have argued elsewhere (Brabant 1991m), the "big bang" approach to convertibility is not feasible for the majority of eastern countries. Simply jettisoning what is in place essentially overnight would infuse the region with even greater chaos than prevails at present, for the beneficial effects of forcefully emplacing the market "solution" are questionable in the short run. To mitigate this, yet nurture along steady progress in marketizing these economies, it might be useful to look again at the EPU's experience, as indicated in Chapter 2.

The opposite of the big bang is gradual progress toward convertibility, in the first instance for authorized merchandise and related transactions. Such gradualism toward current-account convertibility is currently being considered notably in Hungary. The basic strategy consists essentially of putting in place genuine wholesale trading at flexible prices and relaxing the trade regime so that competition can be waged by domestic as well as foreign agents. Monetary stabilization is a prerequisite for such a successful transition to hold without inducing a sharp recession. Usually also privatization, competition, regulation of natural monopolies, and other measures that effectively promote profit-maximizing behavior by management, even in SOEs, must precede moving orderly toward convertibility. Taking government out of the vast bulk of enterprise decision making, particularly short-term management decisions, which may or may not require privatization (Brabant 1990c, pp. 120-38; 1991b, c, l), is required to enact gradual convertibility.

A specific variant of the above route, which at one point was seriously considered by the Soviet Union, is the creation of a parallel currency used in one sheltered segment of the economy, where "hard" economic conditions prevail (Kuzmin and Tsimaylo 1991). The link ("internal exchange rate") between the hard and the soft-currency sectors would be comparatively flexible to enable policy makers to control to some degree the shift of resources under impulse of the pull of convertibility according to a set schedule. But this can be adhered to only by tolerating a fluctuating internal exchange rate that may eventually completely erode the value of the soft currency. The speed of this adjustment process depends chiefly upon the degree of monetary stability with respect to the "old" currency that the authorities are willing - and able - to enforce. As such, it provides an alternative to rapid inflation or outright monetary confiscation prior to macroeconomic stabilization. But experience elsewhere shows that a parallel currency is not likely to delay those events for very long or to mitigate their cost.

Finally, another variant of gradualism, but one that cannot be pursued by one government, is to aim at convertibility through a cooperative solution. That necessarily takes the form of a payment facility. There are many possible variants. The ideal one comprises nearly universal membership, as in the IMF. For reforming Eastern Europe, a payments union such as enacted through the EPU for Western Europe after World War II would appear to be promising, even though initial conditions are very different.[4] This by necessity takes the form of some monetary arrangement in which transactions are cleared in a uniform currency unit but surpluses are not fully available to finance transactions with outsiders and deficits need not be fully settled in convertible currency by transferring earnings from outside the union. Such a payments union, in some sense, combines elements of the three preceding approaches, although its core is gradualism through a cooperative effort. It multilateralizes trade through the big bang and thus seeks to facilitate commerce among the participants. It also creates a dual market for foreign exchange, namely by settling commercial transactions through some combination of currency payments and claims on the clearing agency. The specific proportions will vary over time and for creditors and debitors. Finally, a payments union gradually shifts domestic resources and seeks to modify macroeconomic policies by holding countries to certain rules on payments that have implications for their management.

In the context of the disintegration of the Soviet Union and the postwar CMEA arrangements as well as the desire of Eastern Europe in particular to join forces with the EC, the payments union is also important in speeding up marketization and thus preparing the participants for a much smoother integration into the EC. The central purpose is to accommodate bilateral imbalances by transforming them into multilateral ones. At the same time, it is necessary to ensure that the net surpluses or deficits *vis-à-vis* the group remain manageable. In other words, the clearing agency should have sufficient funds to finance the imbalances. Likewise, the supervisory authority should have ample clout to "guide" partners into mutually reinforcing macroeconomic behavior so that trade imbalances do not get out of hand. This could take the shape either of them remaining too small to invoke surveillance for as long as exchange controls remain in effect or becoming so large because of trade liberalization that the agreed-upon surveillance mechanism in fact breaks down.

Why I deem cooperative gradualism to be the preferred route toward current-account convertibility in the case of Eastern Europe, particularly for their intragroup transactions, forms the core argument of the remainder of the volume. A cooperative approach to moving toward convertibility could measur-

[4] Some suggestions (Nuti 1991) to enact "soft" convertibility, for example, through one of the predecessors to the EPU, notably Finebel or Fritalux (see Rees 1963), for Eastern Europe or multilateral clearing (Michalopoulos and Tarr 1990, Sołdaczuk 1990, Tarr 1991) ignore that relative prices in these countries are still very heavily distorted. Any attempt to swap soft-currency balances under the circumstances is bound to founder.

ably be enhanced in the context of fostering intragroup cooperation, perhaps through a CEEU. The argument for greater regional economic and payment cooperation with western assistance could be enormously strengthened if the Soviet Union or its principal successor republics were to be fully committed to instituting market-oriented reforms. There is some distinct possibility that this may appear on the horizon for the reasons discussed earlier. The same may come to the fore in the case of Yugoslavia for the reasons already analyzed. The international community faces a unique opportunity at this juncture to assist in the gestation of a nearly groupwide solution that will eventually prepare present and future PETs for full participation in regular multilateral commercial and payment relations in the global context. The more general merits and drawbacks of a payments union will be specified, after examining Western Europe's experience after World War II.

4. Western Europe's return to convertibility

Currency convertibility was one of the conditions stipulated in the Bretton Woods agreements to which many countries were party. When Western Europe after World War II sought to find its way back to this policy regime, it quickly turned out to be a much more arduous assignment to manage a convertible currency under disequilibrium conditions than policy makers had anticipated. Indeed, the architects of the postwar economic order had been far too optimistic in their estimate of the time required for the global economy, at any rate its main pillars, to overcome the legacies of the depression of the 1930s and the wartime distortions. This would be a matter of far more than just a few years. Even though the United Kingdom's compliance with its commitment to restore convertibility had been postponed by over a year with the concurrence of U.S. policy makers, its experiment of July-August 1947 was a spectacular failure. The fizzled dash to current-account convertibility drove home the point that the problems of converting the war economy and managing the civilian successor were of quite a different order of magnitude than had been forecast. For a considerable period of time, then, Western Europe continued to adhere to various domestic economic and foreign-exchange controls. Even when the latter were being relaxed as part and parcel of the ERP and the Marshall Plan, including in 1950 formally through the EPU, it still took nearly a decade to reach a modicum of near-convertibility, as Robert Triffin (1957) so aptly called it. Most EPU members formally subscribed to article VIII status only by 1961.

Rather than search with determination for multilateral solutions, the Eastern European countries after World War II embraced bilateralism. For most of the subsequent four decades, they sought to reinforce it by various means. As clarified in Chapter 2, there is presently again the real danger that market-oriented economic reforms, paradoxically enough, are being accompanied by a widespread rebilateralization of intragroup relations, in many cases down to the firm level, even among the PETs. The instruments utilized to strengthen bilateralism in the postwar period were various. One was the inward turning of economic policy. The objective was to innovate autonomous economic policies so as to strengthen the industrial basis of each economy in isolation, while at the same time reserving virtually exclusive control of decision making, including in economic affairs, for the Communist Party and the *nomenklatura* administrative and economic elites that it fostered. The CMEA as the regional organization created in 1949 was expressly set up to buttress this national autarkic bent, although for a short period of time at the organization's foundations some of the Eastern European leaders certainly had more ambitious plans in mind.

For over forty years, no effort at all was made in Eastern Europe to move toward currency convertibility. Certainly, at various times leaders of the area sought to convince western lenders that they were moving toward that status with "great" determination. Hungarian policy makers and their cheerleaders have been extremely skillful at propagating this "systemic disinformation" since the mid-1960s (Brabant 1989c, 1990a). The fact is that under detailed administrative planning or when policy makers in MPEs still desire to maintain pervasive domestic policy autonomy, it intrinsically makes little sense to establish currency convertibility. Any attempt to do so would either have been doomed to failure or remained without implications for resource allocation.

With the decision now to seek assiduously to transform the planned economies into market-based social structures, the multiple issues of the hows and whys of currency convertibility have resurfaced. The present discussion holds considerable promise. The reason is simple: Running an effective ME around economic structures of limited scale of demand or supply, or both, in particular if highly monopolized, is a tall order even without opening up these economies to foreign competition. Moreover, gaining factor-productivity growth through market-based decision making without there being scope to project the economic calculus, at least partly, against the global economic canvas would only lead to costly distortions. From both angles, it becomes necessary to provide a smooth channel between domestic and foreign scarcity indicators. Here an effective and efficient exchange rate can play a critical role. To maintain such a link between domestic and external markets and, moreover, impart it with the wherewithal to discharge its principal function, namely pass on information about external markets and competition, at least some modicum of currency convertibility must be implanted fairly quickly; hence the renewed attention for the issues throughout most of Eastern Europe.

The critical choice for Eastern Europe at this juncture, then, is no longer whether or not to seek currency convertibility. Rather it is how to achieve it and how quickly the transition can be completed. These were the basic questions that Western Europe faced in the late 1940s. Their experiences should, therefore, be relevant, if only because the PETs appear to be even less prepared than the countries of Western Europe were after World War II to create room for anonymous and automatic linkages between domestic and external markets. One of the key questions to be asked is, then, whether it was immanent in the logic of postwar stabilization and transformation of Western Europe into civilian economies that trade liberalization and currency convertibility could be reached only gradually. Related to this is whether Western Europe's experience has more than superficial relevance for Eastern Europe.

The answer to both questions is simply no. Regarding policy options, there certainly were other routes that could have been adopted. However, barring policy errors, these alternative paths were deemed to be too expensive and risky during the postwar transformation. Both qualifiers refer to the magnitude of the adjustment required of the countries seeking convertibility and how quickly this burden could reasonably be worked off. "Reasonably" in this context, of course, essentially refers to maintenance of "law and order" in the broad sense and avoiding the destabilization of the political regimes that emerged from the war with all the rivalries, hatreds, jealousies, settlements of acrimonious accounts, and so on, that had to be overcome. Many of these features prevail at this time in the PETs too.

5. Marketization, transition, and convertibility

To understand the necessary conditions to be met so as to make functional use of a convertible currency, it is necessary to have a full grasp of the exchange, trade, and payment regimes of a typical CPE and how the group attempted to emulate - or accommodate - its typical national conditions onto the CMEA platform as well until 1990. Of course, I cannot examine these regimes or their evolution over time in detail (see Brabant 1987a, b; 1989a). A brief discussion of the key peculiarities may, however, suffice to identify the room for maneuver that the PETs have for moving toward convertibility.

1. The national trade and payment regimes

These emanated logically from two features of postwar developments. One arose from the way in which CPE policy makers conceived their orthodox economic model and growth strategy when they opted for detailed central planning. Also the legacies thereof in various reform attempts undertaken since the late 1950s have shaped the trade and payment system that market reformers, as in Poland, found more and more intact at the initiation of their sweeping reform intentions. The strategy of development aimed, among others, at full employment, a rapid pace of socioeconomic growth, extensive industrialization in breadth as the foundation for steady economic expansion, and a substantial degree of domestic policy autonomy in support of elaborating a more or less autarkic economic complex. For most of postwar Eastern Europe such a development strategy was predicated on emulating the prototype Soviet economic model. Three of its many components are critical to understand the trade and payment regimes. First, central planning in physical detail took the role of orthodox macro- and microeconomic policies centered on indirect coordination. This way of meshing decisions and reconciling conflicts deliberately ignored virtually all indirect coordination instruments and associated policies and institutions in steering resource allocation. Second, most economic decisions were channeled through a complex, fairly bureaucratic administrative hierarchy in which economic considerations formed but one set of issues motivating planners and ministerial bureaucrats, not to mention trade union, Party, and perhaps other interest groups. Finally, this model operated in a dual mode, the dividing marker being the rather rigid separation of the domestic economy from foreign economic influences.

Foreign trade did not play an important role in either the determination of the development strategy or its implementation. Integral to this model was the more or less complete disjunction of the domestic economy from external influences by means of special instruments and institutions. Trade decisions were formulated as a byproduct of economywide central planning and its associated institutions and instruments, rather than through decisions shaped by real microeconomic scarcity indicators. As a result, external economic relations did not form a coherent component of the traditional CPE or any of its variants - here captured under the notion of MPE - and trade levels tended to remain well below "normal" magnitudes for countries of similar size and level of development. There were in addition biases in the commodity composition and geographical distribution of trade as compared to what would have prevailed in a market environment. Especially crucial was the inward turning of foreign trade, it being essentially constructed radially around links with the Soviet Union. Also critical was the concentration of trade on the exchange of industrial raw materials mainly for capital goods.

The institutionalized disjunction between the domestic economy and economic activities abroad was accomplished through the creation of the MFT. This comprised several operational organizations and policies with specific instruments. Regarding its institutional setting, it consisted of various organizational, financial, and ministerial hierarchies. These set the framework for determining concretely what was to be transacted, when, with whom, and at which negotiated or indicative prices. In addition, the MFT comprised separate foreign trade organizations (FTOs) that in essence constituted its operational wing. The latter purchased domestic products destined for export and sold earmarked imports at domestic fiat prices. Differences between domestic and foreign prices converted at the prevailing artificial exchange rate were by and large offset through the so-called price-equalization account. This integral component of the central budget was usually managed by the central bank as monobank. The MFT also embodied total control of central agencies over strategic trade and foreign-exchange decision making, including commercial policy and basic directions for development.

Because trade is by definition a sector that eludes the complete control of one planning center, the CPEs attempted to gain greater stability in the domestic economy by forecasting trade flows as accurately as possible. This was usually accomplished though detailed BTPAs constructed around relatively stable, if artificial, prices. These applied in particular to trade among CPEs. For CMEA relations, a separate TRP regime was innovated (Brabant 1987b). Such organizational accommodations influenced the geographical bias in trade orientation. Because of the minimal role of money, key features of the CPE's trade model were multiple exchange rates in reflection of multitier domestic price systems; currency and commodity inconvertibility as the counterpart of planned resource allocation; bilateralism to facilitate the planned conduct of foreign trade; and exchange controls to insulate domestic from foreign markets.

In assessing the foreign-exchange regime, it is critical to understand that the activities of FTOs were by their very nature guided by other criteria than profit-maximization; if the latter was explicitly included at all, as a rule it did not play a central role in selecting the volume, commodity composition, and geographical distribution of trade. Trading organs were called upon primarily to acquire a certain volume and assortment of imports, essentially goods that could not be produced domestically or not in adequate volumes, and to generate sufficient export revenues to finance such necessary imports. In that narrower sense, then, FTOs were expected to economize on scarce foreign exchange, but only as a very broad guideline. They certainly did not make a major effort to maximize foreign-exchange revenue while compressing outlays to the feasible minimum. Neither did the organs entrusted with macroeconomic regulation of external economic relations, including the Ministry of Foreign Trade, seek to reach an efficient allocation of resources within its ambit.

It is important to recall the substantial degree of domestic policy autonomy coveted in the traditional CPE. This was buffered, indeed bolstered, by the fact that the primary allocation criterion in these economies was not via value indicators. Such a choice was not really surprising given that domestic prices were by and large set by central fiat. That is to say, domestic prices emerged from administrative considerations with the needs to improve resource allocation and efficiency being subsidiary. As a result, they failed to reflect real economic scarcities except by fluke. But FTOs sold and purchased goods abroad at prevailing foreign prices, which they might in some cases influence in view of their market share. The main purpose of this trading mechanism was to insulate the domestic market against foreign transactions interfering with plan implementation, and insulating society otherwise for ideological and political precepts. Price equalization was the buffer that facilitated this disjunction.

However, even in the traditional CPE events abroad could impact on domestic activities to some degree. This certainly applied to the transactions that the CPEs decided to engage in. These repercussions could on the whole be buffered at the macroeconomic level for as long as deviations from plan could be "financed" in some sense (that is, through unplanned export revenues, a draw-down of foreign-exchange reserves, or an expansion in the level of foreign indebtedness). If deviations from plan could not be accommodated in this manner, the MFT initially still attempted to buffer the domestic market by enacting special import controls or instigating export spurts through "storming" - so well known from traditional central planning. These tended to aggravate domestic market imbalances, but they did not perturb domestic prices. Ideally, the CPE hoped to offset deviations from plan through a combination of financing, in the broad sense, and planning for reversing the unplanned imbalances incurred earlier during the next planning sequence.

In this standard planning model, macroeconomic decision makers and especially enterprise managers were only poorly informed about the real cost of their import-substitution policies, in part because they remained physically removed from markets abroad. When growth flagged, central planners demonstrated a natural predisposition to enmesh their economy more in foreign economic relations as a pivotal prop for bolstering domestic growth or at least containing downward pressures on sustainable levels of domestic activity. To face up to the multiple opportunities in domestic and foreign-trade sectors, policy makers began to explore new decision criteria and organizational forms to bolster more efficient commerce. But they did not completely jettison autonomous economic policies. Thus, the link between domestic and foreign prices remained highly tenuous and discrete. These pseudo exchange rates were just that: poor substitutes for an effective exchange rate. It is only when it was decided to move over to comprehensive decentralization that a different environment could begin to emerge. Critical in this transition was the widening room for the indirect coordination of microeconomic decisions, including in trading matters through current-account convertibility or making substantial progress toward putting in place the necessary conditions to move forward with convertibility.

This brief summary of how the foreign-trade components of the CPE and MPE functioned ignores that this system is essentially still intact in countries such as Albania, Cuba, and North Korea. It no longer functions well in countries like Bulgaria, China, Mongolia, Rumania, and the Soviet Union. The distance gained from the old system is more visible in Czechoslovakia, Hungary, Laos, Poland, and Vietnam - and, of course, Yugoslavia. But even in these countries, pervasive legacies of the old system continue to permeate domestic and foreign-trade decision making in a number of respects.

2. THE CMEA TRADE AND PAYMENT REGIMES

The establishment of close economic ties within Eastern Europe after World War II motivated these countries to create trade and payment regimes in support of the expressed needs to pursue their own inward-oriented development interests (Brada 1988). Within this sheltered environment, rules for trading and payments were at marked variance from those prevailing elsewhere. Rather than putting in place an agreed regionwide policy soon after World War II, the distinguishing markers of the external framework in Eastern Europe derived from fairly detailed BTPAs, which formed an integral, at least intrinsic, part of domestic planning of the CPEs.

The CMEA trade and payment regimes consisted of: formal multilateral settlements of bilateral payments imbalances through the TR as accounting unit, but keeping intact bilateral accounting of real trade flows; the establishment of procedures for nominally multilateral settlements in TRs and the management of short-term credit at the IBEC, but maintaining the *caesura* between monetary and commodity transactions, thus prolonging commodity inconvertibility even in intragroup trade; coordination of investment intentions and the promotion of joint investment financing through the International Investment Bank (IIB); the introduction of a relatively autonomous and stable TRP regime in CMEA trade, even though actual transaction prices were in fact set bilaterally; and the elaboration of multiple exchange rates for various classes of transactions that were, at best, poorly interlinked. The CMEA mechanism never embodied clear-cut macroeconomic policies for the region as a whole. Moreover, none of the aforementioned links of the CMEA economic mechanism ever operated automatically. Because of the centrality of BTPAs, economic cooperation could only be fostered within the context of concrete bilateral intergovernmental arrangements. Certainly, in some cases individual firms cooperated directly without the intermediation of the MFT. For example, most notably in Hungary firms were actively involved in CMEA trade negotiations and they may thereby have imparted their microeconomic interests into the process. However, inasmuch as the framework of trade (including volume, broad commodity composition, and trade and payment conditions) was set at a high administrative rung and partner enterprises as a rule did not possess this latitude, the trade deals negotiated yielded scarcity prices only by fluke. In other words, interfirm relations could emerge only if the administrative tiers had made explicit arrangements to that effect.

In spite of national and regional reform attempts, this passivity of the CMEA remained intact until the slow agony of the CMEA's collapse put it in jeopardy in 1990 and rendered it altogether superfluous in 1991. It is only since late 1987 that signs of change began to emerge. But the discussions about reconceiving the TR regime foundered by late 1989 (Brabant 1990b, 1991a), as examined in Chapter 2. Although there is grave doubt at this stage that any intragroup collaboration, even now that the TR is defunct, will quickly get under way, the TR regime continues to exert marked influences. These surface in the macroeconomic, especially trade and payments, stances of Eastern European policy makers. They are also evident in the attitude of those directly involved in trading, paradoxically even in the most reformed PET. It seems almost inevitable that a major impetus from the outside will be required to induce the reforming countries to assess their own intragroup trade opportunities under the new conditions for economic management in a much more relaxed political context than that typical of postwar intragroup cooperation in Eastern Europe.

3. Marketization and convertibility

Comprehensive marketization presupposes the transformation of firms into effective self-accounting agents acting on the basis of their own profit motive. The latter is predicated on the creation of effective domestic markets with flexible prices and quantities, including a direct link to WMPs through the considerable liberalization of the foreign-trade and exchange regimes. This requires managerial behavior that differs markedly from what came to prevail in any of the models of economic management tried earlier. It will hence take time to engineer such a major structural shift. Given the importance of CMEA trade and the persistence of unreformed relations there, the shift in managerial behavior in the PETs will not only require adjusting to competition in world markets. It also must counter the dysfunctional aspects of intragroup economic relations emanating from the lingering aftereffects of the TR trade and payment regimes. This will be so until at least the major practitioners or orchestrator of these arcane arts will foster competition among firms.

One aspect of the marketization under way is moving toward currency convertibility, at least for current transactions, as discussed. To help foster competition on the basis of scarcity indicators, convertibility is inalienably bound up with the existence of discretionary markets, whose operations are guided and coordinated through macroeconomic policies. As such, the automatic and anonymous clearing of some class of transactions, such as by firms, contributes powerfully to efficient resource allocation. Such an exchange regime can be sustained at a fairly predictable exchange rate, which could help to anchor reforms, if the authorities succeed in securing approximate current-account equilibrium with the reserves on hand, including calls on foreign loans. That is, the demand for and supply of foreign exchange must balance at least over the medium term. Putting in place current-account convertibility is a paramount task for PETs for three reasons. One is that their economic structure at the outset of the transformation process is highly monopolized. Furthermore, the market size of most of these countries is too small to permit effective near-atomistic competition among domestic agents. How this potential could best be exploited and to what degree the PETs are prepared to modify their policies are separate issues, however. Finally, becoming firmly anchored in the world economy through transparent policies, institutions, and instruments provides a degree of credibility and sustainability to reform policies that may otherwise be very hard to gain, given the possibility of a sociopolitical backlash of structural adjustments - hence the potential for backtracking on reform commitments.

Convertibility as defined cannot be embraced without promoting effective market-oriented reforms. Key elements of a market environment, especially wholesale trading and flexible prices, are not yet present in most countries of

Eastern Europe. Moreover, they can be emplaced only over time and require perseverence to cushion the adverse socioeconomic costs of adjusting to competition. Furthermore, markets are far from integrated, including in foreign trade. It would therefore seem realistic to envisage a "clean" convertible currency emerging only after some transition during which the price regime is rationalized and trade liberalization is adopted to permit global competition. Its duration is a function of the distance to be traveled and the ability and determination of the leadership to foster swift market-oriented reforms. This depends on two key factors, namely the ability to move forward and willingness of economic agents to bear the associated adjustment burden.

A convertible currency is inalienably associated with a foreign-exchange policy. But "correcting the exchange rate," in whatever sense, is definitely insufficient to move toward currency convertibility. This may easily be seen from the heterogeneity of exchange rates that persists throughout Eastern Europe and why this has been so for over forty years.

4. Exchange rates

Foreign-exchange policies of CPEs are very complex, particularly when the economic institutions, instruments, and policies have been evolving over time toward some MPE status (see Brabant 1987a, pp. 196-268). To come to grips, then, with current approaches to foreign-exchange problems, it is essential to have a good sense of how the system evolved. The reasoning is simple: These countries cannot emplace a newly fashioned foreign-exchange policy in a vacuum, but must develop it on the basis of what is in place.

Recall that arguably the key determinant of the exchange regime established under the traditional CPE model and its evolution under the MPE umbrella since then is twofold. First and foremost, policy makers of the traditional CPE have an overwhelming preference for domestic policy autonomy. This gives them considerable freedom of action in pursuing resource allocation and income redistribution according to their own, at times peculiar, sociopolitical and ideological preferences, including on the strategy and model of economic development. Second, the principal instruments utilized to foster resource allocation domestically and in the international context are not the value criteria so typical in the decision making of MEs. Furthermore, policy preferences are not generally implemented through the habitual macroeconomic (monetary, fiscal, price, and income) policies of MEs. Instead, resource allocation proceeds on the basis of mandatory plan indicators, which themselves are patterned so as to reflect a wide variety of determinants, among which indicators of economic scarcity may have been one - but definitely not the most important - constituent.

Under these conditions, the precise level of the exchange rate is all but irrelevant. There are four exceptions. First of all, a notional exchange rate is utilized in the recording of foreign trade and payment statistics. Also the accounting of the transactions of FTOs, and hence the volume of implicit trade subsidies and taxes, which determine the net transfer from the government budget, can proceed only when foreign prices are "translated" into domestic-currency equivalents. In some cases, the determination of local prices of importables for which no domestic price equivalent exists requires an exchange rate. But this applies only exceptionally. Finally, an exchange rate must be set to permit local spending by foreigners; theoretically one should also provide for local spending by residents with foreign currency, but holding such balances was as a rule unauthorized or even illegal.

Local transactions by foreigners constitute possibly an important category. At the least there are economic activities over which policy makers fail to exercise full control, except by outrightly prohibiting them. They can only seek to discourage such transactions or curb them to the absolute minimum, essentially local spending by diplomats and trade representatives. Indeed, short of physically allocating resources to these economic agents, the local spending by foreigners is by definition settled at domestic prices. They must therefore be in a position to acquire local currency. Consequently, the precise level of the exchange rate determines the real purchasing power of foreign currency in local markets. As such it may influence the volume and composition of such operations individually. It most certainly does so in the aggregate.

Inasmuch as contact with foreign markets and individuals in the first phases of the maturation of the traditional CPE was strictly limited and the exchange rate was generally overvalued, at least in terms of the currency's nominal gold parity and its successor regime, an active foreign-exchange policy was unnecessary. In countries where relative domestic and foreign prices deviated grossly, and hence the exchange rate could not even crudely bridge such divergences, policy makers reverted to market segmentation. That is to say, an attempt was made to keep apart separate categories of foreign operations and to apply in a rather pragmatic fashion different *de facto* exchange rates to each. To the extent that the authorities in CPEs successfully enforced such market segmentation, this exchange-rate policy protected domestic policy autonomy and centralized intervention on the basis of other than habitual value criteria.

To complicate matters further, there has not been a homogeneous foreign market for any individual CPE in which arbitrage could ensure price adjustments in accordance with the relative strengths of demand and supply. This is very important in distinguishing between at least two broad classes of transactions. One referred to commerce among the CPEs themselves, specifically transactions conducted in the context of the CMEA for which special pricing conditions and bilateral clearing in an inconvertible currency reigned supreme. The second involved relations with nonsocialist markets, in which price flexibility in principle ensures balance between demand and supply, perhaps with some frictional adjustment problems. This dual exchange regime was further complicated by incompatible clearing arrangements with most other CPEs and numerous DEs.

The foreign-exchange policy sketched here worked satisfactorily, given the policy objectives in CPEs, until these countries began to express a need to activate their foreign sectors as sources of aggregate growth. This could not be accomplished by highly centralized means, especially because the interest of policy makers for foreign transactions first crystallized in conjunction with a drive toward more generalized economic decentralization. Policy makers in MPEs were, therefore, called upon to formulate a more active foreign-exchange policy. Rather than modify the foreign-exchange regime by revising official exchange-rate policies and letting market adjustments work off the most egregious divergences in relative prices, for all practical purposes the MPEs opted for a further segmentation of markets in each of which different *de facto* exchange rates were applied. It was felt that by creating this plethora of exchange rates when need arose, some modicum of uniformity of relative domestic and foreign prices could be ensured in these specific transactions. At any rate, they succeeded in limiting the most onerous kinds of arbitrage that would have been called for if markets had not been kept apart. However, if that was ensured when the new rates were first introduced, inability to maintain this synchronization mainly for lack of price flexibility as well as because of the forbidding controls over thousands of *de facto* exchange rates, very quickly relative domestic and foreign prices diverged once again, thereby creating opportunities for arbitrage in segmented markets.

De facto exchange rates, in the first place, signal that the CPEs maintain an official rate, which is, however, increasingly relegated to the role of convertor for foreign transactions solely for statistical purposes. These operational exchange rates can assume various forms. They are as a rule derived from a variety of computations and applied under diverse conditions. They are variously denominated. The most important designations are multipliers, internal exchange rates, reproduction coefficients, exchange coefficients, commercial exchange rates, noncommercial exchange rates, exchange rates for organized and unorganized tourism, investment coefficients, joint-enterprise conversion coefficients, convertors for transactions of diplomats and other official representatives, and a whole array of other rates that, to the best of my knowledge, applied only in truly marginal cases (Brabant 1987a, pp. 202-33). In addition, there can be black market and auction rates, the latter being a potentially important instrument on the way to establishing the necessary conditions for moving toward current-account convertibility. Finally, because taxes and subsidies are managed voluntaristically, actual relations between most domestic and trade prices imply a plethora of implicit exchange rates.

Among this diversity, the most important rates to be borne in mind can be grouped into three categories: (1) rates applied directly or indirectly to commercial transactions, (2) rates that are operative in private financial transactions, and (3) miscellaneous rates. Commercial exchange rates and their variants (multipliers, reproduction coefficients, internal exchange rates, and so on) have in common that they are derived by relating over some period of time domestic prices of some categories of export merchandise (usually manufactured goods only) to their foreign equivalents. Prices must be aggregated, of course. To do so, the weights chosen as a rule were based on the commodity composition of the preset basket of traded goods and possibly services during the chosen reference period. In other words, the computations were by definition influenced by past transactions and the decisions that were at their roots rather than geared to linking current domestic and trade prices. It is important to note three things. One is that the coefficient is an average, rather than a marginal one. Furthermore, it is computed for a given commodity composition and geographical distribution of only part of overall trade, let alone foreign transactions. The reference period usually stretches over several years. Finally, these rates of various foreign currencies are as a rule modified in accordance with fluctuations in international currency markets. But the local currency is only infrequently reset against the value of the basket.

Noncommercial exchange rates can be determined in various ways, possibly for different kinds of the relevant transactions. These include foremost tourist operations, usually split into organized ("prepaid") and other flows. But there are other noncommercial transactions, such as transfers of honoraria, student and research stipends, alimony transfers, social-security payments, earnings of workers abroad, unrequited transfers, and domestic foreign-currency shops. The most important of these rates, hence the largest component of noncommercial operations, is undoubtedly for tourist transactions. In the traditional CPE bent on fostering tourism as a source of foreign exchange, tourist exchange rates were usually set rather crudely by declaring a bonus over the official rate. When first established, this magnitude may have been estimated by relating retail prices for tourist transactions during some reference period. More often than not, however, the premium was selected impressionistically with a view to enacting a sharp devaluation of the official exchange rate and thus to deter foreigners from fueling the black market.

In the more sophisticated determination of noncommercial exchange rates, authorities generally made an effort to compare domestic and foreign prices of goods and services selected for the typical tourist consumer baskets. Because domestic relative prices are very different from those abroad, tourist exchange rates for inconvertible and convertible currencies were determined separately. This distinction was important. Whereas in many cases the tourist exchange rate for convertible currencies dominated all kinds of so-called noncommercial transactions conducted chiefly by foreigners, for the TR regime noncommercial transactions were as a rule further segmented into noncommunicating classes, or at least types of transactions that interacted only on the margin, poorly, or not at all. This follows from the fact that consumer prices in traditional CPEs are rather immobile and relative consumer prices differ sharply from country to country. Because of the important claim on domestic resources reserved for CMEA tourism and the divergence between the basket of goods and services consumed by tourists and that representing other noncommercial transactions, countries have as a rule imposed restrictions on the aggregate volume of tourist transactions, on tourist exchange rates, on the allocation of such transactions between organized and unorganized tourism, and oftentimes on the amount of foreign exchange that individual tourists may acquire.

But even for convertible-currency transactions, there were as a matter of course separate noncommercial exchange rates. This applied in particular to the direction of the transaction. Thus, quite apart from restrictions on the volume of foreign currency that could be acquired under some well-specified conditions, the tourist exchange rate for a resident bent on obtaining a dollar, say, was very different from that applicable to a nonresident.

The third group refers to a miscellaneous category of foreign-exchange transactions that interact poorly. Examples are the rates applied in domestic foreign-currency shops, for the conversion of unrequited transfers or the repatriation of profits in joint ventures or foreign-owned enterprises, to harmonize the interests of two or more CPEs or MPEs in setting up joint production or service enterprises, to foster direct interenterprise transactions in the CMEA, and others.

With the drift toward broader market-oriented reforms, Eastern European countries have felt the need to overcome the excessive division of foreign-exchange transactions. Although it may have provided useful makeshift arrangements at one point or another, pervasive market segmentation very quickly debilitates the potential contribution of foreign transactions to spurring on domestic growth that policy makers were looking for. It certainly obfuscates which foreign-trade transactions contribute positively to growth and welfare. This has gradually been leading to a major shift of emphasis in foreign-exchange policies. Prior to the initiation of the transition toward markets, the more reform-minded countries aimed at gradually unifying exchange rates for merchandise and other transactions, at least separately for convertible and clearing currencies; subsequently, the harmonization of exchange rates in convertible and inconvertible transactions, possibly first in the commercial sphere; and finally moving toward a uniform exchange rate. These stages, in some sequence and combination, amount to a set of necessary conditions, not necessarily preconditions, for gradually moving toward meaningful currency convertibility. But the suggestion is manifestly not that there should invariably be substantial time intervals between the various stages. By advocating this stagewise approach I do not, of course, endorse sequencing over a long period of time. Policies announced well ahead of implementation tend to lose credibility, if they embodied it to begin with. But some phasing is required, especially to the degree that foreign transactions remain largely influenced by special conditions prevailing in intragroup relations. Now that at least the spirit of the TR regime has been put to rest, the paramount task for PETs is to establish a uniform exchange rate in convertible-currency transactions that can be domestically supported and sustained through widespread liberalization of foreign-exchange and external commerce.

Key to any such transition, unlike in the case of the market segmentation explored in many MPEs since the late 1950s, is the degree of price flexibility condoned. In the domestic economy, the latter is essential to attain uniformity of exchange rates in convertible and inconvertible currencies. Price flexibility is also required to unify the exchange rate. It is critical in generating the effective support of a convertible currency in influencing domestic resource allocation in the broad sense. Inasmuch as prices in many MPEs have been kept constant for many years, relative prices of goods and services are generally widely out of truck with relative WMPs.

With the current reform drift, virtually all countries of Eastern Europe have expressed a need to rationalize their exchange rates and indeed to overhaul their traditional foreign-exchange regime as part and parcel of liberalizing economic activity. But some countries, including Hungary, still prefer to move ahead with radical reform first in the domestic context and go somewhat slower in trade and payments. Their attention is primarily on improving the exchange rate as domestic firms are granted greater financial autonomy. Others, including Poland, have seen trade and foreign-exchange liberalization - hence reform in the exchange rate - as an essential component upon which further radical reforms in the domestic economy are predicated. This includes in particular the promulgation of rather drastic changes in industrial structures.

As a result, the foreign-exchange situation in Eastern Europe at this juncture is very varied, if not downright confusing. Presumably once the transition gets fully under way, particularly in Central Europe, in part as a result of coming under the IMF's monetary regime, rationalization of the plethora of exchange rates and the management of the exchange regime is bound to occur. Even now that measurable progress toward marketization has been made, multiple exchange rates are still the order of the day in Rumania and the Soviet Union. Elsewhere considerable progress toward unification and convertibility has been made, even though measurable exchange restrictions remain in effect. The range of effective exchange rates and deviations between transaction and black-market rates are considerable, even though sizable changes in quotations have come to the fore over the past year or so. These gaps reflect the differences between prevailing relative and scarcity prices for the specific category of goods and services that dominate, say, the black market. Purchasing-power parities would, of course, be very different, owing to the disarray in relative prices. In some cases, these more realistic rates, whether official or already adjusted, are applicable only for transactions that "legal" economic agents other than FTOs engage in. The overvaluation in some cases is not too bad, but in others it is very substantial indeed. Among the latter, the Soviet Union figures prominently. Any realistic rate for trading purposes would have to be a multiple of the present commercial exchange rates.

It bears to stress that all of these countries have had some experience with currency auctions. Thus far, however, enterprises have had authority to earmark only a comparatively small proportion of their foreign-exchange earnings for these auctions. Furthermore, in several countries participants are allowed only to enter the market for specific pre-approved procurements from abroad or for earmarked currency only from certain sources. It would be of considerable interest if these auctions could be quickly expanded so that the bulk of foreign exchange would be allocated at a fairly uniform exchange rate at any moment of time. Once reached, the stage is set for declaring current-account convertibility at least for merchandise and related transactions.

6. Toward a payments union for Eastern Europe?

I have deliberately circumnavigated a detailed discussion of the multiple exchange rates in TR transactions. On the one hand, that regime was abandoned in principle in January 1991; it will, in fact, be phased out during 1991, according to current expectations. Yet, the existence of *de facto* multiple exchange rates in relations among the Eastern European countries, especially the Soviet Union, has not ceased with the discontinuation of the TR regime. This will not occur until these countries genuinely move toward market-clearing prices and settlement of imbalances in convertible currency. I contend that this can be effectively accomplished only if there will be some payments facility to foster such a direct widening of the participation of these countries in the multilateral trade and payment regimes.

Because several Eastern European countries are presently bent on marketizing their economies there is now a good chance that their mutual relations too can soon be placed on the basis of prices negotiated by firms. For that to work well, macroeconomic authorities need to take care of exchange-rate and settlement matters. A subregional integration scheme propped up by a transitional mechanism for moving toward convertibility for current merchandise and related transactions appears to offer a constructive alternative to pervasily intransparent trade and payment restrictions. The desirability and mechanics of such a transitory prop could usefully be explored in the context of the western assistance efforts currently being entertained for Eastern Europe.

I have been arguing the merits of creating a regional payments union for the PETs as one critical instrument on the way to currency convertibility. Central is that it could help these countries to revamp their intragroup economic cooperation as a buttress for transiting to effective decentralization and marketization. This, of course, should in no way be understood to imply advocacy of maintaining the "old CMEA" or encouraging further petrification of the economic structures in place; quite the contrary, as I shall argue in Chapter 7. The very essence of a payments union is predicated on independent firms acting in competitive markets that are or are being sharply liberalized. But there are other arguments that favor the elaboration of a payments union that I should like to elaborate on in the following chapters. At the same time, I shall attempt to explain what is required to make such a payments union work. Two pivotal elements are the capital requirements as well as the mechanics of clearing, on the one hand, and the associated macroeconomic policy adjustments that will have to be monitored closely by an impartial body, on the other. Although I deem such a facility promising in assisting the reform, I readily admit that there are, possibly substantial, downside risks.

Among the elements that have motivated me to elaborate on the payments union, five stand out. First and foremost has been concern about the viability of Eastern Europe, or components thereof, as an integrated economic zone. Whether that should take the form of a customs union, as advocated in Chapter 3, or be more ambitious and aim at economic and political union is not the issue here. All I contend is that the destruction of intragroup trade beyond what is clearly unprofitable is unwise policy making. This is especially so once policy makers ostensibly wish to divorce microeconomic interests from the macroeconomic framework of economic management. It would seem inherently contradictory to encourage exporters to move into, say, DMEs as rapidly as possible when at the same time they are discouraged from exploiting existing and emerging intragroup trading opportunities.

Second, with the budding radical reforms in Eastern Europe, a (pro-western) European sentiment has come to the fore in the sense that the "lost" countries of Eastern Europe would like to "regain" their anchor in "European" culture. Also the Soviet Union has stressed this, but only to gain admission into a European common house. Many structural changes will be required to realize this. A payments union would prepare the participants for smooth accession on equal terms into the EC. It would also stave off the problems of diverting a sizable volume of trade formerly conducted among these countries in the CMEA trade and payment frameworks to the EC, something for which these markets are hardly prepared, given the adjustment problems noted earlier.

Third, the most immediate and painful problems faced by Eastern Europe in general and the PETs in particular are pressures on external payments or the shortage of liquidity to conduct market-oriented trade with minimal interference. If these are not alleviated, external constraints are likely to inhibit the implementation of the desired economic and broader sociopolitical reforms and may in effect undermine the achievements booked since mid-1989. It would be a tragedy if such a setback were to occur for lack of a proper international response, given the past forty years of stalemate and the relatively small cost compared to the gains to be reaped, including for those eventually asked to put up the capital.

Fourth, I have no illusion that a payments union could be run without a hitch. Among the many objections that I have been confronted with two are important. One is that intragroup trade is such a "small" part of the total trade of these countries that constructing a CEPU would not be worth the effort. Of course, if these countries could start trading in convertible currency, there would be no point in elaborating a CEPU as distinct from a CEEU. In this it is usually forgotten that trade with other socialist countries and the bulk of trade with DEs is dealt with on clearing accounts. Hence the extra demand for convertible currency, if the "small" part were to be placed on such a basis, would not be negligible at all. Perhaps more important is the argument that without the Soviet Union there would be little point in elaborating a CEPU. I agree but only if the CEPU is seen as a static vehicle and if trade and payment flows are homogeneous. For one, the share of trade transacted within Central Europe is small because these countries have not been able to exploit their reciprocal comparative advantages. The example of the Benelux after World War II could usefully be invoked here once again. In addition, the current environment favors east-west cooperation, including in assisting Soviet market-oriented reforms. If the latter were to become a viable promise, the argument based on the "smallness" of Central Europe would disappear. It would be further eroded if Yugoslavia were to become a member. Without orderly arrangements, all kinds of arrangements are being introduced that, in fact, substantially raise the various bilateralized trade flows over and above half the number of possible bilateral channels, as detailed in Chapter 7.

For now, however, another solution will have to be found to come to grips with the dependence of these countries on trade with the Soviet Union. A more positive attitude toward genuine regional integration may be very constructive in this regard. Its success depends, of course, critically on the Soviet Union placing its reform on a market-oriented last. That is, unfortunately, not yet in sight. To the extent that negotiators can detect promise with market-oriented Soviet reforms, given the time it takes to negotiate a CEPU, a good case can be made for designing the CEPU from first principles with eventual Soviet participation as well as the potential accession of the rest of Eastern Europe and Yugoslavia built into the scheme.

It has to be borne in mind that a payments union is strictly a temporary device to be utilized for a very narrowly defined technical set of issues and, in the process, to be wielded as an instrument in pursuing broader socioeconomic and perhaps also political goals. But it certainly cannot help the PETs, or any other group of countries for that matter, with the structural payments problems that are currently commingled with the transitory payments problems that could be addressed in a union, as discussed in Chapter 2. One could intellectually separate the issues at stake into two groups. One refers to predictable balance-of-payments problems, such as those deriving from the erosion of the terms of trade. This is different from the issues connected with seeking security against unpredictable imbalances arising from the liberalization of trade, especially the separation of trade policy making from actual trading conducted by autonomous firms acting on their own account.

It bears to stress from the outset, however, that a payments union does not and cannot provide an ironclad guarantee that the objectives - basically the easement of payments problems stemming from trade liberalization and economic decentralization - will be reached in the envisaged time frame. There are, of course, also negative implications of setting up a payments union that should be mitigated as much as possible by both the architects and even more the supervisors of the payments union. Financial diplomacy, as Jacob J. Kaplan and Günther Schleiminger coined it in their history (1989) of the EPU's management, will be critical in guiding reformers. Special precautions may therefore have to be taken from the outset. If not properly supervised, a payments union may lead to a dangerous easing of reforms. How to design the right blend of encouraging incisive reform while making those changes tolerable for these fragile societies remains a major assignment.

Finally, reforms in the PETs must find mutual support not only to exploit more fully existing comparative advantages and generate dynamic advantages through the reform process. Also, it could help to facilitate the enormous shift in managerial attitudes, marketing, legal trading arrangements, and the other wherewithal of markets that will have to be learned the hard way, namely in the process of practicing the virtues of market-oriented decision making.

5

Technical aspects of a payments union

In Chapters 2 and 3 I argued the substantive case for establishing a payments union for the PETs, and the rest of Eastern Europe, the Soviet Union, and Yugoslavia under some conditions. This proposal can be credible only if details of the conceptualization and functioning of such a union are cogently addressed. This chapter first looks at the salient features of such a payments union, making the connection with the EPU's example drawn in broad brush strokes in Chapter 2. Next it examines one basic problem associated with the ongoing or desired economic reforms and the emerging current-account problems. Section 3 points out several technical issues and how they could possibly be resolved. Details regarding minimum capital requirements of a regional payments union under various assumptions on modalities of settlements and participants are discussed next. The issue of macroeconomic surveillance is, of course, a critical one, and for that reason I defer it to Chapter 6. In the last section, I deliberate on whether it would be wise to conceptualize a CEPU without involvement of the Soviet Union or its successor republics for that matter.

1. Overall conceptualization of the CEPU

The "thoroughly bilateral solution" for relations among the Eastern European countries, following the demise of the TR regime, might have been avoided. For that to have happened, the reforming countries would have had to identify common ground on how to restructure their reciprocal economic relations in a meaningful way, that is, one dovetailed with their own domestic reform blueprints or aspirations. A CEEU could have contributed significantly to desirable reforms. If strengthened with a mechanism that offered some protection against unanticipated payments imbalances that could potentially derail the reform, or at least set it back, such an economic union would have been highly desirable. In its absence, countries must individually come to grips with balancing their external accounts by curbing absorption, borrowing abroad, or cooperation.

Any cooperative solution involves mounting a payments facility for the countries involved. As noted in Chapter 3, this can take on various dimensions. One extreme would in essence bribe the reforming countries into enacting current-account convertibility forthwith, at least for merchandise and related transactions. The other would essentially involve the construction of a mechanism to guide these countries toward convertibility through a payments union.

In both cases, a considerable degree of international surveillance would have to be exercised to ensure that the facility remains manageable and the countries embark on and progress with market-oriented reforms. If successful, these reforms will render the payments facility superfluous after a comparatively brief period of time.

Efficient market relations in support as well as in emanation of domestic and foreign economic reforms in the PETs cannot be secured without moving decisively toward current-account convertibility in virtually all trade relations. As discussed in Chapter 4, there are several ways of reaching that target. In my scheme of things, a cooperative approach is the most desirable route to be taken, given the realities of the PETs. That would seek to resolve external payments problems in such a way as to safeguard desirable structural reforms, which in part will be required to implement meaningful - credible and sustainable - current-account convertibility. By proceeding in this fashion, macroeconomic managers must ensure that the commitment to gradualism does not get dissipated under force of circumstance. A clearing institution with some external supervisory muscle would seem to offer the preferred route. But there are admittedly other options, depending essentially on how big a payments facility can be mounted for the PETs (see Chapter 8).

The fundamental features of such a payments union would be the following eleven. First and foremost, all participants via their central banks extend each other automatic credit as transactions are conducted in local currency via transfers at the national bank. That is to say, in each member the central bank maintains accounts of exports to and imports from every member of the union by its residents. Whether or not books are kept bilaterally is immaterial.

Second, periodically all bilateral imbalances incurred by the members are immediately multilateralized. This could be done once a month as in the case of the EPU. But with modern telecommunications, clearing could be executed almost instantaneously, thereby reducing the automatic crediting mentioned under the first point. Whatever the reporting periodicity, each country tallies up its deliveries against all its obligations toward all members of the union. The net balance is reported to the technical institution entrusted with the accounting tasks. In what follows, I call this the Clearing Agent. The latter translates these reports into one common currency unit and facilitates the settlement of imbalances. This should preferably be the European Currency Unit (ECU), with participants for now managing exchange rates themselves.

Third, all members are granted a certain quota against which they can draw or must grant credit to the union. Quotas are set in proportion to some realistic recent visible and, if possible, invisible turnover levels. The size of the quotas should be sufficiently large not to discourage countries from undertaking agreed-upon reforms, including in particular the promotion of steady liberalization of trade and foreign-exchange regimes. At the same time, the quotas should not be too substantial for then the discipline on macroeconomic behavior, on which more below, will only rarely be exercised. Large quotas will in all likelihood be associated with substantial creditor positions. If creditors can divert their trade to nonunion partners, it may be difficult to bolster and prop up intragroup trade - the primary objective for launching the scheme. But even if creditors are not in a position to divert trade, large surpluses tend to discourage export promotion - another worthy objective.

Fourth, given the reluctance of PETs to incur deficits in trade that used to be denominated in TRs, quotas are split up into one or more tranches that consist of various combinations of credit and actual cash payments, at least for the debtor country. Asymmetry in settlements to encourage countries to export and obtain a net surplus, yet not compel the country ending up with a deficit to pay a substantial part of it immediately in convertible currency would be useful. The Clearing Agent keeps imbalances in a cumulative fashion. The particular combination of loans with cash payments will be evaluated in accordance with the tranches reached for the cumulative imbalance, utilizing the principle of "last in first out." This means that a debtor recently at a high tranche (that is, with a large share of cash payments) who is now reversing the imbalance into a surplus position gets access to the high tranche of loan and cash receipts.

Fifth, to make this asymmetry function well, a common fund is required from which the Clearing Agent can finance net claims on the union, if any. The size of the common fund depends on the degree of settlement asymmetry that the participants are keen on introducing. The larger the asymmetry, for any volume of trade turnover, the larger the capital fund must be, owing to the fact that the potential net claims on union resources rise. This common fund could usefully be contributed by an outside partner, in particular the EC. In exchange, the funder obtains some leeway in monitoring settlements and indeed in surveilling the entire operations of moving toward convertibility, hence trade and foreign-exchange liberalization. The settlement and surveillance mechanisms should guarantee that, on balance, the demand for resources from the central fund for the orderly conduct of trade decreases over time as a steadily rising proportion of the cumulative imbalance is being paid in convertible currency.

Sixth, some solution needs to be worked out to come to grips with current TR imbalances as well as TR debts existing prior to the CEPU's inception. These need to be worked off outside the union or be revalued at a more realistic exchange rate, something that is now a distinct option.[1] This is necessary because the imbalances were incurred at relative TRPs that were far from even moderately consistent, thereby inhibiting transferability. If ways could be found to temporarily finance such revalued imbalances outside the payments facility, it would help matters. Otherwise, the principal parties themselves would have to work out a *modus vivendi*. Also with respect to the outstanding convertible-

[1] Hungary converted its trade surplus with the Soviet Union at a rate ($0.92 per ruble) that is between the then official dollar-ruble (0.6) and dollar-forint (2.36) rates. Czechoslovakia reportedly did likewise in December 1990 by agreeing to a one-to-one exchange rate, which is also between the two cross-rates.

currency debt, some solution will have to be found outside the provisions of a payments union. These debts and their servicing requirements pose structural payments problems that cannot possibly be resolved from within a payments union. Forcing participants to service their convertible-currency debt is tantamount to undermining the potential salutary effects of a payments union, and indeed may altogether threaten the process of marketization.

Seventh, the Clearing Agent acts essentially as a bank charging interest on loans and granting interest on deposits. Any excess funds are to be wisely invested with the net returns accruing to the capital base of the facility. These interest charges should soon be approximate those applicable to international short-term interbank lending.

Eighth, an agency must be entrusted with surveillance. This I refer to as the Surveillance Board. Its task should be to maintain the connection among reform intentions, trade liberalization, currency convertibility as a policy goal, and facilitating external settlements. It should be clearly understood by all parties involved that a clearing scheme that does not allow for the rapid emergence of more rational trade - and domestic - prices will undermine any kind of multilateral clearing, regardless of how sophisticated the technical accommodations laid down may in the end be. This is particularly relevant in the case of the PETs. Disparities among relative prices not justified by some scarcity criterion have been the bane of all previous attempts at multilateralizing TR trade and payments (Brabant 1987a, pp. 273-8). Selection of the members of the Surveillance Board would, of course, be the privilege of those financing the scheme.

Ninth, owing to the complex technical issues of guiding the transition of PETs, particularly from the point of view of weathering external imbalances, moving forward with currency convertibility, enhancing trade liberalization, and underpinning market relations, it would be desirable to constitute the Surveillance Board mainly with, say, half a dozen to a dozen professional macroeconomists; some should be well versed in the problems of the legacies of central planning and the issues of transition in PETs. These individuals would derive their authority from, and hence be responsible to, the funders or their designated oversight agency. One could imagine, for example, the EC as funding organization to select the members of the Surveillance Board; but the Board would owe ultimate accounting to the Council of Ministers, the Commission of the EC, or the European Parliament. Other modalities can be readily explored provided they promise greater credibility and efficiency.

Tenth, membership in the union should be open to all countries of Eastern Europe that adopt credible market-oriented reforms. Under certain conditions, this might include Yugoslavia and the Soviet Union or their successor republics.

Finally, the scheme should have a clear-cut time path by the end of which all intragroup transactions will automatically be conducted in convertible currency, though not necessarily immediate cash payments. Clearing in convertible currency would economize foreign-exchange reserves. If managed expeditiously and at minimal cost, it would for all practical purposes be equivalent to current-account convertibility. Once the latter stage is reached, provisions will have to be made on what needs to be done with outstanding loans and the remaining "liquid assets," namely the original capital contribution plus investment earnings that over the lifetime of the union.

Acceptance of these broad guidelines on the institutional structure and clearing procedures of the CEPU does not, of course, answer all questions. Indeed, every single element set forth above elicits one or more technical queries pertaining to the clearing fund and what needs to be safeguarded against to prevent its premature demise. These include questions on quotas, what to do with the existing debt and current imbalances, the clearing authority, credit tranches, asymmetry in allocating quotas to creditors and debtors, the exchange rate utilized for transactions, the capital fund, surveillance, duration of the agreement, and so on. Most of these ingredients of the mechanics of creating and technically operating a payments union can be explored in some depth. Other elements that complete a payments union must necessarily emanate from compromise solutions thrashed out in negotiations about what are essentially matters falling within the purview of foreign commercial policy and financial diplomacy. The most desirable outcome of such negotiations cannot, of course, be intimated by an outsider. Rather than try to second-guess in advance how such deliberations might unfold, I shall confine the discussion of these issues to proposals or options of what might be most useful and what is feasible. Whether that will indeed be borne out in concrete negotiations among the various parties involved remains to be seen.

Given the urgency of coming to grips with balancing the external payments of the PETs and the intricate problems that have to be faced to keep the reform moving along without debilitating these economies, it would be useful to leave as few parameters as possible for detailed negotiations among the parties directly involved in the union. In other words, it would be useful if, say, the EC as funding organ would come forth with as detailed a proposal of the CEPU as can be reconciled with the need to avoid any impression of a *Diktat* for eastern policy makers. Without laying any claim to arrogating for myself the EC's latitude in putting together the details of a clearing scheme, I shall consider in Section 3 several elements that could usefully be embedded in the proposal to be tabled for the participants. But first a brief look at the nature of the PETs' external-payments problems and whether it would be wise to resolve them through a payments union in preference to some other payments facility.

2. Payments problems and a regional payments union

One of the potentially more serious problems associated with any scheme designed to tackle imbalances in regional payments revolves around the current-account target. In principle, a country's balance-of-payments problems should be looked at from the point of view of its payments to and receipts from *all* partners (Balassa 1990). As such, any regional-clearing scheme suffers from a fundamental weakness: To require, in principle, that all countries balance their current account with the clearing system, and, if not, that they will be persuaded through the macroeconomic surveillance facility to take steps to achieve precisely that, is tantamount to assuming that they balance at the same time their accounts with countries that remain outside the system. Without this, participants are tempted to react in an asymmetric fashion to surpluses and deficits, depending upon the addressee of the particular position. Countries with a favorable balance with the union will tend to utilize their surplus to offset deficits with outside partners; but those in deficit with the clearing agency do not want to repatriate their outside surpluses. This is certainly a theoretical conundrum. It may have serious repercussions in practice too.

Innovating a payments facility that seeks to preserve as much as possible the desirable features of multilateralism, nondiscrimination, and convertibility, or, at the very least, moving in that direction, should in principle be preferred over a payments arrangement such as the EPU. However, rarely do serious constraints on payments arise for countries operating in a multilateral world with minimal trade and exchange inhibitions. A moderately flexible exchange rate or participation in near-universal clearing unions, such as, in fact, the Fund, will as a rule suffice to come to grips with payments problems (Bofinger 1991a, b). Enacting the "GDR integration" scenario for the rest of Eastern Europe, as Bofinger advocates, would simply be disastrous (Bergsten and Willimanson 1990, p. 47; Protzman 1991). There is simply not enough "integrated flexibility" available to achieve the required adjustment at a tolerable cost, including its distribution over time. Countries may face serious problems with their bilateral or subgroup payments, perhaps because distinctions between alternative partner groupings have deeply drawn systemic roots. That is to say, the nature of their inherited trading world for now leads *de facto* to different payments problems because most goods cannot be switched from one "market" to another, at least without incurring sizable costs. To mitigate this dichotomy or even more complex fragmentation of the trading world, it may be desirable to institute, what on the face of it is, a discriminatory arrangement. This would seem to be Eastern Europe's case.

Eastern Europe's trading world is hardly fully integrated with minimal trade and foreign-exchange constraints. This applies to some degree to their intragroup trade. It holds even more with respect to their commerce with third parties. Practical considerations, if nothing else, therefore argue for dealing separately with partners that honor a fairly transparent foreign-exchange system from relations in which countries find it difficult for technical reasons to move away from severe constraints on balancing their external payments. That is to say, when the realistic policy choice is manifestly *not* between a payments union and a multilateral trading world, then another intermediate option could usefully be innovated. This fundamental choice between bilateralism and the EPU was the case with Western Europe after World War II. In my view, for Eastern

Europe the choice is essentially between some payments facility and a full rebilateralization of intragroup relations. While theory would argue against a clearing union because of the asymmetry of surplus and deficit countries with respect to outside partners, the practical task is to mitigate the adverse implications thereof through careful monitoring and fine-tuning of macroeconomic, including trade, policies through commercial and financial diplomacy.

In the case of the EPU, the temptation to deal asymmetrically with surplus and deficit positions outside the union was on the whole not very significant, although the issue in and of itself caused a number of management crises (Kaplan and Schleiminger 1989, pp. 136-53; Rees 1963). There are several reasons for this. One was the size of intragroup trade. Most participants at the outset conducted about half of their external commerce among themselves (including their extended monetary areas). These proportions rose rapidly once the currency devaluations of 1949 took hold and the process of solid recovery was well on its way, including most notably on account of the rapid expansion in the western zones of Germany and the quest of the emerging FRG to integrate itself quickly into the global economy. Furthermore, by the early 1950s, these countries had gained reciprocal trust and confidence. They were, therefore, on the whole bent on nearly scrupulously observing the agreed rules of the game. Even so, some cajoling on the part of the guarantor, especially through the ECA and later the Managing Board (Kaplan and Schleiminger 1989, Rees 1963), proved at times necessary. As a result, each was willing to pay some price for making the EPU and the transition to currency convertibility work. This helped to reach consensual solutions for otherwise intractable technical problems. Also, trade and payment flows with countries outside the union were overwhelmingly with the United States, hence in a convertible currency. This country had been the key sponsor of the EPU to begin with and had little interest in draining its own currency from the fund.

Critical in this respect was that the United States explicitly allowed Western Europe to discriminate against dollar trade through the payments mechanism rather than through tariffs, quotas, or even less transparent instruments of commercial policy. In fact, the United States had been one of the pivotal champions of economic integration in Western Europe. It saw such a realignment of economic linkages as a paramount instrument not only for economic recovery there, but also to maintain the peace and form a strong bulwark against the eastern adversaries. To further this, it had been willing to tolerate a somewhat faster reduction of quantitative restrictions within the EPU area than of the member countries *vis-à-vis* outside partners. Indeed, policy fine-tuning required temporary reversals of the trade-liberalization schemes when no other option remained (see Chapter 6).

A similar support for the CEPU, this time extended on behalf of the EC, would be very important indeed. Some positive discrimination in currency matters, rather than by encumbering existing tariffs, quotas, or less orthodox commercial-policy instruments, would unquestionably help to solidify the foundations of the CEEU and persuade potential members that it would be in their own interest to first transit through the CEEU, including on the way to entry into the EC as soon as practically feasible.

Are the conditions under which the EPU succeeded likely to be replicated in Central or Eastern Europe? Given the present disarray in the area, it is hard to envisage these countries in some combination autonomously being imbued with a great deal of mutual trust in the near term. Such may emerge once the uncertainty about where to go from here, including in the Soviet Union, dissipates. This lack of confidence is much less pronounced for some of the smaller countries, however. Thus, a payments union for Central Europe would cater to shared political interests and commitments "to making it work," although the degree of overt commonality for now admittedly remains rather shallow. Lingering social and political revendications even in that subregion may pose unusual obstacles, but these could be overcome through a concerted policy.

The existing distrust would argue for strong leadership in managing the union. In the case of the EPU, management was essentially entrusted to a Managing Board consisting of financial experts appointed in their personal capacity. But all had strong ties to their respective governments, chiefly through positions in the central banks and ministries of finance, but also the ECA. Such could not possibly be envisaged for the organ surveilling the CEPU's mechanics and policy adjustments. One reason is the desirability of bolstering credibility for reform policies through the European connection (see Chapter 8). Another is that many policy makers and administrators of PETs are simply unfamiliar with the workings of the market or the inner logic of international trade and finance. As I argue in the next chapter, this is a fruitful area for broader cooperation in Europe. More specifically, I see essentially a role for more active involvement of the Commission of the EC, the Council of Ministers, or even the European Parliament as the ultimate sponsor of the scheme and authority to whom the Surveillance Board owes accounting. This would provide an element of credibility to Eastern European reforms and expectations around them that would otherwise scarcely be available.

German unification poses its own problems. For one, the GDR used to be the second-largest trading partner of Eastern Europe. Its industrial prowess, however much it may have lagged behind that of DMEs, is intimately linked to the needs of the rest of Eastern Europe, including because of the machine park in place. Such transitional requirements could have been met only if a unified Germany had not forcibly precluded gradual restructuring of the former GDR's industry. Indeed, a good deal of trade could have been maintained through bilateral loans or government guarantees as in the case of the Soviet Union, something that observers have been advocating (Kenen 1990, p. 29). Such a proposal has apparently been floated confidentially by the FRG and some follow-up measures may have been emplaced in December 1990 (Schill 1991).

I do not deem such loans very desirable for the same reason that the substantial lending of the 1970s turned into a fiasco of major proportions. It would have been more constructive to accommodate the former GDR's trade within the CEPU. German traders of properly identified goods would have paid for imports from Eastern Europe in *Deutschmark* and exporters would have obtained full payment. Identification is necessary for otherwise there would be too great an opportunity to arbitrage between the *Deutschmark* and the combination of *Deutschmark*-and-clearing claims, perhaps as a result of special agreements in effect at the time of unification or those negotiated during the transition. Such transactions could have been taken care of by a special office at the Bundesbank, perhaps the successor to the intra-German clearing agency, as participant in the CEPU. The Eastern European counterparts would have settled their obligations or obtained payment for their exports through the CEPU mechanism. Without such an accommodation, as it happened, eastern partners find it impossible, at least for now, to place their trade with the former GDR on a convertible-currency basis. As a result, the viability of the ex-GDR's industry has been jeopardized far more quickly and extensively than need have been the case (Protzman 1991). Such additional trade volumes would have helped to "force through" the process of moving to convertibility. Of course, the former GDR could realistically no longer form a constituent part of a CEEU.

3. Technical issues of a payments union

Any payments union has two sides. One is the generally politicized type of cooperation that the national leaders entrusted with the negotiations and ratification of proposals will inevitably engage in, if only to gain short-term benefits for themselves. The other consists of a sequence of highly technical aspects of how settlements can be arranged. Of necessity, these will be resolved either during arduous negotiations among the potential participants in such a union or beforehand by those financing the institution. For comparison's sake, the concrete negotiations around the EPU, after a fleshed-out proposal drafted by Richard M. Bissell and Robert Triffin had first been tabled by the United States (Kaplan and Schleiminger 1989, pp. 31-32), took more than nine months. Even then numerous technical problems had subsequently to be overcome.

It should be recalled that the EPU proposal was designed for countries that had been collaborating very closely, had engaged in makeshift payments arrangements for several years, and were comparatively well prepared for adopting a cooperative solution to relaxing the constraints on their external payments and moving toward convertibility. Even so, numerous technical issues arose in the EPU's initial stages and many practical obstacles had to be settled subsequently as well. This suggests that it would be hopeless even to try to sketch a blueprint for a ready-made payments union. Instead, I confine myself to the technical aspects of a union. The more sticky issues can only be resolved through accommodating compromises among the parties involved.

1. The Clearing Agent

Inasmuch as the Clearing Agency performs highly technical tasks, identification of such an institution should be guided by technical norms. Modern computerized telecommunications are a prime requirement, aside from the organization's integrity. Because the BIS was the EPU's accounting agency and has conducted clearing in a number of schemes, including interbank clearing of transactions denominated in ECU, it embodies some store of expertise regarding the type of transactions envisaged for the CEPU. It could be entrusted with the accounting and technical supervisory tasks once the members agree upon an acceptable mode of clearing without too many problems.

2. Techniques of accounting

The essence of a payments union is twofold. One is to cut down on the transaction demand for convertible currency. Periodically, partners simply tally up their reciprocal transactions. In the meantime, they automatically extend technical credits to each other. It also makes available to participants a combination of loans and actual payments, within agreed-upon limits, for settling net imbalances *vis-à-vis* the union. This reduces the precautionary demand for foreign-exchange reserves because the CEPU compresses settlements requirements, hence the magnitude of the potential outflow of reserves to cover deficits.

Practical procedures could be set up as follows. Any trader in a participating country obtains a license for the acquisition of goods from any other participant. The exporter receives and the importer pays the local-currency equivalent. These transactions are reported to the national correspondent of the Clearing Agency, where claims and payments are accumulated in one currency unit, preferably that of the union itself, until the net balance has to be reported to the union. Once that is done, the Clearing Agent verifies at which tranche the net claim needs to be settled. In case the upper tranche is surpassed, it will have to refer the matter to a higher authority.

In the envisaged CEPU, participants are reforming countries. By definition, they have made some progress toward current-account convertibility for merchandise and related transactions. Czechoslovakia and Poland claim to have reached domestic convertibility in the above sense. Hungary has gone a long way to liberalizing its trade regime. These features apply, if at all, only to trade that used to be conducted in convertible currency, including through clearing that simply provided a framework for the conduct of actual transactions; it is obviously not for other forms of clearing (see Chapter 7). For that reason, in the CEPU, there is no need to institute foreign-exchange controls that are more discriminatory than the *status quo ante* position. All that is required is that the licensing for individual transactions with countries with whom formerly trade was largely conducted bilaterally within the TR regime, or its successor nonframework, from now on be replaced by licenses for any transaction with any partner, although reaching that type of intragroup trade liberalization itself may well require some transition. This is unlike in the EPU, where participants maintained foreign-exchange controls, even *vis-à-vis* dollar transactions, at least on the import side. However, to the extent that not all clearing arrangements with countries that did not apply the TR regime can be replaced with convertible currency, some form of discriminatory licensing will have to be maintained. Key is however that this would *not* forcibly exacerbate absolute discrimination. This topic is addressed in greater detail in Chapter 7.

Accounting requires some rules on the clearing unit, the conversion of various currencies into that unit of account and *vice versa*, the publicity given to the statistical status of the operations, and the follow-up, if any. Regarding the currency unit of the CEPU and the exchange rates to be used, there is no ideal solution. Convertible-currency exchange rates are flexible, the present currencies of the CMEA countries are inconvertible, and there is simply no ideal - let alone fixed - exchange rate that could be selected for the CEPU members. A pragmatic solution, therefore, recommends itself. This could place, for example, the ECU at the heart of the CEPU scheme.

The ECU is attractive because it is becoming the invoicing currency of a rising share of Eastern Europe's trade with the west. It is also more stable than other currencies, including the dollar, because it is a currency basket and especially the FRG, the pace maker of the ECU, has been pursuing low-inflation policies. Furthermore, it is a currency unit that does not solely depend on one country's national monetary policy. Moreover, it is a currency that governs integration relations in the EC, membership of which is being coveted by PETs. Also, the EBRD, which is to play a critical role in the transition, will keep its books, hence lend, in ECU. Finally, the ongoing debate on the Economic and Monetary Union (EMU) and further progress with integration in the EC framework holds out the prospect of there eventually emerging a single currency managed by a responsible European monetary institution; the reforming Eastern Europe would certainly wish eventually to be part of this as well (Brabant 1991f). Seen against that backdrop, the ECU should be as attractive, especially for the creditor, as the real 1950 dollars used by the EPU were. The members of the CEPU themselves would have to take care, for the time being, of managing the rates at which their trade gets translated into domestic currency.

This solution not only suggests that CEPU participants gradually manage their foreign exchange regime in tandem with that of the European Monetary System (EMS). If so, it would also subject them increasingly to the discipline of the EMS - a useful learning tool (Pons 1990). Of course, such a choice would invite the EC to assume a major role in financing the CEPU's initial capital. It would also compel the EC or a designated agent to see to the success of the union over some period of time. If carefully worked out in the context of firm stabilization policies with steady growth reasonably assured after some interlude through supply actions, regaining stability may prepare the CEPU participants for *de facto* or *de jure* entry into the EMS. This could, of course, work only if potential participants are prepared to subscribe to and abide by the EMS's monetary policy. As such, the envisaged CEPU, instead of being a fairly simple "decompression chamber" (Agnelli 1990) toward full convertibility, would constitute the *antichambre* to the EC. It would be reached by passing through the CEPU tunnel lined with the EC's promise and properly shored up through the EC's capital and authorized surveillance (Brabant 1991f).

3. Prior imbalances and loans

When a payments union is set up, participants usually have outstanding debts and current imbalances to contend with. Those referring to reciprocal claims may directly affect the operations of the union. But even imbalances with other partners may aggravate the problems ensuing from the asymmetry discussed in Section 2.

International debts pose a serious challenge for the CEPU. Particularly Hungary and Poland are heavily indebted. If the union were to be wider, also Bulgaria and the Soviet Union have substantial convertible-currency debts and the Soviet Union has some TR debts to as well as claims on Eastern Europe. The convertible-currency debt cannot but drain currency balances. Countries will be induced to divert surpluses with the clearing union to offset current-account deficits with nonmember countries. Of course, several of the potential members have mutual loan arrangements (of which the Polish-Soviet one is by far the largest). It would be useful to design a solution for the debt problem with respect to both the Soviet Union and MEs. Certainly the experience with bringing outstanding debts into the EPU (see Kaplan and Schleiminger 1989, Rees 1963) suggests that it would be preferable not to commingle this issue with problems pertaining to current payments within the context of a CEPU. To achieve this, it would be useful to identify a mechanism to allow these countries, at least for now, to focus on current trade (and perhaps nondebt services), while the apparently insoluble problems stemming from their inherited external debts are addressed by other means.

I have no ready suggestion on what could be done. However, in the context of the initiative of the Group of Twenty-four in general and the Paris Club in particular, there may now be some inclination to find a mutually agreeable *modus vivendi* on the issues concerning outside debt. It is now almost universally agreed, given the precedent with partial debt forgiveness to sub-Saharan Africa and Poland, that any pragmatic solution in fact entails a substantial write-off of the debt. Such should ensure the separability of the stock of debt from current payments for trade and services other than debt service. Also with respect to the Soviet Union some willingness to cooperate will have to come to the fore. One vehicle would be to have the Soviet Union join the IMF as a creditor either as a full member or as a "concerned observer." Some of its windfall oil gains, if they indeed materialize (that is, if oil production does not sharply contract and WMPs remain high), that cannot now be profitably invested in the domestic economy could be rechanneled to Eastern Europe through the Fund's good offices. I am, of course, aware that the politicized aspects of the relations between the Fund and the Soviet Union have soured sharply as a consequence of the military repression in the Baltic states. But the opportunity for undertaking such a cooperative facility with the Soviet Union fully into the picture may recur at some future date.

The second type of claims that may disturb a payments union refer to current imbalances that need to be rectified or accommodated before the payment regime can be altered. Several CMEA countries have recently involuntarily sustained fairly substantial intragroup trade and related imbalances stemming largely from unexpected terms-of-trade shifts, supply constraints, and abrupt changes in demand leading to cancellation of previously placed orders. Some solution should be found for these TR imbalances. As shown by the Hungarian-Soviet agreement reached in March 1990 and the Czechoslovak-Soviet agreement of December 1990, it is now possible, although by no means easy, to negotiate a mutually agreeable means of converting TR into convertible-currency balances that may be earmarked against future deficits. Owing to the very different relative TRPs at the roots of these imbalances, it would be desirable to work toward a political compromise that does *not* encumber the CEPU. Again, the EPU's negative experience in this respect is instructive (Rees 1963).

4. Publicity

Regarding publicity to the evolving nature of clearing, a low-key, technical approach recommends itself. The Clearing Agent essentially informs each member of its position purely from an accounting point of view. This information is also transmitted to the Surveillance Board as basic input for its macroeconomic policy assessment and remedial advice, on which more below. There is certainly no need to publicize the activities of the Surveillance Board in great detail.

5. The question of asymmetry

Even if a solution can be found for the inherited imbalances, it remains true that Central Europe conducts most of its external payments with countries that would be outside the CEPU. The single most important partner in the east is the Soviet Union, whose participation in a CEPU is problematical, to say the least. Since early 1991, this trade has in principle been placed on a convertible-currency basis and conducted at imputed WMPs. In practice, however, it is being conducted at several unsynchronized levels. These include pure barter, clearing in convertible currency, transactions in convertible currency, and combinations of the preceding three modes with multiple variants. With respect to genuine convertible-currency trade, Western Europe constitutes the paramount partner. This might tempt participants to erode the clearing fund's base by appropriating surpluses to settle convertible-currency deficits with outsiders. As noted in Section 2, only concerted action on the part of the major MEs, chiefly through the Commission of the EC, but also on account of the trading interests of a united Germany, could help to stem that tide. Remains, then, the variety of clearing with chiefly DEs but also a number of former CPEs.

There should be no doubt that, even with the Soviet Union participating in a payments union, Eastern Europe is aiming mainly at full integration into world markets. This can materialize only if these countries come to grips with convertible-currency imbalances. If no solution is found for the lingering external debt, the temptation to earmark convertible currency from the fund to settle imbalances with third partners will be insuperable. This incentive to drain resources from the common pool can be mitigated only through western support and some self-denial by forgoing potential trade substitution in the short run. In other words, the sponsor(s) of the union may voluntarily defer some of the benefits expected from trade liberalization and trade creation in the PETs - they will probably not be called upon to tolerate trade diversion for the reasons discussed earlier - through their own actions as financial sponsors, advocates of strict surveillance, and coordinators of payment stances with desirable reform policies. This temporary abstinence could be appropriate for the same reason that Western Europe after World War II was actively encouraged by the United States to discriminate explicitly against dollar imports through the payment mechanism rather than through more orthodox commercial-policy instruments. Net exporters to the union would prefer to conduct their trade with union participants only if they could not divert trade without incurring terms-of-trade losses exceeding the potential cost of granting credit to debitors. A similar support for the CEPU, this time extended on behalf of the EC, would be very important indeed to solidify the foundations of the CEEU, as discussed in Chapter 3, and persuade potential members that it would be in their own interest, including in their endeavor to link up with the EC, to first transit through the CEEU.

Of course, there are considerable obstacles to a successful CEPU. Even so, policy makers should carefully ponder the range of options in their exchange regime and its ramifications from among which the PETs can realistically choose at this juncture. None of the alternatives is very attractive, without downside risks, or promises swift movement to markets at a tolerable cost. A gradual approach would embody at least a commitment to structured success in freeing up trade and domestic competition at a tolerable cost, including the time required to attain current-account convertibility. It is against this backdrop that I stress the benefits of setting up a capital base to support the PETs in their moving in a relatively short period of time toward current-account convertibility. Of course, as argued, this will be so *only* if participants cannot or will not establish current-account convertibility all at once or very quickly, or they are unable to divert trade to the west without incurring sizable terms-of-trade and export-revenue losses. The financial, intellectual, and managerial support required could usefully be mustered from within the context of the assistance currently being provided, such as from within the Group of Twenty-four. This would be of the utmost importance if the Soviet Union and remaining Eastern European economies, including Yugoslavia under some conditions, would be included too. The sums involved are not at all substantial, as documented later.

6. Quotas and access to credits

With respect to the financial benefits of a payments union, one salient task is to establish quotas against which participants can draw in case of a net deficit with the union or give credit in case of a net-surplus position. As a rule, the quotas are divided into several combinations of loans and convertible-currency payments. That necessarily involves negotiations about the very heart of not only the facilitation of payments but also the kind of macroeconomic policy surveillance associated with "excessive" use of the facility. A high quota leaves leeway for bold trade-liberalization measures, whose adverse imbalances can partly be cushioned through loans. But it might invite members to go slow with the underlying trade-liberalization and restructuring efforts to correct external imbalances. A creditor may, however, get discouraged by virtue of the fact that he does not immediately obtain full currency payment. As already intimated, this will be so only if the cost of giving credit exceeds the cost in terms of negative terms-of-trade effects incurred upon diverting trade to nonunion partners. A low quota, on the other hand, would call for quick macroeconomic policy adjustment, including rapid trade-liberalization and restructuring efforts. This might make the scheme rather attractive to creditors. But sociopolitical realities and unacceptability of some kinds of austerity may slow down the process rather than enhance these measures because it will deter potential debitors from moving swiftly with trade liberalization for fear of draining reserves.

In the case of the EPU, quotas were drawn up against total visible and invisible trade among the EPU members for 1949. Fifteen percent of that trade was set as the quota, of which at most 60 percent could be drawn in credit and the rest had to be effected in convertible currency. The shares of actual payments and loans varied with the degree to which agreed-upon quotas were utilized at the end of each trading month. These shares resulted, however, from two or more tranches with various combinations of currency payments and claims on or loans obtained from the union. Over time, the requirements on actual convertible-currency settlements for a given use of quota rose. At the conclusion of the EPU, that share reached 100 percent, of course (Kaplan and Schleiminger 1989; Rees 1963; Tew 1967, pp. 111-12; Triffin 1957, pp. 170-2).

Whether these are the proper parameters for the PETs remains to be seen. Nonetheless, the overall features of the quotas, the tranches, the asymmetry for debitor and creditor, and the periodical reporting of net claims would be desirable for the CEPU too. Certainly, one major consideration would be the traditional rather low level of imbalances incurred in the bilaterally controlled trade and payment relations. Another important consideration is how much outside money will be forthcoming and to what degree members will be willing to extend automatic credit. The potential impact of alternative quotas and tranche arrangements will be discussed below together with the order of magnitude of the capital required to make it all work.

7. Adjustment rules

Inasmuch as a payments union is a comparatively simple technical device to enable participants to smooth balance-of-payments disturbances that may be due to structural problems or to problems of the transition, or both, the adjustment rules regarding macroeconomic policy must be clearly understood. In essence, they should not differ measurably from those traditionally adhered to for MEs (Brabant 1987a, pp. 115-7; Corbo 1990; Rodrick 1990; Spitzer 1969) by the Fund and the International Bank for Reconstruction and Development (World Bank or Bank). But they must be tailored to the specific problems of the transition in Eastern Europe (Dembinski and Morisset 1990). Critical is that these countries exhibit multiple legacies of central planning, including notably in the fields of foreign trade and low elasticities of supply, certainly at the outset of the structural-adjustment process. Radical and fairly rapid action is required to alter supply, something that has not figured prominently in traditional Fund adjustment programs. These are to a significant extent based on the assumption that market forces will almost automatically respond to demand restraint. This cannot be applied to Eastern Europe because of pervasive rigidities in supply.

However the multiple adjustment tasks are tackled, there is no alternative to weathering persistent external-payments deficits but by lowering absorption and shifting resources toward export-promoting sectors. Similarly, the stylized facts for a persistent surplus country call for raising levels of absorption, including stimulating import competition in domestic markets. In the case of the PETs, the weight of the adjustment advice should probably fall as much as possible on trade-promoting measures rather than bolstering aggregate demand, although the latter's fine-tuning cannot be dispensed with altogether. However, because intragroup imbalances may exhibit the opposite sign of imbalances with outsiders, special balancing procedures will need to be formulated. These will, by necessity, call for disciminatory trade-liberalization measures, if still possible, or even temporarily backtracking on reform commitments, as detailed in Chapter 6.

8. Macroeconomic surveillance

A natural question to ask in this connection is who will formulate such macroeconomic surveillance and through which mechanisms it can be enforced without unduly interfering in the domestic policy autonomy of the participants. Recall that in the case of the EPU the Managing Board formulated proposals for the Council of the OEEC, which then sought to influence a member's macroeconomic policy (Vries 1969a). In principle, this should on the whole not have been a satisfactory solution, inasmuch as the OEEC's power to impact upon decision making on members was highly confined.

The traditional perception of how the EPU functioned is that it had a rather perfunctory Managing Board essentially subordinated in its recommendations to the weak kind of coordination that could be achieved through the policy machinery of the OEEC. However, the comprehensive analysis recently presented by Jacob J. Kaplan and Günther Schleiminger (1989), and indeed by Brian Tew (1990), casts serious doubt on that widespread assumption, although their account is not free of criticism either (Milward 1990). If true, the role of the Managing Board was vastly more important than had earlier been suspected; the only upbeat account until recently had been the study by Graham Rees (1963). Whatever its role in influencing macroeconomic policy stances may have been, there is no longer any doubt that "quiet" commercial and financial diplomacy exerted through the Managing Board persuaded countries to adopt the kind of adjustment policies required to avert excess surpluses or deficits, and, when they occurred, to work them off while minimizing adverse effects on relative, and exceptionally even absolute, discrimination. That is not to deny that some participants were at times recalcitrant and threatened to undermine the union altogether. Belgium was notorious and so was Germany after it weathered the negative implications of the monetary reform of 1948. Critical in having this influence exerted through the Managing Board was the confidence that national governments vested in key Board members. Most members were in or were intimately linked to the national governments or central banks and on the whole enjoyed broad ministerial support (Kaplan and Schleiminger 1989, Rees 1963).

To keep a scheme such as the CEPU's manageable, as in the EPU's case, tight surveillance over macroeconomic policies must be exercised. This could best be done by the party bringing in the capital because of its interest in seeing the marketization approach succeed in Eastern Europe. If the CEPU's capital fund were to be provided by the EC, it would stand to reason that the macroeconomic Surveillance Board would report to the Commission of the EC, the Council of Ministers, or the European Parliament. This would not only strengthen the position of the Board in allocating the capital fund, managing reciprocal adjustment, and sustaining outside support for temporarily exacerbating relative discrimination. It would also permit the ultimate oversight agency to influence the CEPU's participants through its leverage in the context of its broader assistance efforts. Particularly important in this respect are the resources amassed under the so-called PHARE (*Pologne/Hongrie: assistance à la restructuration économique*) program and related initiatives, a program that is now open to all reforming countries.

For reasons clarified in Chapter 6, I advocate entrusting surveillance mainly to a small body of perhaps half a dozen to a dozen professional macroeconomists, some of who need to be specialists in Eastern European economic affairs. Their primary task would be to monitor the situation in the participants on an almost continuous basis and to prepare technical options from among which policy makers will be asked to choose. Each option would be tied in with the delicate questions of how best to resolve excessive deficits and surpluses.

9. Interest-rate policies

A payments union as a rule seeks to implement favorable - possibly zero - interest rates for settlements among partner countries. In the EPU they were very low: 2 percent for creditors; the same for debtors the first year, 2.25 percent the second year, and 2.5 percent the third year (Rees 1963, p. 109). I do not see the advantage of underpricing foreign exchange. Negotiators should agree to anchor the union's interest-rate policies to levels customary in financial markets. Claims on the union should be treated in the same way as holdings of convertible currency. There might initially be some reason to marginally favor depositors simply to ensure flexibility in the union. This is desirable at the beginning when the size of bilateral imbalances is likely to rise and uncertainty prevails as to the sustainability of these imbalances. But the discrepancy between deposit and credit rates should, perhaps after a fairly brief transition phase, not surpass customary levels. The BIS could be instructed to apply international rates. This could be the London Interbank Offered Rate (LIBOR) plus a small fixed margin for deposits and a somewhat larger one for loans.

10. Capital cost

Intragroup trade of the European CMEA countries expressed at official exchange rates amounted to some $82.3 billion in 1989, with the absolute sum of imbalances *vis-à-vis* the group totaling some $4.2 billion, largely on account of the Soviet Union. If the payments scheme were to be mounted initially for the most reform-oriented countries, the volume of trade among Czechoslovakia, the ex-GDR, Hungary, and Poland in 1989 was roughly $15.8 billion with absolute imbalances *vis-à-vis* the group amounting to $291 million. Imbalances on so-called noncommercial account (transactions for tourism, unrequited transfers, transfers of royalties, alimony payments, stipends, and others), whose magnitude is unknown, probably offset part of the trade imbalances. These sums could easily be accommodated through a payments facility.

True, the lifting of bilateral constraints on trade among these countries would in all likelihood initially entail greater intragroup imbalances. But it would not necessarily result in larger absolute claims on the region; the ceiling would probably not exceed $1 billion per year in the short run, other things being equal, in the CEPU with reforming countries. Of course, if the Soviet

Union were to join the capital base would have to be more substantial or the quotas for imbalances more restrictive. However, instead of the deficits incurred by the Soviet Union with Eastern Europe in recent years surpluses, if allowed to emerge, will materialize over the next several years. If the transition to convertibility were to be envisaged over a five-year period, as argued, the clearing fund's capital base could be stretched out accordingly.

If the west were to put together a capital kitty to support a CEPU, how much would it cost? The answer is simple: not much in comparison to the magnitude of outside support that is currently mooted by way of aid to Eastern Europe, certainly when the Soviet Union is included. Precisely how much depends critically on what is to be accomplished. The central guideline, in my view, should be that the CEPU must ease the intragroup payments problems of these countries yet also nudge policy makers into adopting proper macroeconomic policies, not just trade stances. Only then can the solid groundwork for current-account convertibility be laid over the envisaged life of the union, the process of marketization move rapidly forward, and the countries continue to undertake modifications so as to enhance participation in the global economy.

Given the above conditions, it is very difficult to predict the magnitude and sign of imbalances that will emerge with the devolution of trading decisions to autonomous firms in an emerging market environment at home and abroad. Current external imbalances among the Eastern European countries are reached under constrained trade conditions, not only from the side of foreign-exchange management but also from the point of view of who engages in trade and for what particular motive. They can therefore not provide a solid basis for estimating the kinds of imbalances that may have to be supported once trading arrangements are sufficiently loosened to enable firms to negotiate under competitive conditions for market access and procurements on the basis of their profit motive.

11. DURATION

The duration of the union depends on how soon participants will be able to switch to - or will be cajoled into adopting - convertible-currency trade. This may be more difficult to achieve in Eastern Europe, given the size of the adjustment burden and how quickly it can be borne, than was the case for the west after World War II. Eastern Europe not only needs to introduce market-oriented reforms but also to restructure external trade and payments, literally almost from the ground up. The task of maintaining trade volumes, while effecting radical changes in the commodity composition thereof in line with comparative-advantage indicators, is a daunting one. The assignment becomes even more complex when it is realized that the restructuring of the domestic economy along rational economic criteria can proceed only by revising the traditional prices and ensuring that the necessary structural changes materialize by knitting meaningful linkages among domestic and trade sectors. This is a very tall order indeed, even under the most favorable set of domestic and external circumstances.

The process of moving to trading in convertible currency might take as much as a decade to cement in the foundations of these tasks. More time is required to subsequently encourage their further refinement through the self-motivated behavior of economic agents under centrally issued policy guidelines. Some Eastern European policy makers are more optimistic, and would like to dollarize trade in a matter of two to three years. Others are more cautious. Perhaps a common commitment to reach convertibility in trade among the reforming countries over a period of five years could offer an acceptable compromise. I am suggesting such a more realistic target because the EPU's experience with successive two-year renewals of the payments arrangements (Rees 1963; Triffin 1957, pp. 189-99) was not really the most constructive solution. If countries want to move toward convertibility faster than forecast, they should be enabled to do so, of course.

4. A hypothetical capital fund

Forecasting current-account imbalances especially for emerging MEs is intrinsically a hazardous enterprise beset by all kinds of uncertainties. It would nonetheless be of interest to have an anchor for the capital support that may be required for a CEPU, if only because of the cumbersomeness, if not outright impossibility, of revising the capital fund on any regular basis. As a starting point, it may be instructive to ponder the magnitude of the capital fund required if the same or similar parameters as those used for the EPU were imposed (Triffin 1957, pp. 170-2). In addition to the parameters on the magnitude of quotas and the maximum share of loans and currency payments, multiple tranches of drawings were adopted. Credit was automatically available on a symmetrical basis for the first 20 percent of cumulative imbalances at the end of each month, taking into account that some outstanding imbalances had been brought into the EPU. For creditors, half of the imbalance exceeding that share was made available in convertible currency; their credit position would thus be maximally 60 percent of quota. Debitors had to pay in convertible currency (or gold at the time) one additional fifth for every twenty percent bracket over the first one. For example, 60 percent of quota for a debtor would require payment in convertible currency amounting to 12 percent (that is, no payment for the first tranche, 20 percent for the next tranche, and 40 percent for the third tranche). The maximum credit for debtors was thus also 60 percent of quota.

For imbalances exceeding the credit line, the management of the union, in principle, encouraged surplus countries to pursue more expansionary policies, including through further trade liberalization, and deficit countries to compress domestic absorption, but preferably not through exchange and trade controls. The 100 percent convertible-currency trigger should have been implemented more strictly. But this issue was a matter left to some degree at the discretion of the Managing Board (Kaplan and Schleiminger 1989). They generally sought to arrange for "stretching" voluntarily quotas through so-called *rallonges* (literally extensions like the leaves of a table), provided arrangements could be made for debtors to correct policy; they also sought to help out creditors through extra payments of ERP funds. There were a number of revisions of the size of the quotas as well as the proportions of currency and claims, especially in 1954 and 1955. The purpose was gradually to "harden" the payments system, that is raising the proportion of settlement in convertible currency or gold. The need for a capital base arose essentially from the fact that negative imbalances could be spread over most members of the union, possibly holding individual imbalances to less than the first tranche, whereas one or a few creditors would surpass that tranche, thus laying net claims on convertible-currency payments. The reverse is, of course, also possible in which case the union would end up with a growing surplus. To finance net claims on currency, the United States had appropriated $500 million from ERP funds, of which $350 million was paid into the union (actually, because of "initial balances" the funds available to the union amounted to some $271.6 million - about 7 percent of the total quotas of $3.95 billion) and $150 million was left at the discretion of the Managing Board to come to grips with "exceptional" circumstances.

Utilizing the initial EPU parameters, it should in principle be easy to compute both the quotas and the kind of imbalances that might have had to be supported if trade among reforming countries in recent years had been cleared in a payments union. Whether the results yield magnitudes of the capital required in the 1990s under different conditions for reforming countries will be discussed later. Actually, matters are not that simple. Perhaps the most mundane reason is that exchange rates of the Eastern European currencies in the late 1980s were disequilibrium rates and cross-rates to convertible currencies were far from approximately uniform; most lacked a solid economic foundation in any case. As a result, the available trade statistics, let alone the inconsistencies in mirror statistics, are not a good guide to what might emerge in a more market-oriented environment. Some are undoubtedly overvalued while others are undervalued. But nobody knows the order of magnitude of the exchange rates that will approximately clear markets. Second, present trade has been attained under heavily constrained circumstances. If 1989 as the most recent year for which detailed data are available is taken as anchor, the vast bulk of trade was still conducted under orthodox intergovernmental BTPAs. Under such arrangements, imbalances occur in principle only when countries agree *ex ante* to grant loans, succeed in evading part of their assumed obligations, or raise their net export over and above levels foreseen in the agreement. If trade will now be conducted by autonomous firms, earlier magnitudes of the level, geographical distribution, and commodity composition of trade are unlikely to be a good guide to what can be expected to emerge under more market-oriented criteria. Finally, recent trade years have been rather unusual for reasons that stem in part from gradual CMEA reforms and the inability of these countries to come to grips in a structured manner with the volatility of terms of trade induced by marked shifts in WMPs, as discussed.

These caveats are of sufficient weight to dissuade anyone from estimating the capital requirements of a CEPU. Nonetheless, some magnitude may still provide a useful reference. Utilizing reported visible trade data of the various Eastern European countries ranked in English alphabetical order and taking half of reporter and mirror statistics for 1989 and an average for 1987-1989 yields the magnitudes of trade turnover and possible quotas and credit lines listed in Table 5.1 for various combinations of membership in a CEPU; because only annual statistics are available, the implicit assumption is that participants in the hypothetical union grant each other automatic credit during the calendar year. I have kept the former GDR in some of the computations because the trade of the eastern part of Germany with the PETs could have been handled through the union. The data listed refer to six different unions: Central Europe in the strict sense (Czechoslovakia, Hungary, and Poland) without (EE3) or with the Soviet Union (EE3+S); Central Europe in the broader sense, including the ex-GDR (EE4 without the Soviet Union and EE4+S including the Soviet Union); Eastern Europe without the Soviet Union (EE6); and Eastern Europe with the Soviet Union (EE7). For each of these reference bases, five different quotas were defined. The most generous provided for 25 percent and the most restrictive for only 5 percent. For example on the basis of 1989 visible trade data and the 15 percent quota, Table 5.1 shows that the maximum credit allocation ranges from $620 million for EE3 to $16.7 billion for EE7. The comparable data for the three-year average are $0.6 and $17.3 billion.

The reasons for computing these alternative quotas are several. But two stand out. One is that the trade and imbalance patterns of the late 1980s were generated under constrained conditions. They are, therefore, unlikely to be indicative of what might emerge when trade decisions will be increasingly based on effective market-clearing criteria. To allow for the latter the credit line should be made larger, but not so large as to enable debitors to avoid having to pay in convertible currency for too long. For that reason I computed quotas at 20 and 25 percent of turnover in the base year. Likewise, if stricter trading and macroeconomic policy surveillance were to be imposed, it would be necessary to keep the credit line relatively low. To make for a more stringent arrangement, I computed scenarios with only 5 and 10 percent of trade in the reference years being made available as quotas. In all cases, I kept the other EPU parameters (that is, 60 percent credit and the various initial credit-payment tranches) unchanged, although many variations on these fixed points could be considered. A case could be made for accelerating settlement, hence forcing debtors to pay a larger proportion of cumulative imbalances in convertible currency. On the other hand, that might not be the most productive way to get political approval for a payments union. In any case, as argued, these and other paramters need to be negotiated among policy makers. The alternative

Table 5.1: Trade turnover, quotas, and credits (in million current dollars)

	EE3	EE3+S	EE4	EE4+S	EE6	EE7
			1989			
Trade turnover						
Bulgaria					5588	24156
CSFR	3709	12357	5771	14419	6926	15574
GDR			4633	12673	5978	14017
Hungary	1422	5729	2551	6857	2959	7266
Poland	1753	6508	2809	7564	3415	8170
Rumania					3746	9133
USSR		55635		77600		107205
Total	6884	80228	15764	119113	28612	185521
Quotas						
25 percent	1721	20057	3941	29778	7153	46380
20 percent	1377	16046	3153	23823	5722	37104
15 percent	1033	12034	2365	17867	4292	27828
10 percent	688	8023	1576	11911	2861	18552
5 percent	344	4011	788	5956	1431	9276
Credits						
25 percent	1033	12034	2365	17867	4292	27828
20 percent	826	9627	1892	14294	3433	22263
15 percent	620	7221	1419	10720	2575	16697
10 percent	413	4814	946	7147	1717	11131
5 percent	207	2407	473	3573	858	5566

Table 5.1: Trade turnover, quotas, and credits, ct.
(in million current dollars)

	EE3	EE3+S	EE4	EE4+S	EE6	EE7
			Average 1987-1989			
Trade turnover						
Bulgaria					6068	25137
CSFR	3615	12739	5774	14898	6990	16114
GDR			4539	12903	5878	14242
Hungary	1629	6747	2770	7888	3308	8426
Poland	1973	7641	3102	8770	3899	9567
Rumania					3916	9483
USSR		57400		80279		109213
Total	7217	84527	16185	124738	30059	192182
Quotas						
25 percent	1804	21132	4046	31185	7515	48046
20 percent	1443	16905	3237	24948	6012	38436
15 percent	1083	12679	2428	18711	4509	28827
10 percent	722	8453	1619	12474	3006	19218
5 percent	361	4226	809	6237	1503	9609
Credits						
25 percent	1083	12679	2428	18711	4509	28827
20 percent	866	10143	1942	14969	3607	23062
15 percent	650	7607	1457	11226	2705	17296
10 percent	433	5072	971	7484	1804	11531
5 percent	217	2536	486	3742	902	5765

Source: Trade data converted at official exchange rates are from official statistical releases. Quotas are calculated as the indicated percentage of trade turnover. Credit lines are 60 percent of the respective quotas.

quotas are listed in Table 5.1 for both 1989 and for the average of 1987-1989 turnover data computed as explained earlier.

In the context of these alternative quotas, I investigated the implications of applying the EPU-like parameters given earlier to the various trade groups in 1989 and the average for 1987-1989. From the many alternative computations that could be investigated, I decided to explore three in some detail, namely 1989 imbalances and quotas, average 1987-1989 imbalances and quotas, and 1989 imbalances applied to average 1987-1989 quotas. The results of these alternative quotas in terms of capital requirements are listed in Table 5.2.

If the pattern of trade in 1989 were to be representative of what might emerge under conditions of a payments union, Table 5.2 demonstrates that the net claims on the union in 1989 would have been on the order of $5.9 million under EE3 and $1.7 billion under EE7; the comparable data for the three-year 1987-1989 average would have been $20 million and $0.7 billion. These sums would have had to be financed from outside the union inasmuch as surplus countries could have taken out of the union more than the deficit countries paid in. That explains the need for a capital fund. Looking first at the more stringent requirements with 1989 as reference, drawings on the capital fund rise to $15.2 million for EE3 and to $1.8 billion for EE7 in the case of a 10 percent quota; the corresponding data for a 5 percent quota are $17.1 million and $1.7 billion, the latter decrease being due to the fact that countries hit their credit ceiling earlier and will therefore have to provide 100 percent convertible-currency payments from their own reserves. Under the most liberal quota allocation, the claim on the capital fund decreases to zero for EE3 and to $1.3 billion for EE7; the corresponding data for a 20 percent quota are zero and $1.5 billion.

The data computed with the average for 1987-1989 as reference are naturally slightly different. Under the more stringent requirements, drawings on the capital fund rise to $24.2 million for EE3 and to $0.8 billion for EE7 in the case of a 10 percent quota; the corresponding data for a 5 percent quota are $21.5 million and $0.9 billion. In this case, a decrease in calls on the capital fund results from the fact that the imbalances in 1987-1989 were smaller than those for 1989. Under the most liberal credit allocation, the claim on the capital fund decreases to near zero for EE3 and to $0.3 billion for EE7; but it increases to $0.4 billion for EE3+S. The corresponding data for a 20 percent quota are $9.9 million and $0.5 billion.

Claims on the union when imbalances for 1989 are settled against quotas computed for 1987-1989 are, of course, slightly larger. They range from 0 to $14.4 million for EE3 under the most generous and restrictive quota, respectively, to from $1.2 to $1.7 billion under the most generous and 10 percent quota, respectively.

From these hypothetical computations, two suggestions emerge. One is that imbalances relative to overall trade have been limited in Eastern Europe. This is true even in 1989, which was the most unbalanced reference year, for virtual-

Table 5.2: Hypothetical net claims of a payments union (in million current dollars)

	EE3	EE4	EE6	EE7	EE3+S	EE4+S
Based on 1989 reference data						
5 percent	17.07	22.48	89.20	1655.41	1090.25	1266.65
10 percent	15.17	44.81	103.33	1809.39	1291.46	1389.82
15 percent	5.86	31.34	76.06	1744.94	1172.44	1238.80
20 percent	0.00	19.72	36.58	1505.57	1059.82	1069.44
25 percent	0.00	1.88	2.14	1332.74	928.45	864.67
Based on 1987-1989 reference data						
5 percent	21.51	49.65	124.15	926.01	772.50	720.66
10 percent	24.24	58.18	117.79	769.27	559.87	511.43
15 percent	19.76	50.33	92.02	705.87	530.18	443.32
20 percent	9.89	42.42	49.51	490.21	468.72	360.03
25 percent	0.03	22.43	20.11	274.56	396.78	276.74
Based on 1987-1989 quotas and 1989 trade data						
5 percent	14.38	24.31	90.96	1586.13	1059.12	1243.12
10 percent	10.53	42.84	103.11	1729.67	1179.76	1333.88
15 percent	2.75	32.76	71.31	1597.06	1065.80	1127.38
20 percent	0.00	21.61	30.18	1368.88	917.63	950.79
25 percent	0.00	4.22	0.00	1238.05	853.14	802.98

Source: The data were generated by applying the initial EPU tranches to the imbalances as referenced and the credit lines detailed in Table 5.1. These amounts would have to be financed from external resources to keep the union manageable at the observed moment of time.

ly any combination. This is unlikely to remain so once trade liberalization in the payments union gets under way and firms will be called upon to capitalize on their perceived comparative advantages. This suggests that the capital fund be set generously. Second, it is also evident that the Soviet Union is *the* major trade partner in substantial deficit in 1989, but at a relatively low level of currency payment, given its quota. To make any prediction, then, about imbalances in a union with Soviet participation, it is necessary to gain some handle on the future trade pattern of the Soviet Union. Unfortunately, there is simply no way of doing so. All we know is that current imbalances are bound to change dramatically in favor of the Soviet Union in 1991 and beyond, provided the Soviet Union can maintain its export volume. But that will only remain so if the Soviet federation holds together. If it were to disintegrate into numerous sovereign republics, autonomous areas, and perhaps even big cities, the magnitude of imbalances to be settled might considerably deviate from any of the scenarios set out here. Again, to make the payments scheme attractive and afford leverage over the transition phase, the more liberal arrangement might be instituted *ab initio* with a more prominent role for the Surveillance Board.

However shaky the above data are, allowing for persistent lobsidedness on the part of chronic debtors (or creditors) and implementing the most generous alternative, the amount of money required to finance the pattern of trade typical of the late 1980s would on the whole have been rather small. It would have been only several million dollars in unions that do not include the Soviet Union. With the Soviet Union as participant, the amount of money required in the worst case would have been on the order of perhaps $1.5-2 billion. Worst means that surplus countries would immediately withdraw their holdings. If the EPU's experience is any guide, the ratio of the capital fund ($271.6 million) to the maximum to be financed ($1.58 billion) was less than one fifth. Utilizing the data in Table 5.1 for a 15 percent credit quota minus the 60 percent credit allocation, the maximum to be financed (inclusive of the Soviet Union) would be less than $2 billion. A capital fund of that magnitude, say $2.5 billion, would provide a sufficient base to move decisively forward, provided the Surveillance Board could obligate chronic debtors and creditors to adjust in such a way that absorption would be contracted or expanded, respectively, with minimal adverse effects on pursuing the other goals associated with the payments union.

This comparatively small commitment needs to be seen against the constructive benefits a clearing scheme is likely to yield, apart from guiding participants to current-account convertibility and trade liberalization in a structured manner. Perhaps most important, it would reinforce the trade relations among the PETs, especially if those were to be buttressed through a CEEU, and assist them with the industrial restructuring to be undertaken in any case. Not only would it support the reform trends from within and strengthen intragroup relations, it would also transfer assistance in a form that least interferes with the emerging economic incentives for microeconomic agents and the macroeconomic framework being elaborated; by moving toward convertibility it would in fact facilitate such progress. Furthermore, it would ease the pressure on Western European markets to accommodate significant trade diversion for Eastern Europe. In the medium to long run, it would open up new opportunities for trade not only for those countries financing the transition in Eastern Europe, but also regional cooperation and strengthening the competitive position of many DEs. Finally, it could sharply reduce the magnitude of the contraction in levels of activity in the PETs during the restructuring process, given supply rigidities there and the anticipated sharp deterioration in the external-payments position of all Eastern European countries.

5. A payments union with the Soviet Union?

When in early 1990 I first proposed the creation of a CEPU as an instrument to assist the radically reforming Central European countries in coping with the problems resulting from opening up their reciprocal markets, I deliberately excluded the Soviet Union from the scheme. The CEPU was meant as an inducement to support market orientation of the PETs by allowing these countries to maintain warranted trade levels while the composition of profitable trade would be gradually restructured under impulse of the self-interest of autonomous agents yet to be created, of course. They should be able to exploit their comparative advantages as discussed in Chapter 3. Moving decisively forward with making their reciprocal trade relations as convertible as trade with western partners was one technical motivation.

None of these criteria or objectives permitted including the Soviet Union as it was then most unclear, to say the least, whether Soviet policy makers had reached a consensus on the establishment of financially autonomous firms within the discipline set by emerging markets. Of course, the politics of the situation, including the then jelling east-west assistance efforts within whose scope the CEPU had been placed; the very substantial proportion of the PETs' trade with the Soviet Union; and the large imbalances with the Soviet Union argued for conceptualizing some facility with the Soviet Union included. One option would have been a dual-track payments facility.

Since then, of course, fuel markets experienced some upheaval, which jeopardized the buoyancy of DMEs. Hence the payments position of the PETs is being very sharply aggravated in the near term on account of both terms-of-trade as well as export-revenue losses. Of course, the Soviet Union would stand to gain significantly, which would change the sign of the imbalances incurred by Central European countries and hence to be financed. Likewise, the Soviet federation now appears to be in serious jeopardy. If it were to crumble Eastern Europe's trade would no longer be settled with the Soviet Union but with the sovereign units, many of which would in effect be in deficit with the Russian Federation as well as non-Soviet partners. This could not but seriously worsen the payments problems of all involved.

Given the prospect of a significant aggravation of the balance-of-payments position of the reforming countries because of the switchover in TR trade and payment regimes and the expected deterioration in east-west terms of trade and export earnings, a comprehensive solution for the payments problems of reforming countries cannot be found without the cooperation of the Soviet Union or simply within the confines of a payments union. The latter can work only if anticipated imbalances are "manageable" within the context of the capital fund and surveillance mechanisms in place. Neither would seem to apply to the case at hand. However, now that the crisis in the Persian Gulf has subsided and genuine marketization in the Soviet Union may get under way, we find ourselves in the starting position of early 1990, when I first proposed the CEPU, but with it now being clear that the Soviet Union should usefully be included in the scheme of things, at least hypothetically.

Including the Soviet Union in a payments union inevitably raises political stakes. Yet, I rest my case for an expanded payments union on technical grounds and a sense of optimism as regards economic buoyancy in DMEs and the Soviet Union (or its successor republics) soon adopting a market-oriented reform - a central precondition for participation in the CEPU. Also the politics of agreeing on a payments union and the danger of deliberately keeping the Soviet Union out of any east-west arrangement are to be taken into account.

Once a case can be made to usher the Soviet Union into such a payments facility, one might just as well take in the two remaining Eastern European countries (Bulgaria and Rumania), as well as eventually Albania, and indeed conceptualize the facility in such a way that any backtracking with current-account convertibility in Yugoslavia, perhaps because of the tight monetary stance adopted by federal authorities being undermined at the republican level or because of the irrevocable breakup of the federation, would be an opportunity to bring the country into the CEPU. But obtaining access to the settlements facility should be made conditional on a modicum of market-oriented reforms being pursued and a commitment to move resolutely forward in that direction. Likewise, all potential members of the union, be they the Soviet Union or individual republics, *must* subscribe to rules and regulations on the utilization of macroeconomic policy adjustments when chronic deficits or surpluses become evident. This has delicate political implications that will require circumspection and a good dose of commercial ingenuity well exceeding what was required during the EPU's existence. Some of the tangents of this situation are addressed in the next chapter.

6

Macroeconomic surveillance and the transition

Now that the unrealistically optimistic expectations about the revolutions in Eastern Europe have subsided, there is no doubt that the process of marketizing the region will be exceedingly painful and protracted. There are many reasons for this. Surely one important bundle stems from the fact that markets have to be created from first principles in an environment burdened by a great deal of economic, political, and social uncertainty, which in turn is aggravated by institutional instability. In several countries of the group, admittedly, these first principles are at least available in some rudimentary form. Past experiments with administrative reform and economic devolution have contributed measurably to this environment. They could, therefore, at this juncture lessen somewhat the uncertainty besetting decision making. Elsewhere, including in the Soviet Union, even the fundamental principles have yet to be hammered out and agreed upon at the purely conceptual level. This generates unease on the part of economic agents, to say the least, and creates more uncertainty than is already embedded in the fluid situation. These disconcerting expectations are furthermore burdened by other instances of profound irresolution that pervade the economies of Eastern Europe.

Western technical assistance could potentially be of critical importance in rendering the drawnout transition process tolerable. At the same time, western sponsors have to see to it that the easement they provide is introduced in such a way that the determination to move over to the market setting as the core mechanism for allocating scarce resources is introduced as expeditiously as possible. Any setback incurred in the process should not be used as an excuse to slow down or reverse the reform effort. On the contrary, these adverse experiences should be fully analyzed as a means of fine-tuning the reform effort, hopefully in full cooperation with western donors and the assistance of international organizations. Yet, at the same time, the adjustment process should not be pushed beyond the limits to the tolerance that for now provides a social consensus. Any major setback in that respect cannot but exert deleterious consequences for policy credibility. It certainly would further destabilize these economies.

There is little doubt that one of the more painful constraints on moving ahead with marketization will be the worsening of the current account, at least in an *ex ante* sense, for reasons discussed earlier. An external facility, perhaps in the form of a regional payments union, could constitute one mechanism to structure the burden of adjustment inherent in moving to markets, to weather to some degree the impact of unforeseen shocks in the global economy, and to be prepared to counter any adverse development that may crop up in the course of the reform process. As argued earlier, such a union makes sense only if there is a minimum of macroeconomic surveillance exercised over the revolving disbursement of funds provided by outsiders keen on promoting some objectives related to marketization in Eastern Europe.

Exercising macroeconomic surveillance poses delicate tasks not only for economic policy, particularly in the areas of trade and payments, but also for financial diplomacy. These issues form the core topics of this chapter. Section 1 sets forth the kind of desirable macroeconomic policy responses to transitory payments imbalances. These are being complicated by pervasive legacies of the planned environment which are examined next. Section 3 investigates how the standard adjustment policies for MEs could be adapted to the PETs. Because so much of what might come to the fore under a payments union remains unknown, the following section addresses some contingencies that should be allowed for. The delicate matter of outsiders meddling in the adjustment efforts of the PETs is the subject of Section 5. The framework adopted there should be applicable to all outside advisers, be they representatives of countries or regional or international organizations or persons acting relatively independently under someone's general authority. There are numerous issues of macroeconomic management that go beyond those inherent in steering toward currency convertibility through a payments union. These are tackled in the last section.

1. Macroeconomic responses in a payments union

Provided the external-payments scheme is set up in such a way that policy makers are compelled to take positive actions to keep imbalances within certain agreed-upon bounds, two sets of questions need to be explored. One refers to the matters discussed in Chapter 5. That is to say, a payments facility should not be so generous that it enables participants to forgo structural adjustment and pursuit of the reform, including in particular through trade and price liberalization. At the same time, neither should the facility be so stringent that it inhibits orderly macroeconomic adjustment. Critical in this respect is to increasingly allow economic agents to engage autonomously in commerce on their own account without passing through various trade and exchange licensing.

The second set of questions refers essentially to the nature of the response to emerging imbalances that in time cannot be financed. Apart from analyzing the process by which these substantial imbalances emerge, some authority in the payments union will have to formulate more appropriate policy options and see to it that the leadership of the country in question revises its policy stance accordingly. The prime purpose of adjustment to both chronic surpluses and deficits should be such that the trade-liberalization process is interrupted only after all other avenues of adjustment have been thoroughly explored by policy makers of participating countries acting in consultation with the Surveillance Board.

Adjustment policies in the above sense, in a way, are quite similar to the traditional advice embraced by the IMF to come to grips with transitory payments imbalances in MEs. But the issues go well beyond the stylized demand-management framework that is the hallmark of the Fund's policy advice. There are many reasons for this. One is that structural payments imbalances will have to be tackled. Also, at the same time that deep-rooted payments problems need to be addressed, the entire framework of economic decision making in the PETs is being placed on a last that differs in numerous details, as well as in overall form and content, from the features of balance-of-payments adjustment and steering a CPE or MPE for that matter. Not the least is that these changes will have to be sought in an unstable environment that is furthermore clouded by profound uncertainties emanating from several corners. Expectations in such an environment are inherently fluid, complicating any attempt to make them explicit for policy purposes. Finally, conflicts may be evident in terms of the policy stances required to keep the union manageable, yet address global balance-of-payments problems.

As argued earlier, there is not much sense in creating a payments union for countries that either do not invoke the policy responses or that constantly run against the barrier of formulating advice designed to elicit modifications in policy stances. In the former, movement toward currency convertibility could be accomplished simply through national macroeconomic management. It is also possible that the country in question is not sufficiently relaxing the constraints on its trade and payments. If the limits of the payments scheme need to be constantly invoked, two endemic obstacles may be at work. One is that the settlement framework might be too restrictive for the problems at hand. Alternatively, participating countries face many more adjustment burdens in coming to grips with their external-payments situation than can be taken care of through a fairly simple technical arrangement encompassing short-term financing, such as a payments union, for regulating imbalances.

However, there may be circumstances in which adjustments in trade and domestic economic structures are such that expansionary or contractionary macroeconomic policies can be implemented with some degree of credibility. Under these conditions, policies that react to emerging events can be pursued while yielding fairly flexible adjustments in demand and supply. If so, any country that exceeds its credit ceiling either as a debtor or creditor will have to be induced to adopt policy measures that would remove the circumstances, either policies or institutional arrangements, that are at the roots of it hitting repeatedly the outer limits of the payments scheme.

For creditor countries, this would imply that more expansionary policies need to be adopted. Since the facility is emplaced to expand trade levels and ease payment problems, adjustment policies should in the first instance attempt to raise trade by eliminating import restrictions or export subsidies. Expansionary policies can be adopted that affect government, enterprise, and household sectors in a way that is most conducive to raising import demand, provided this injection remains compatible with the basic objectives of the reform, including progressing toward currency convertibility. These measures could be emplaced by lowering interest rates to encourage demand, further relaxing any remaining import restrictions, pursuing more expansionary fiscal policy, or any other encouragement to raising domestic absorption, hence demand for imports including from the partner countries in the payments mechanism.

For chronic debtor countries, the reverse response is required. Here the objective should be to foster exports while avoiding cutbacks in import levels. Restricting absorption in the end cannot altogether avert a compression of import levels. But first efforts should be made to compress as much as possible domestic demand, thereby freeing up resources for exports. In other words, macroeconomic managers should try to curtail domestic absorption, including by lowering import demand if no other option is left. These objectives can be reached through various means. One would be to adopt a more stringent monetary policy with a view to discouraging borrowing for investment as well as consumption purposes. This might be combined with a more restrictive fiscal policy, cutting in effect disposable incomes of the population. A devaluation would make imports more expensive in terms of domestic prices and hence curb import demand. The same could be accomplished through various nonprice import controls. However, such a policy response runs squarely counter to one fundamental objective of the payments union, namely the relaxation of the trade and exchange regimes so as to facilitate currency convertibility.

In other words, seen from within the context of the fundamental aim of the transition to marketize the former CPEs and MPEs, policy advice under external supervision in a payments union should encourage chronic surplus countries to adopt more expansionary macroeconomic policies that bolster in the first instance imports from union members. To the extent that no egregious current-account conflict erupts, it should also encourage progress toward more general trade liberalization. Likewise, it should persuade chronic deficit countries through policy advice to seek contractionary policies. This should be phrased in such a way as to limit overly adverse impacts on import liberalization, particularly as they affect participants in the union.

The two situations sketched out here refer to the easier type of policy choices to be made when the boundaries of financing in a payments union are reached, namely when there is no conflict between regional and other payments. Such a straightforward policy choice may in fact prevail. More usual, though, is that a payments union is instituted for countries that run a deficit with one group of countries and a surplus with others, but for one reason or another cannot combine the two to regain overall balance. It may also address a situation where balance reigns with outsiders, but participants are reluctant to disturb this by placing intragroup trade on a convertible-currency basis.

There is therefore bound to be a greater chance for a conflict to arise between intragroup imbalances and imbalances with nonparticipants than for a common adjustment policy to do the trick. These issues are specifically addressed in Section 5. However, the overall framework of how surveillance can work in the context of east-west economic assistance efforts, including in case the Soviet Union were to be included in such a payments union, forms the core of the rest of the chapter.

As suggested by the above examples, there are multiple options to reduce aggregate (including import) demand and boost aggregate (including export) supply, and hence engineer a macroeconomic situation that would be conducive to sustainable partial imbalances. Some require deliberate policy choices and careful fine-tuning. The more desirable combination of policies and institutional adjustments under a regime with chronic surplus or deficit countries depends very much on the features of the country and society whose imbalances need to be rectified. This is especially important in economies that have not known the market environment for a long time and whose markets, when created, are exceedingly weak in part because of the legacies of central planning. To understand the complexity of formulating adjustment programs for such countries, it is useful to recall briefly how they used to enact adjustment in the past.

2. Adjustment under traditional and modified planning

Adjustment in the traditional CPE and MPE proceeded through institutional mechanisms and policy instruments (see Brabant 1987a, pp. 117-26) that are, of course, no longer unambiguously present in the PETs. In that sense, the current economic environment for adjustment differs greatly from that typical of CPEs and MPEs. Even so, it would be counterproductive to seek macroeconomic adjustment in PETs without heeding the pervasive legacies of over forty years of central planning. Especially during the earliest phases of the transition, it will be critical to come to grips with these matters in a comprehensive technical framework. But I recall here only its principal features.

1. Adjustment in the traditional CPE

Policy instruments in a pure CPE are overwhelmingly variants of direct administrative intervention. In the best case, the instruments are fully embedded in comprehensive physical planning. More common, however, is that stabilization is pursued through administrative intervention, including the intermittent revision of plans by injunction. However, even in the traditional planned environment, such stabilization could also be pursued through monetary means, provided the latter were actively manipulated. This can be easily seen by briefly recalling the orthodox approach to correcting current-account imbalances chiefly through demand management.

The familiar monetary approach to the balance of payments focuses on accounting identities and behavioral relationships. From the accounting point of view, given a stable demand for money, an improvement in the balance of payments is equivalent to a change in the money supply minus any change in net domestic credit. Thus, by controlling credit, autonomous adjustments in prices and the balance of payments occur so that the desired demand for money set by those in charge of monetary policy is satisfied. The physical adjustment process is mirrored in an increase in domestic savings by the household sector, the government, and enterprises. Since these categories exist in a CPE too, it has been argued that progress with adjustment efforts in a CPE can be monitored "through the use of financial indicators in broadly the same way as in [MEs]" (Allen 1982, p. 417). Demand must be lowered by cutting private consumption, investment, or government demand.

The financial aspects of a reduction in household demand in a CPE, at least *ex post*, could follow a pattern quite comparable to the typical adjustment process of MEs provided money commands goods legally and in practice. By virtue of the fact that asset accumulation is on the whole the privilege of the state and state-controlled cooperative sectors, the authorities in principle control aggregate investment and its distribution, foreign-exchange mobilization, wage rates, to some extent overall employment, the allocation of intermediate goods of domestic and foreign origin, and domestic prices. They do so either directly by regulating commodity prices or indirectly by setting the rules by which firms are entitled to determine their prices. In theory, then, administrative instruments provide planners the tools they need to control the macroeconomic aggregates of key concern to those entrusted with monitoring or regulating adjustment and to allocate resources accordingly.

In the stylized ME model, demand adapts instantaneously to supply and *vice versa*. Full knowledge and timeless adjustment assures balance in markets. This is clearly not the case in reality, when lags in adjustment may be very considerable. Similarly, if the planner were omniscient he or she would know exactly the desired reallocation of resources. Adjustment would then simply be a question of political will and the administrative infrastructure. Production and uses could accordingly be restructured by simple administrative means. In practice, however, the authorities of a CPE do not have this comprehensive information any more than actors in an ME. They must, therefore, resort not only to direct intervention in the reallocation of resources but also influence the behavior of economic agents with a view to inducing them to bring about adjustment rather than circumvent it. Unsatisfied *ex ante* consumer demand, while having little effect on supply and retail prices in a CPE, may eventually discourage workers, thereby contracting the effective supply of labor. In addition, it may also have adverse social consequences. Similarly, in the socialized sector planners do not possess full information about all alternatives available at the microeconomic production level from among which economic agents may choose. The timely manipulation of an appropriate incentive system to enable enterprise managers to initiate various adjustments with a salutary impact on the economy as a whole affords CPE authorities crucial sources of initiative and information.

In principle, stabilization in a traditional CPE is a fairly simple operation: The authorities mandate in the plan the shift of resources needed to foster exports, to promote import substitution, and to cut back total domestic absorption in some combination through changes in production and distribution targets, including inventory formation. Because planners do not fully control trade prices, the extent of the required adjustment in export and import targets is a function of the terms-of-trade effect engendered in the process. This package of measures is almost certainly embraced on an emergency basis with immediate repercussions on trade with MEs, because in these relations exists the greatest flexibility. The impact on partners with whom detailed BTPAs have been signed may be delayed, although violations of agreed trade protocols have by no means been exceptional in Eastern Europe. Whether the measures have a more permanent influence on economic behavior and will in the end help to forestall the recurrence of the external imbalances that initially called for the formulation and implementation of the stabilization program depends critically on the nature, origin, and depth of the disequilibria.

Among the instruments that are wielded most intensively in comprehensive adjustment are those that help to promote greater efficiency in the allocation of resources. Through the planning process, resources are reshuffled with the traditional instruments of the command economy by changing the level and structure of output targets. But direct policy actions leading to different plan instructions and prescriptions need to be coupled with incentives, such as wage bonuses, taxes, and capital levies. Only in this way can the authorities ensure that the immediate improvement in output and exports that is feasible can be sustained for some time through "normal" policy means as well. Such improved incentives in conjunction with better targeted sanctions for violations of plan instructions may be exploited also in a more general way to boost production quantitatively as well as qualitatively. Profitability guidelines, elimination of undesirable taxes and subsidies, stressing financial discipline, and utilizing the profit lever more intensively for enterprise decisions can be very important alternative or supplementary instruments to foster adjustment.

On the other hand, the behavioral relationships associated with monetary policies in a CPE are much less clear than they are in an ME context. Given the prevalence of administrative controls, there is asymmetry in the effects of restricted and excessive liquidity. If liquidity is sufficiently restricted, consumers reduce their purchases and enterprises may be unable to engage in transactions they might otherwise have wished to undertake. Thus, financial stringency may have an effect on real behavior. Since excess liquidity in the hands of consumers and enterprises cannot spill over to the foreign sector, the balance of payments may be improved without the elimination of excessive domestic liquidity. To the extent that consumers and enterprises are obliged to hold larger cash balances than desired, financial discipline tends to be undermined with adverse effects on output performance. In other words, at a given level of economic activity there is a certain minimum demand for money. Credit ceilings can thus serve to ensure that monetary expansion, on balance, does not undermine the other measures taken to alleviate pressures on ways to equilibrate external payments.

The abovementioned financial levers can promote greater efficiency only if prices, broadly defined, are not too distorted. If properly set these scarcity indicators may play a pivotal role in the enactment of an adequate adjustment program. In any case, the better the structure of prices mirrors underlying opportunity costs, hence relative scarcities, prevailing in the economy, other things being equal, the more efficient and effective the adjustment process tends to be. Most CPEs have ample access to foreign markets so that these provide the ultimate source of information on real opportunity costs. An appropriate price structure should therefore reflect WMPs to some degree, even if policy makers for reasons of domestic policy autonomy desire to forgo the creation of a direct link between domestic and trade prices.

Introducing effective opportunity costs can be accomplished in several ways. One would be by letting prices fluctuate freely to levels compatible with WMPs. But this can scarcely be a satisfactory solution since preferences in a CPE diverge measurably from those molding demand in world markets. Another avenue might be to parametrize exactly the desired differences between domestic and trade prices, to maintain this separation in line with policy priorities, and to let prices adjust freely otherwise.

The proper selection of the level and structure of prices is undoubtedly important to enact structural adjustment. However, the price system of a typical CPE is usually so distorted that regaining broad economic balance is a task intimately bound up with fairly comprehensive economic reform. A period of emergency adjustment, perhaps because of sudden external or internal constraints, as enacted throughout Eastern Europe in the early 1980s, does not normally provide the proper setting for such an undertaking. But emergency adjustment measures of the above type may well help to stabilize the CPE's economy, even if at much less than maximum efficiency. Once reached, the authorities may tackle more fundamental issues with a greater portent. Such a comprehensive positive adjustment program could be directed at a variety of socioeconomic objectives of managing and steering the CPE. These could include incipient kinds of economic reform by which I mean (see Brabant 1989a, pp. 179ff.) major modifications in the economic model of the CPE, perhaps accompanied by shifts in the orthodox socialist development strategy as well.

2. Adjustment in an MPE

Prior to the revolutions of late 1989 most countries of Eastern Europe had gathered at least some experience with major and minor administrative reforms and economic devolution. The key aspect was widening the scope for interaction through indirect policy instruments, although the authorities invariably shied away from thinking this through to its logical end. Regardless of how far policy makers went in installing an indirect coordination mechanism, the role of traditional administrative regulation remained pervasive also in the MPE. Everywhere, the MPE functioned with elaborate controls over enterprise behavior that severely limited the action radius of agents in the productive sphere. These included extensive interferences in enterprise affairs through a host of tax and subsidy schemes. Of course, there were also direct controls over investment, employment, wage, and output decisions. Under the circumstances, enterprise profit remained by and large a function of government prescriptions rather than of own production and investment decisions motivated by considerations about maximizing the net value of assets entrusted to the SOE. As such, that category of enterprise performance failed to provide an indication of how well the firm was doing or in what directions it should aim its prospective strategy for enterprise reform and adaptation.

This administrative environment of "neither plan nor market" posed serious conceptual problems for economic agents, including notably those operating outside the administrative environment of the MPE. Conditionality conditions worked out, possibly by private or official financial institutions, in the context of explicit or implicit adjustment programs based on the underlying assumption that an MPE behaved like an ME yielded unexpected, in some cases even perverse, results. Since actors did not respond to price signals and prices in any case did not react to market pressures, as they are presumed to behave in the neoclassical paradigm, alternatives to market incentives needed to be explored. Variants of conditionality that were better attuned to the economic structure, policies, and institutions of the MPE about to undergo adjustment were therefore in order. Unfortunately, they were rarely placed within a comprehensive framework that diverged more than trivially from the standard demand-management prescriptions.

What MPEs had in common is considerable. But there were palpable differences in institutions, policy priorities, and social systems as well. It would be a serious mistake to assume that all MPEs operated in the same way. For example, though policy makers in the MPE were in principle fully in charge of investment decisions both at the aggregate and sectoral level, the experience with externally driven macroeconomic adjustments notably during the early 1980s clearly demonstrated that effective control remained far from absolute and that it moreover could be exercised to a varying degree in individual countries. Indeed, the bout of adjustment programs enacted in the 1980s proceeded chiefly by administrative fiat and accomplished very little by way of protecting viable and desirable projects at the expense of uneconomic ones. Instead, projects in motion were delayed and potentially high-yielding new ones were blocked and dispersed. Thus the squandering of investment funds on account of local and regional sociopolitical interest groups was not at all halted. In some cases, it was even exacerbated in an egregious way.

This brings me to the point of adjustment programs embraced for other reasons than emergency external constraints. The efforts of the past two decades in MPEs demonstrated that it was far easier to agree upon temporary stabilization policies, even if through Draconian administrative or policy measures, than on more fundamental changes in the functioning of the economy. More specifically, in most countries policy makers eschewed desirable adjustments in key economic categories such as prices, exchange and interest rates, wages, and mandatory minimum returns on capital. External regulators therefore faced formidable obstacles in attempting to design and enforce conditions that could render resource allocation in MPEs more flexible and efficient without taking sides in domestic political squabbles over the scope, content, and implementation of reform attempts.

The presumed greater room for maneuver available to the authorities of an MPE with respect to wage regulation and the decreased reluctance to alter relatively frequently administered prices in some sense facilitated the introduction of adjustment programs. Reduced government intervention, more comprehensive enterprise autonomy, and greater emphasis on financial discipline raised at least the possibility that authorities could pursue a more active monetary policy than in a CPE, where it was frequently designed to "accommodate" the lending system's assets in accordance with real and fiscal variables.

With few exceptions, the enterprise and household monetary sectors did not interact, however, thereby lessening the impact of any policy with flexible interest rates on restoring equilibrium in various parts of the economy. Furthermore, the downward inflexibility of the money wage, all but absolute job security, and retail price stability, combined with the enormous problems encountered by central administrators in quickly undertaking the required changes in wages, employment, and prices, placed a disproportionate burden of adjustment on the consumer sector. Without essential freedom of modifying interest rates and prices of consumer goods, however, it was difficult to imagine how household consumption patterns, saving preferences, and enterprise profitability calculations could be dovetailed effectively so as to yield equilibrium simultaneously in markets for consumer and investment goods. Providing for smooth intermediation between enterprises and households through the banking system at market-clearing interest rates could significantly lessen the authorities' control over the basic "proportions" of the economy. It could also widen social inequalities and fuel excess demand if such movements were not closely monitored through firm policy prescriptions.

The MPE normally paid considerable attention to foreign trade as a source of output growth and regulator of a more efficient pattern of resource allocation. But with prices and interest rates still set largely voluntaristically through administrative fiat it proved rather difficult to dispense with physical controls on external trade and payments. Continued expansion of the scope for flexible pricing of tradables was required. The exchange rate of an MPE played some role in price formation and the allocation of resources, but only on the fringes of economic decision making. Although it thus became a potentially significant instrument of macroeconomic stabilization, because it could in principle relieve the burden placed on credit and fiscal policies, the effect of exchange-rate variations was widely blunted by administrative and other buffers between domestic and trade prices, including because of the disarray in relative TRPs as compared to WMPs.

The instruments by which authorities attempted to move an MPE to internal and external balance differed in nature from those used in a CPE. Parametric approaches were to some extent possible. However, given the less direct nature and possibly ambiguous effects of such approaches in the *quasi* markets of the MPE, the authorities were tempted, at least temporarily, to revert to the more direct, interventionist instruments of quantitative control typical of the orthodox CPE. This option was invariably embraced in preference to fostering rapid progress with economic reforms centered on indirect economic coordination. When the crunch came during the enforced adjustment bouts of the 1980s, rather than improve the arsenal of policies, institutions, and instruments required to engineer indirect economic coordination, the authorities on the whole resorted to dirigistic intervention. Of special importance in this stance was adherence to a multiple exchange-rate regime (Brabant 1987a, pp. 196ff.), including on account of the divergences between the trading conditions of CMEA and world markets. In fact, as noted in Chapter 4, the MPE sought to further segment its variety of economic transactions into noncommunicating compartments rather than set in motion the necessary conditions for the unification of the exchange rate. The weak commitment to establish eventually a direct linkup between domestic and foreign transactions, in the first instance for traded goods and services, afforded the authorities with some degree of domestic policy autonomy. But it deprived them of the means to enact adjustments that would be sustainable and lead the economy back to solid growth.

Because of inertia on the foreign-exchange front, including on account of the dichotomy between the TR trade and payment regimes and the conditions governing east-west economic relations, the authorities of MPEs could not really adhere to standard prescriptions for macro- and microeconomic adjustments. Outside regulators were hence forced to seek instruments and policies to complement the standard prescriptions on how to overcome structural balanceof-payments difficulties. As is well known, the latter include changes in relative prices, expenditure reduction, and, especially, expenditure switching by changing one or more key exchange rates, even though the sphere of operation of the exchange rate in the MPE remained highly confined. In this connection, several pointed questions immediately spring to mind: Since the MPE normally operated with a wide variety of exchange rates, which rate should be targeted for adjustment purposes? Since none of these rates really operated freely, what was the precise room for maneuver reserved for manipulating the exchange rate? and How was adjustment to proceed in an environment that segregated rather rigidly between TR and convertible-currency transactions?

Without trying to answer these questions (see Brabant 1987a, pp. 125-6), suffice it to recall that the administrative setting for policy adjustment in the MPE was rather complex, certainly far less integrated and transparent than in most MEs. It was characterized by divided interest groups without any effective central control with whom outside authorities could credibly negotiate about desirable modifications in macroeconomic policy stances. This certainly applied with respect to imbalances stemming by and large from changes in the environment of the TR regime.

The experience with forced adjustment in the early 1980s demonstrated quite clearly the limits of weak market-type instruments in helping to nurse along desirable economic adjustments, especially in the external sphere. At the same time that the advantages of adjusting in the short run through traditional central planning were being appreciated, the rather pronounced drawbacks of the inflexibility of the entire wherewithal of central planning in a longer time perspective came to the fore much stronger than before. In other words, these experiences underlined once again the need for reforming these economies from within without further delays, preferably against the backdrop of greater integration into the global financial and trading networks.

To overcome imbalances and especially to stimulate economic growth, buoyant trade was perceived to be a crucial component of adjustment programs in MPEs. Precisely because foreign-trade operations exhibited far greater uncertainty than any domestic sector, authorities were reluctant to broadly relax administrative controls over the foreign sectors, whether real or monetary. Although the MPE did not seek to maintain full market segmentation, its wavering policy stances certainly did little to abolish that regime altogether. This feature was true not only in "real" terms but also with regard to indirect decision-making criteria, especially effective surrogate exchange rates. But they at best provided useful overall guidelines in drawing up essential plan proportions; in the planning by lower-level administrative organs; in the establishment of new fiat prices; possibly in the clearing of foreign transactions by FTOs, even though the latter did not always have discretionary authority over the volume of traded goods or prices; and, under some conditions, in formulating meaningful indicators for choosing appropriate trade volume and determining profitability. These surrogate exchange rates could provide some help in resolving trade problems in planning and management if the effective allocation of economic resources in the MPE were to be realigned with relative world scarcities. But this was never really the planner's true policy intention.

3. Standard adjustment policies and the PETs

The new political leaderships presently entrusted with the formulation and implementation of economic policy in Eastern Europe are, of course, in many ways very different from the ruling cadres of the erstwhile CPE or MPE. In more than one respect, however, prevailing economic institutions, policies, and policy instruments, let alone the behavior of economic agents, do not - at any rate, not yet - differ much from the situation as it existed prior to the revolutions of 1989. In time, one may anticipate major changes as these economies become more and more oriented to and by the market. In the meantime, however, there are pervasive legacies from the central-planning framework that have to be reckoned with in steering economic policy.

Although the collapse of the TR trade and payment regimes may eliminate some strong determinants of plan bias, the new external regimes are not yet fully or even comfortably in place. These factors will also have to be taken into account by any outsider trying to come to grips with macroeconomic policy advice. This goes to the heart of what the Surveillance Board of a payments union could engage in and how its strategy for adjustment should be linked, on the one hand, to existing realities and prevailing and emerging constraints on external payments and, on the other hand, to desirable institutional and policy reforms away from the behavior molded under the policies, institutions, and instruments of administratively centralized planning.

Prior to the changes in trade and payment regimes in the CMEA, it would have been all but impossible to enact uniform policy adjustments. Indeed, trying to tackle problems in relations with countries that conducted their trade in a convertible currency without taking fully account of the pervasive dependence of the PETs on trade conducted at TRPs and settled in TRs would have spelled failure. Inasmuch as a sizable share of each PET's total trade and the bulk of imported industrial inputs will continue to be transacted with each other, at least for the foreseeable future, the adjustment problem faced by the PET leadership is far more complex than simply changing one or more applicable "prices." Domestic price liberalization and harmonization of domestic prices with WMPs are both incompatible with trade prices negotiated in some BTPAs, especially those revolving around some variant of pure barter. The only exception prevails when volume and price of all three elements of the equation (that is domestic, TR, and world trade) can be adjusted. But this is a trivial exception for it would make at least the BTPA altogether superfluous. So, synchronization of adjustments through prices is evidently not an option for the bulk of transactions of the PETs with economies that are still far removed from effective transition to market orientation. Under the circumstances, opening up these economies to international competition, exposing them to the vagaries of the international business cycle, will have to take place under circumstances that will remain quite intransparent for some time to come.

The continuing dependence of the PETs on trade relations with each other and former CMEA members that have not yet embarked on radical economic reform is one thing. Another is that the measures to be inaugurated in each PET must be directed not only at correcting aggregate absorption through policy measures on the demand side. Especially in countries that continue to exhibit considerable supply rigidities, it will be particularly important to formulate policy advice and buttress policy actions also on the supply side. Only in this way can policy makers, and possibly external advisers, ensure that structural changes are introduced in line with the basic requirements for the coveted market orientation.

Demand-management policies would be typical for the market approach of Fund and Bank policies. Fostering indirect or market incentive mechanisms - epitomized by the slogan "getting the prices right" - will be very important in countries whose prices have been distorted for so long. Various forms of demand management to reduce expenditures by cutting purchasing power and to switch expenditures to bolster exports and discourage imports need to be explored. But no adjustment program can be expected to work well if supply rigidities are ignored.

Supply measures of the adjustment package can take on various forms. In the case of the PETs they could usefully enhance resource allocation by direct and indirect policy means. Direct instruments are in the sphere of tariffs, exchange rates, interest charges, and, in many cases, key product prices, including of energy and foodstuffs but also of services. Indirect instruments are contingent on changing the underlying institutions, such as the systemic liberalization of foreign trade and payments; promoting compatibility between domestic and foreign conditions; introducing efforts to corporatize SOEs and provide for more effective monitoring of management, whose behavior itself is more and more geared by commercial considerations; fostering the private sector, including through the establishment of clear-cut property rights and the rapid introduction of a competitive commercial-banking sector; or the imposition of controls over nominal variables. Better management of aggregate credit and the money supply also improves the setting of financial markets and thus indirectly affects aggregate investment and inflation.

Of course, as outlined earlier, a CEPU would not only be directed at managing external payments because of limited liquity. This is especially so because I envisage it as a vehicle to have the participants encourage their emerging autonomous firms to explore fully on their own account all opportunities for making profit within their national and intragroup markets. For that trade-promoting measures should be allocated even greater weight than I did earlier. If in addition the payments union is to facilitate moving toward currency convertibility and preparing the participants for smoother integration into the global economy and, in the case of the PETs, also into the European economy, the macroeconomic policy package, hence the task of surveillance, that may be designed should be quite varied.

4. Fund-type adjustment programs and the PETs

The role of the Fund in the world economy and the possible benefits of Fund membership to PETs are not the subject proper of this volume (see Brabant

1991g). It bears to recall, however, that in the past the relationship between CPEs or MPEs and the Fund, and to some degree also the World Bank, was at times beset by serious conflicts. This situation may have had various origins. As far as technical matters are concerned, however, friction occasionally arose because the standard type of adjustment policies recommended by the multilateral financial institutions did not mesh well with the environment for administrative planning. I hasten to add that *in se* the task of adjustment under planning or market conditions is identical: Expenditure reduction and switching must be accomplished to eliminate deficits on external account. But the way in which these adjustments are introduced under planning differ in many respects from the demand-driven programs suitable to integrated MEs.

Because PETs hope to reach the status of a full-fledged ME as quickly as possible, prospectively the conflict with standard policies of the Fund and Bank will presumably become much less pronounced. At any rate, these countries will seek to avoid problems to the degree that macroeconomic surveillance and outside policy advice remain compatible with overall domestic socioeconomic precepts. Nonetheless, a program for adjusting to external or domestic pressures in the PETs must necessarily be phrased differently from the way in which this has traditionally been accomplished in either CPEs or MEs. There are two fundamental reasons for this. One refers to the pervasive legacies of central planning. The other recognizes that, in part because of these legacies, macroeconomic management must include active intervention on the supply side to sensitize economic agents into undertaking the kinds of structural changes required to install the rudiments of the coveted ME. For the near future, adjustment even in the PET will require a much more varied policy regimen and institutional setting than envisioned in orthodox policies.

A few stylized aspects of adjustment policies typically embraced by MEs under Fund conditionality at this juncture may help to gain a robust understanding of what Fund-type adjustment policies are all about and the problems that may arise during the transition. For one thing, virtually all western assistance, other than that rendered for emergency and humanitarian reasons, has been made contingent on the potential beneficiary country in Eastern Europe reaching an "agreement" with the Fund. This holds even with respect to disbursements of funds in support of various kinds of technical assistance with the transition, not just providing stabilization loans or more general support for external payments. In the case of countries not yet in the Fund (such as Bulgaria and Czechoslovakia prior to September 1990, when they acceded to the Articles of Agreement, and Albania and the Soviet Union until today), assistance efforts were conditioned on the country seeking accession. This involved, among other instances of synchronization, coming to a working arrangement with the exploratory Fund mission that normally recommends changes in trade and payment practices, recommends the Fund quota assessed in special drawing rights (SDRs) to the Board of Executive Directors, and may smooth the way to the signing of the first standby agreement with the Fund. In any case, in the course of these exploratory exchanges of views on macroeconomic policies, as well as considerations about the underlying efficiency of the microeconomic sphere, potentially leading up to accession there is ample scope to pass Fund precepts on to local decision makers.

The second reason why a rounded comprehension of Fund-type policies is desirable follows from usances. Upon the creation of any type of external-payments facility with western financial support, sponsors will be tempted to entrust surveillance either to the Fund or to the executive directors representing the donor countries. With all due respect for the professionalism of Fund staff, I would not advocate this. For one thing, the nature of the transition in Eastern Europe is uncharted territory for the Fund as much as any other institution or commentator, including the reformers themselves. The tasks ahead require considerable imagination on how to reactivate supply, something that Fund surveillance has not been very good at. The Fund certainly does not have ample experience in assisting reforms of former CPEs and whatever knowledge has been accumulated, to the extent it is still relevant to the PET, has not been very encouraging (Assetto 1988, Dembinski and Morisset 1990). The risk of imposing Fund orthodoxy upon a delicately balanced, if not outrightly precarious, domestic sociopolitical situation virtually without precedent does not seem advisable, given the problems faced by the PETs. It certainly would not necessarily afford the Surveillance Board with the wherewithal and commitment to manage the payments facility with a view to generating the best results for the beneficiary countries. Neither would it provide management with the means to synchronize as much as possible the movement toward structural reform with trade and price liberalization as well as buffering the potentially adverse impact of the fragile situation with external payments. Furthermore, the task of guiding Eastern Europe to convertibility through a payments facility is vast and requires nearly continuous monitoring. Any advisory opinion being prepared would by necessity touch upon delicate issues of political autonomy in economic policy making. By its very nature, adopting discriminatory measures for one group of Fund members - the PETs in this case - would inevitably give rise to problems in a near-universal institution. Finally, providing assistance to Eastern Europe is on the whole a European issue.

These are not idle charges derived from subjective motivations. Rather, they reflect a constatation based on the attitude taken by the Fund toward the EPU in the early 1950s (Kaplan and Schleiminger 1989, pp. 41-51 and 339-41; Vries 1969a). This stance is presently being resurrected (Kenen 1990, Polak 1991). In an uncanny, almost verbatim, set of arguments, the Fund appears to oppose putting together any kind of payments facility, however slightly discriminatory, for Eastern Europe whose features would diverge to some degree from the mainstream, rather stereotypical, policies that it routinely advocates. Whether this attitude derives from the intrinsic demerits of a payments union or because such a facility challenges the Fund's authority, I shall leave in the open for now.

The common adjustment measures of Fund and Bank policies focus on austerity so as to cut demand through a variety of shifts in policy stances, changes in instruments, and perhaps modifications in economic institutions that are intended to promote indirect or market incentive mechanisms, as noted, epitomized by the slogan "getting the prices right." A typical adjustment program in an ME consists of a combination of measures aimed at improving the current account through stabilization policies and efficiency through target adjustments in domestic production, distribution, and foreign trade. Usually such a program is supported by financing from abroad arranged by official institutions, at varying degrees of conditionality, or private banks (or a combination of the two) and comprises three phases: the implementation of the preconditions for adjustment, otherwise banks would not be inclined to lend enough for smoothing the adjustment process; the fulfillment of quantitative and qualitative policy targets upon which further disbursement of the loans agreed upon in the adjustment package is conditioned; and actions that governments commit themselves to undertake, although these are not normally accompanied with stipulated sanctions for noncompliance. These areas for policy action are primarily concerned with demand management, although over the past decade or so both the Fund and the Bank have increasingly turned also to stimulating supply.

The above suggests that there is normally a tie-in between additional loans and the implementation of adjustment measures under international economic cooperation within the context of the Fund. To some degree, incidentally, this also explains why so much of the promised western economic, technical, and financial assistance has been committed subject to the potential beneficiary reaching an understanding with the Fund on desirable adjustments. Participants in the negotiations normally select a quantum target as well as a time sequence for improving the current account. The decision on the amount by which the current account needs to be corrected over a given period of time is a function of the volume and timing of the inflow of official and private capital. Because it is constrained by conditions in international capital markets, the Fund does not have complete discretion in choosing the depth and speed of a country's adjustment, of course. But it can nevertheless exert considerable leverage over the concrete terms on which commercial banks may be willing to keep lending, especially when the potential beneficiary is heavily indebted or faces problems with the orderly servicing of the debt. The second step in an adjustment program revolves around issues pertaining to domestic macroeconomic balance, especially in fiscal and monetary affairs, and economic stabilization. Domestic demand needs to be set at a long-term sustainable level without aggravating imbalances and inflation. If prices are not moving flexibly in response to shifts in demand and supply, inflationary pressures tend to be disguised or repressed. But they leave an imprint on the economy just the same. Stabilization as a rule requires a cut in total absorption so that real expenditure shrinks. Austerity usually has a disproportionate impact on investment, which by lowering the growth of capital reduces the capacity to produce over time.

Stabilization and adjustment policies need not necessarily depress levels of economic activity, unless the imbalance originated in the first place from output being at a level exceeding long-run capacity. Nevertheless, recent experience has corroborated the long-standing conjecture that Fund-mandated adjustment programs entail a contraction of economic activity. In some cases, this may in fact counteract the improvement in economic efficiency that the adjustment program was intended to bring about.

This conflict between economic efficiency and the need to improve the current account may stem from a variety of sources. The most important can be captured under four headings. Perhaps foremost is policy "overkill," or excessive adjustment measures causing a contraction in economic activity that may be quite dysfunctional in the sense that it further aggravates the ability of the country to bolster its external revenues. Second, many programs are implicitly conditioned on rather optimistic assumptions of flexibility in the domestic market, thus overstating the potential for expenditure switching to narrow the gap between revenues and payments. Third, because import cuts affect not only final consumption but also intermediate and capital goods for which no substitutes from domestic production are available in the short run, the sustainable level of economic activity will be adjusted downward. Finally, the compression of domestic absorption levels may fall disproportionately on investments rather than consumption. This may stem from policy makers opting for protecting consumers for social or political reasons. Whatever the cause, a sharp and sustained contraction in investment activity cannot but weaken future production capacity levels, hence the potential for generating export revenues.

Adjustment programs such as those enacted in the 1980s under the aegis of the Fund and the Bank rely overwhelmingly on policy instruments that are appropriate in a setting with integrated markets and that have their largest impact on aggregate demand. The recent bout of externally induced adjustments suggests that, in an environment where there are serious rigidities in markets or where markets are not fully free by policy design or legacies of policies pursued in the past, output losses result that far exceed any efficiency gains from better resource allocation. There is, therefore, a real trade-off between the two that is often neglected. This would seem to apply in particular to the PETs. Indeed, macroeconomic problems and stabilization programs in PETs can satisfactorily be assessed and monitored only if the specific policy and systemic antecedents of these economies in the classical CPE and MPE, as discussed in Section 2, are clearly understood.

5. CEPU adjustment, commercial policy, and diplomacy

A payments union can be set up under various arrangements as regards the financing of imbalances. Under some circumstances, it may even be conceived without there being a common capital pool. But then the chances of successfully moving forward with currency convertibility remain decidedly confined. A capital pool can be constituted by the members themselves. But here the possibilities are also limited as a payments facility is as a rule set up precisely to alleviate the external-payments problems of the participants. Remains then the option of soliciting funds from outside, as in the case of the EPU.

Even under the most congenial conditions, outside capital has an opportunity cost to the donor and will therefore need to be mobilized as effectively as circumstances permit. That is to say, the means available should be employed to bring about the pivotal goal of the payments union to begin with, namely the implementation of policies, institutions, and policy instruments that will permit countries to balance their current account in the medium run. The sponsors of the payments union may decide to leave all substantive decisions up to the recipients. This solution is rather unrealistic, given the opportunity cost of financing the envisaged facility. It is also one that cannot but fail to inspire confidence in the payoff of the sacrifices that the reforming countries necessarily have to incur to succeed with their transition to the ME environment. Under most circumstances, then, donor countries will wish to exercise some macroeconomic surveillance over the operations of the payments union. This will be directed in the first instance at monitoring progress with the domestic policies of the participants aimed at mitigating or easing the constraints on external payments.

Although there are many motives that outside surveillance may wish to serve, the core objective should be making the payments union manageable. Indeed, participants must be encouraged to adopt proper macroeconomic policies. They should also be induced to foster more rational trade and domestic product and factor prices. But a payments union should not directly be concerned with domestic economic or broader reforms. Given the context in which such a scheme for Eastern Europe would be set up, however, a clear understanding among sponsors and beneficiaries about the latter's eventual market orientation and commitment to price and trade liberalization are necessary preliminaries to ease the constraints on external payments as effectively in support of reform as possible. Because the nature and size of future imbalances in Eastern Europe are essentially unpredictable, it is difficult to determine the precise magnitude of the problems that a payments union will have to come to grips with in the context of evolving reform. Some authority associated with the clearing scheme must, therefore, exercise surveillance. This should encourage chronic surplus countries through macroeconomic policy to adopt more expansionary policies, particularly by encouraging imports, but not solely from within the union. Likewise, it should induce chronic deficit countries through policy advice to seek contractionary policies, particularly in levels of domestic absorption so as to free up resources for export promotion, but not necessarily solely to participants in the payments union.

The policy advice to be formulated here is fairly straightforward if the imbalances of participants in the payments union are unambiguous. This is not

Table 6.1: Macroeconomic policy responses to chronic imbalances

Sign of imbalance			Policy response
Total	*Union*	*Rest*	
+	+	+	Expansionary policy, especially import promotion
-	-	-	Contractionary policy, but stimulate exports
0	0	0	No change required
0	+	-	Liberalize union trade
0	-	+	Liberalize nonunion trade; possibly fund union deficit from outside
+	+	-	Expansionary policy, but liberalize union trade
+	-	+	Expansionary policy, but liberalize nonunion trade; possibly fund union deficit from outside
+	+	0	Expansionary policy and liberalize union trade
+	0	+	Expansionary policy and liberalize nonunion trade
-	+	-	Contractionary policy, but liberalize union trade
-	-	+	Contractionary policy, but liberalize nonunion trade; fund union deficit from outside
-	-	0	Contractionary policy and stimulate union exports
-	0	-	Contractionary policy and stimulate nonunion exports

normally the case, however. To see this, Table 6.1 lists the various logically plausible combinations of imbalances with union members and outside partners that can occur. There are only three occasions in which adjustment policies in a payments union will be unambiguous. One is trivial, namely when balance is reached in relations with the union as well as with outsiders. The best policy advice in those conditions is to endorse the *status quo ante*, provided trade liberalization is not being forcibly held up.

The other two refer to overall balance being either in surplus or in deficit at the same time that the balance with union members and with nonmembers is of the same sign. The advice in these cases is as described earlier. Chronic surplus countries should be encouraged to pursue expansionary policies, including notably by liberalizing their import regime. The measures embraced may have to be discriminatory if the surplus is chiefly with one partner group. The discrimination should, of course, lessen the degree of absolute discrimination and contain the extent of relative discrimination. Likewise, chronic deficit countries should enacted contractionary policy, but preferably while enacting measures to bolster exports. Once again, if the deficit is primarily with one country grouping, discriminatory measures may be in order. Absolute discrimination, if possible, should be reduced in the process, however.

Any of the above variants will prevail only by coincidence. More normal will be a conflictual situation, as already intimated in case the overall imbalance is disproportionately on account of trade with one group. Easiest to deal with are the cases in which the imbalance prevails only on account of one group of countries. In that case, one-sided discriminatory policy measures may be required. These should preferably be confined to trade-policy actions, such as relaxing exchange constraints with union members faster than with other partners. The policy prescription in a case of surplus is roughly as already discussed. Expansionary policies are recommended with attention being paid in the first instance to efforts that bolster imports, especially from union members if that is where the surplus prevails. Likewise in case of a deficit, when contractionary policies are in order. Under the circumstances, attention will need to be paid in particular to efforts to bolster exports on a discriminatory basis, if necessary, to the area with which the deficit occurs.

Under normal trading conditions, countries will tend to run imbalances of opposite sign with union members and other trading partners. Under such conditions, the question arises what macroeconomic policy should be all about once the quota of participants in the union is exhausted. It is evidently impossible, on logical grounds, to formulate a singular response for it could at best correct one, but not both, imbalances. Clearly, instituting general trade-liberalizing measures or inducing an expansion of macroeconomic absorption would only aggravate the intragroup imbalance. It would, therefore, be important to pursue discriminatory trade-liberalization measures. Under some conditions, these policy choices may no longer be feasible, perhaps because countries have already earlier made rapid progress with trade liberalization, possibly upon the creation of the payments union. If discriminatory trade liberalization is no longer feasible, the Surveillance Board may wish to recommend some temporary backtracking with opening the economy. In the case cited, this would require restricting intragroup trade relative to trade with outside partners. The other combinations with desirable policy responses are illustrated in Table 6.1.

However, discriminatory trade restrictions, especially if they entail a retrogression in trade-liberalization policies, are as a rule hardly acceptable to those who believe in a free multilateral economic system. This would normally hold also for those sponsoring the payments scheme for PETs. In the event of policy conflict, the Surveillance Board will have to resort to more subtle instruments. In the case of the EPU, these could take on any form that was negotiable through commercial-policy advice or financial diplomacy. Frequently explored were two means that, by their nature, violated the very principles of the payments union. One was to persuade chronic creditors to accept *de facto* a larger quota or to make otherwise more room for granting additional loans to the deficit countries than they would have by the strict rules of the union. In the EPU, these so-called *rallonges* were very important, especially in holding the FRG within the EPU (Rees 1963). Another instrument used especially with respect to debtor countries was to create for them larger credit quotas. Either or both were in some cases pursued through funneling payments from outside the union to chronic creditors. ERP funds were very important in this respect, especially during the earlier stages of the EPU (Kaplan and Schleiminger 1989, Lamfalussy 1989, Rees 1963, Tew 1990). Such flexibility in commercial policy and financial diplomacy would be highly desirable in a CEPU as well.

6. Other issues of managing a payments union

There are a few remaining technical issues of surveillance in a payments union of the kind advocated here. These include the selection of the members of the Surveillance Board and by whom, the authority of the Surveillance Board and to whom it will be responsible, where the Surveillance Board should be located and whether it should be institutionalized, and how best to dovetail its assigned activities with broader east-west economic assistance.

The Surveillance Board that I advocate consists essentially of a fairly small number of professional macroeconomists and specialists in the policy choices and options available to PETs. Among the members, there should be some individuals from the PETs, preferably outstanding professionals who enjoy the confidence of their governments. But they need not necessarily form part thereof or owe otherwise allegiance to their government. This raises two critical questions. One deals with whether key economic matters can be entrusted to economists. Would it not be better to mobilize government specialists in economic and financial affairs who enjoy the confidence of the respective governments in place and can, if necessary, personally persuade national decision makers of the desirability of following one reform course rather than another? Of course, there is no assurance at all that a group of economists will invariably find the right solution to complex macroeconomic problems. But neither is there certainty that government bureaucrats or international civil servants will be able to distance themselves sufficiently from their national or institutional "interests" to try to come to grips with the issues at hand in a payments union. I would give the benefit of doubt to a group of professional macroeconomists capable of formulating technical answers to technical questions, if necessary in a very pragmatic manner, provided their behavior is sufficiently monitored by some political institution, such as advocated here.

The second question revolves around the delicate issues of national economic sovereignty and the administration of surveillance. Clearly, macroeconomic surveillance cannot avoid exerting an influence on the reform process in member countries. This calls for a common understanding on the vital issues of the comprehensiveness of reform measures, the sequencing of policies measures in the broad sense (policies as such, market-conform institutions, policy instruments required for coordinating economic decisions indirectly, and changes in the behavior of economic agents), and the speed at which reform measures must be introduced. There is no agreement on these issues within any given reforming country at this time. Neither is there such an unambiguous gospel in the international organizations currently assisting the PETs. That is to say, the Surveillance Board will have to negotiate a common understanding on what reforms should be all about, subject to the alleviation of external-payments constraints, and persuade policy makers in countries that are exhausting their quotas as creditors or debtors to introduce modifications in the comprehensiveness, speed, or sequencing of the reform strategy. Under the circumstances, it would be impossible to leave the reform fully up to national policy makers. Delicate commercial and financial diplomacy with a lot of *ad hoc* pragmatic intervention, as it were on the spot at the heat of the moment, will necessarily characterize the operations of the Surveillance Board. This is one of the reasons for my advocating that the Board be made up chiefly of independent, highly skilled macroeconomists, some of whom must have the necessary diplomatic acumen to overcome the potential difficult intermingling in economic sovereignty of the countries participating in the envisaged payments union.

Because the vast bulk of activities of the Board will involve a good dose of intelligent macroeconomic engineering, issuing commercial-policy advice, and engaging in delicate financial diplomacy, I would argue for a substantial degree of autonomy for Board members. Of course, they must be responsible to some authority. If the European Parliament were to be strengthened, as currently envisaged, that would be the proper authority. In the interim the EC's Council of Ministers could take this role upon itself. The job could also be undertaken by the Commission of the EC. But I find this the least desirable of the three instances for potentially granting authority over supervision. For one, the Commission is preoccupied with a myriad of other tasks in the coming years. Also, it has been trying hard to carve out a great-power political status for itself. Applying these precepts to relations with the reforming countries in Eastern Europe would, in my view, be highly misplaced.

Nonetheless, there would seem to be little point in having a Surveillance Board formulate desirable policy modifications without it being involved to some degree in the broader context of east-west assistance. At the very least, the latter will exert an impact on the institutional and behavioral setting of the kind of policies that PETs will gradually be able to pursue. Inasmuch as this assistance is essentially being coordinated on behalf of the Group of Twenty-four by the Commission of the EC, this would provide one logical instance in which a Surveillance Board acting under the EC's aegis could for now interface with the broader western assistance efforts. This would come into play especially if and when the Soviet Union or its successor republics were to join the union. Such a mutation could not but pose real problem for the Surveillance Board. Firm stewardship on the part of a group of economists would probably be ignored unless a stick were associated with the carrot of external financing. In this case, the Commission of the EC - or the surrogate European patron of the payments facility - would assume a paramount role in keeping matters on an even keel.

Because of the relatively small size of the Surveillance Board and the fact that technical supervision over the payments arrangements will be exercised by the BIS, there is no need to establish another full-fledged institutional layer. What is required, however, is some link between the Surveillance Board and national governments called upon to modify their macroeconomic policies. Especially in the initial phases of the payments union it will be essential to pursue developments in the PETs on a nearly continuous basis. It would, therefore, be preferable to locate the Surveillance Board in the heart of the area participating in the scheme. I would suggest Prague as a venue for the Surveillance Board. If that would be objectionable to other participants, Berlin or Vienna could be selected. The first alternative might mollify objections on the part of the FRG and induce it to facilitate maintenance of the traditional commercial ties between key enterprises in the eastern part of the country that are still functioning, or can be resurrected in a viable manner, and the countries of Central Europe. Vienna might be a desirable locale given the city's traditional role in the east-west economic and political context, Austria's aspirations to membership in the EC, and the fact that Austria joining the EC would probably induce the remaining EFTA members to do likewise.

7

Downside risks of a CEPU

The creation of some kind of economic union supported by a payments facility to ensure transferability in the prospective trade among the reforming countries of Eastern Europe is not, of course, without a number of drawbacks. These emerge first and foremost when the current environment for economic reform is viewed against the backdrop of fostering the speedy integration of the PETs into the multilateral framework for international trade and payments. There are also considerable risks in terms of successfully nursing along the reform process and obtaining the objectives set at the outset of the payments union. If not properly implemented and monitored, unduly delayed adjustment in economic structures and policies is bound to be counterproductive.

Many observers have shown considerable apprehension about the above-mentioned aspects. Some have based their stance against any cooperative solution on inadequate or even faulty information. Others do not seem to have grasped the essential features or even the purposes of a payments union. Whatever the attitude taken, virtually all variants of proposals that envision encouraging Eastern Europe in general and the PETs in particular to come to grips with the problems of disturbances in their balance of payments, other than those structural in nature, through a cooperative but discriminatory framework have met stiff resistance. This holds for many policy makers, the leadership of international organizations, academics, and other commentators on Eastern European economic affairs. Some of this outright opposition, to my proposal in particular has been well taken, reflecting essentially inherent weaknesses of any pragmatic payments scheme in contrast to the inherent elegance of neat theoretical solutions. Other arguments must be attributed to views that I do not at all share.

This chapter has a dual purpose. It categorizes the various criticisms made against a payments union and clarifies some of the mysteries that may surround the stances taken by many, if not all, observers. Section 1 sketches briefly the backdrop to the proposal for a CEPU and its evolution, elaborating somewhat on the condensed clarification of the genesis of this book given in the introduction. Next I briefly restate the options available to the PETs to make steady progress with marketization in the wake of various disequilibria, especially those in external payments. Section 3 sketches the most important overall arguments invoked against the creation of any regional payments union. The key points tabled against the creation of a payments union for part or all of Eastern Europe are examined next. In this review, I shall confine myself largely to the comments made with respect to the proposals that I have formulated over the past year or so. I take up these arguments in the last section.

1. Backdrop to the debate

The motives that led me to advocate the creation of a payments union for Eastern Europe in early 1990 were briefly recounted in the introduction. Initial versions of these ideas sought to lay bare the grand outlines of the scheme and its parentage, which has all along been the EPU; but I have never contended, as Kenen (1990) suggests, that a CEPU could be equally successful in terms of trade creation, regional cooperation and integration, and global trade liberalization. These views were published anonymously in two major publications of the United Nations and two contributions circulated under my own name (Brabant 1990c, f). The proposals have been examined from various angles in international fora, in many of which I was allowed to participate, and in numerous informal meetings in east and west with academics, government advisers and officials, civil servants of international and regional economic organizations, and enterprise managers and bankers involved in trade and finance with Eastern Europe. Invariably they all have helped, perhaps unwittingly, to hone my present thinking on a payments facility that could best suit the PETs and be least costly for donors and potential other beneficiaries, given the environment in which the transition is perforce placed. Several others, however, have perplexed me if only because of the sheer muddle and convolution that can so utterly deflect from the thrust of a comparatively simple suggestion, thereby nullifying the very conditions upon which any payments union, and the CEPU in particular, is necessarily predicated (see Oppenheimer 1991 and Schrettl 1991). Nonetheless, even these exchanges of views and reflections have been very constructive in refining the original scheme, including through papers presented at seminars and conferences, all listed in the bibliography.

Taking stock of the negative and positive reactions, not counting queries for clarification, I end up with over two dozen critical arguments designed to puncture one or another substantive or technical angle of the CEPU. Some of these comments refer to the intrinsic merits of a payments union. Others question the tactics of fostering economic reform through western assistance or argue that my proposal is way behind the times, given the aspirations and achievements of the PETs at this juncture. I dare say that none of these arguments has been very persuasive. This reaction is not because of pique or obduracy. Rather, most critiques rest on stances that have at best a tangential relevance to the aspirations and possibilities of the PETs at this juncture or create for themselves an environment for the transition that varies radically from the precarious situation that has characterized the PETs from the outset.

Indeed, these critical deliberations and exchanges of views that the proposal has elicited have only strengthened my views regarding the desirability of erecting a CEPU. I take this seemingly inflexible position not to deny that some comments have been highly constructive. Other arguments against the proposal can be attributed to the fact that the original scheme was presented without adequate detail on the techniques of the envisaged clearing and the type of macroeconomic control to be exerted through tight surveillance. But those involved in the ongoing debates on the economics of transition are rarely sufficiently patient to go with a fine-tooth comb through the technical aspects of a payments union. Moreover, most ignore critical elements of the situation that prevails in the PETs. This stems from a number of peculiar circumstances that owe a lot to the way in which the problems of central planning and its transformation have traditionally been shunned by mainstream economists, who are now suddenly attracted to the intellectual challenge of "the economics of transition," whatever meaning they may wish to impart to that task.

It is sad to observe that many newly found converts to the problems of Eastern Europe continue to deal in their ivory-tower approach with theoretically challenging - but in practice highly abstruse - issues for which policy implications are derived for Eastern Europe. Others feel called upon to issue recommendations for the transition that ignore the fact that the PETs are existing societies to be remade, not entities to be erected onto a *tabula rasa*. There is no malice intended, of course. The point is that many commentators have had, at best, a fleeting glimpse of the situation in Eastern Europe. Others simply project a straw man onto the arrangements for the transition that has little chance of being even remotely close to reality, and for that reason can be easily downed.

This lack of understanding for the plight of Eastern Europe as a whole or individual countries in particular on the part of many commentators must be held responsible for much of the sheer confusion about both the CEPU and the CEEU. Some arguments have been based on faulty information with respect to what the PETs really are, the scope of their current ambitions and possibilities, the ideology of unfettered marketization and multilateralism that neither reflects the real world outside the PETs nor the possibilities of the PETs, and the degree to which potential western donors are prepared to see to these countries becoming full-fledged MEs that can soon take their "rightful" place in the world economy.

Another set of charges essentially question my motives and purposes in advocating the scheme, although at no point did I leave any doubt that my CEPU proposal was formulated strictly as a transitional mechanism to assist the PETs with their most egregious intragroup external payments problems prior to the convolutions engendered by the crisis in the Persian Gulf. In particular, I have never left any doubt that this transitional arrangement should be wound up relatively quickly - better yesterday than today, if such were feasible at all. There are also commentators who prefer simply to impute ideological, prejudicial, or political motives to my proposition that I had earlier not even divined at. I must say quite frankly that I find the vast bulk of these allegations utterly rejectionable. Still another category of comments has merit in the sense that there are obviously dangers and risks involved in setting up a CEPU. My counterargument is essentially based on second-best grounds, taking into account that the world economy is far from transparent.

Of course, events in Eastern Europe have been progressing very quickly and the international environment for reforms in the PET has changed dramatically in more than one respect since I first proposed the creation of a CEEU and CEPU as transitional arrangements. One factor has been the sharp turn toward pervasive sociopolitical and economic crisis in the Soviet Union. Also the stalemate over significant further reform in several Eastern European countries has to be factored into the equation. So does the much slower response to reform efforts in the PETs than had been anticipated and indeed the prominent slowdown in intensity and pace of implementation of envisaged reforms. Prevailing macroeconomic policies are indecisive and incoherent. Furthermore, the institutions and instruments of central planning are no longer available, yet there simply is not even a moderate coordination mechanism to take the place of central planning. The economic questions around German unification became very pointed in mid-1990. For many Eastern European countries, as distinct from the Soviet Union, the resulting adjustment problems have thus far remained unresolved. The utter disintegration in a highly disruptive manner of the TR trade and payments arrangements in the course of 1990, the formal abolition of the CMEA in April 1991, and the vacuum in terms of successor trade and payment regimes, pending the adoption of full "world conditions" have also influenced the environment for which transitional solutions are to be designed. Finally, the potential disintegration of the Soviet federation needs to be heeded in pondering assistance efforts. It is necessary to weave those realities and potential complications into the frame of reference for the CEEU and CEPU. They can only sharpen the arguments for and underline the urgency of exploring with an open mind cooperative solutions to common trade and payment problems.

As I argued earlier, the proposal for erecting a payments union simply assumed that the crisis in the Middle East would be short-lived. Now that oil prices are again around $20 pb and the international ambiance for coming to grips with convertible-currency debts for several PETs is favorable, the advocacy of a payments union essentially entails an examination of what might be undertaken for and by Eastern Europe to counter transitory difficulties with their external accounts, especially in intragroup group. In that case, the main consequences of adjustment to market conditions emanate from the shift in the TR trade and payment regimes, the dissolution of CMEA arrangements for production specialization, and the desire of some PETs to raise their economic interaction with MEs, even if at the express expense of intragroup trade, whatever the opportunity costs may be.

Briefly put, in sum, my basic point of departure is that in transiting toward market conditions, especially the PETs are encountering a range of problems, among which a severe liquidity shortage constitutes but one constraint. This is making policy makers wary of moving swiftly with trade liberalization or marketization, thereby delaying the reform or sharply decelerating its implementation. Failure of reform, after the enormous political and other sacrifices some PETs have already absorbed, would be most regrettable indeed. To facilitate progress with radical economic reform by relaxing the foreign-exchange constraint, I propose to create a payments facility. Another objective is to encourage the radically reforming countries *not* to deny their emerging independent firms the opportunity to exploit their advantages in neighboring countries (including goodwill and market knowledge as detailed in Chapter 3) on the grounds of potential foreign-exchange shortages. Also, the transition is bound to be protracted. There is, therefore, no way in which these countries can quickly integrate themselves with the mainstream MEs without running into severe problems that the former by themselves cannot solve for the PETs, be it for financial or other reasons. Finally, any dash to current-account convertibility that is not credible, and therefore cannot possibly be sustained over some period of time, would be highly disruptive. Moving toward such convertibility requires that the underlying economic infrastructure can maintain current-account balance at least over the medium term. This is not now the case. A payments union would help these countries to work off the sacrifices required to adapt economic structures to competition, including among themselves.

2. The rump order of priority

Establishing current-account convertibility for the domestic currencies forms an indispensable tool of the process of establishing full-fledged markets as quickly as possible in Eastern Europe. Reaching that stage while making progress with structural change is being complicated by several factors. The first and foremost is the dislocation caused by massive structural change. Second, modifications in traditional policies are bound to entail inflation, unemployment, and austerity. Third, the demise of the CMEA and the disintegration of the TR trade and payment regimes are derailing external relations that have traditionally accounted for the lion share of trade. Fourth, with the crisis in the Persian Gulf, also the trading relations with MEs were temporarily perturbed as a result of which Eastern Europe incurred sizable terms-of-trade and revenue losses. Finally, key elements of a market environment, especially wholesale trading and flexible prices, are not yet present in most of Eastern Europe. They can be emplaced only over time and with perseverence to cushion the adverse socioeconomic costs. It would therefore seem realistic, as argued in Chapter 4, to envisage a convertible currency emerging only after some transition phase, during which the price regime is rationalized and trade liberalization is adopted to permit global competition. How protracted that process will in the end turn out to be depends crucially on the policy flexibility prevailing in these countries.

If the reforming countries could immediately make their currency convertible, at least for *all* merchandise and related transactions, and maintain some semblance of exchange-rate stability and current-account balance, perhaps with western financial support, some of the adjustment problems currently arising in particular from the replacement of the TR regimes would be easier to handle. If outright convertibility, including for intragroup commercial transactions, cannot be ensured, substantial diversion of trade to convertible-currency markets could be explored. Even if MEs were prepared to allow eastern countries to penetrate their markets on the basis of their competitive strengths, or perhaps even more favorable, preferential, arrangements as have been discussed for some time in the context of the EC and EFTA, the accommodation of the trade-diversion efforts would require working off the implied terms-of-trade and export-revenue losses. This may be difficult to accomplish in the short run, given all other transition costs. In other words, Eastern Europe for the foreseeable future will have to maintain traditional trade links. Whatever imbalance may arise at this juncture somehow needs to be financed. Most useful would be a mechanism that minimizes the austerity to be taken into account for lack of more flexible commercial arrangements.

If the countries of Eastern Europe must continue to trade with each other and are unable, for whatever reason, to conduct that trade at WMPs and in convertible currency, then it would seem logical *not* to encourage these countries to explore all kinds of nonmarket deals, ranging from bilateral clearing all the way to pure interfirm barter, sometimes of questionable economic rationale. But many eastern (Luft 1991, UNECE 1991a) and western (CEPR 1990, Tarr 1991) economists disagree with this. Under those conditions, it would seem preferable to explore a cooperative solution to alleviate that particular constraint on external payments. Those attributable to longer-term structural problems must be tackled differently. At least, this would permit making further orderly progress with industrial restructuring at a tolerable sociopolitical cost, even though such a payments facility would call for discriminatory treatment of foreign partners, on which more in Section 3. The external-payments facility could take on various characteristics, ranging from outright financing of the expected deficit in the balance-of-payments to multilateral clearing. Neither of these extremes is likely to be available. Even if the former were temporarily feasible, there would still be a need to exert surveillance over PETs so as to avoid repeating the misguided financial recycling exercise of the 1970s.

In my view, then, a realistic cooperative strategy should envisage the creation of a restricted payments facility. This has two principal features. One is to provide partial funding to transfer bilateral imbalances into multilateral ones to permit the maximum volume of economically warranted transactions. The other is external supervision to keep imbalances manageable by guiding partners into adopting macroeconomic stances that ensure that trade imbalances do not get out of hand and that the reform process will move forward as expeditiously as circumstances allow. Such a union would assist Eastern Europe in maintaining existing trade links that have an economic rationale and expanding intragroup trade on the basis of the profitability interests of autonomous firms as they emerge with reform. It would also facilitate the marketization of these economies and hence prepare them to compete in global markets. At that point a request for accession to the EC would be far more credible than it can possibly be at this juncture. Finally, it would nurture along the introduction of convertibility without imposing immediately massive adjustment costs.

My favorite variant of a payments facility is a regional payments union for the reforming countries of Eastern Europe with financial support from the EC and surveillance conducted under the aegis of the Commission of the EC, the Council of Ministers, or the European Parliament. Setting up a payments union with an operational surveillance mechanism is not at all straightforward. Aside from the many technical issues involved (as discussed in Chapter 5), exercising surveillance of the kind dealt with in Chapter 6 is by definition a political matter, particularly in the case of Eastern Europe. The clearing scheme has to ensure that payments imbalances remain manageable while the countries promote more rational commerce and domestic prices. Without these, any multilateral clearing is bound to fail. Whereas the latter task may be daunting for the smaller countries of Eastern Europe, it will be a Herculean effort to exercise meaningful surveillance over Soviet marketization. Nonetheless, I deem it politically wise and economically farsighted to conceive the clearing union with the Soviet Union counted in so that with a commitment to create markets (in either the federation or key successor republics) the problems of regime switch could be adequate tackled; I am less sanguine about proposals that would bring the Soviet Union in immediately but without allowing it access to loans (Ethier 1990, Pant and Tarr 1990). If such an attitude is taken, the union might just as well be conceived for all countries, old and new, of Eastern Europe, including Albania and Yugoslavia (or its successor states) if dinar convertibility were to falter. But activation would be contingent on participants adopting economic decentralization and enforcing hard-budget constraints for all.

3. General arguments against payments unions

To tackle the general theoretical comments against the creation of a payments union, the core aspects of the advocated facility, the starting conditions of the potential participants, and the directions of fundamental change in institutions and policies into which the surveillance associated with the payments facility should help to move the participants must be clear.

1. Key aspects of a payments union

A payments union essentially embraces four components. First of all, it automatically clears bilateral imbalances among the participants. Second, it encompasses a credit mechanism that extends loans on a *quasi*-automatic basis, because there is a predetermined credit ceiling within preset quotas. Third, it must be associated at least *de facto* with a coordination mechanism to facilitate the transition to current-account convertibility through global trade liberalization. This may initially call for discrimination, which may or may not be desirable to reach the objectives set in concurrence with the facility's main sponsors. Finally, the coordination mechanism must be supplemented with explicit macroeconomic surveillance. Only in that way can it be ensured that weak adjustment mechanisms emanating from incipient market relations are supplemented with macroeconomic intervention, possibly of the dirigistic or discriminatory kind, to maintain some degree of coherence between external payments and domestic structural adjustments. All four are essential in any kind of payments union. Especially the latter is critical in guiding the PETs to the market environment and helping them to overcome the deleterious legacies of central planning. Let me briefly recapitulate the role of each component in a more theoretical framework than I could invoke in the earlier discussion.

Very often, when considering payments facilities, the question of surveillance is dealt with at best implicitly. Thus, in Bofinger's (1990b) scheme of things, only the first three are clarified because his (1990a, b, c; 1991a, b, c) favored disciplining tool is emulating the integration of the GDR for all of Eastern Europe by submitting the latter's monetary policy in effect to that of the EMS. Kenen (1990), Polak (1991), and Williamson (1990), to cite only the more prominent commentators on the CEPU, implicitly favor the Fund's discipline as sufficient for a *de facto* regional payments facility. This is shortsighted for the reasons adduced in Chapter 6. But it is pertinent also because the role of managing surveillance, as in the EPU, is often pooh-poohed. Yet that does not concord with actual experience. Kaplan and Schleiminger (1989) as well as Rees (1963) suggest that the EPU's Managing Board, in fact, did play a very comprehensive role in the coordination of national macroeconomic policies through effective surveillance. Both were steered through policies available within the OEEC's framework, which might suggest that these claims are rather exaggerated. In a personal conversation with J. Kaplan on 24 October 1990, he confirmed in fact my impression of the book, and emphasized it several times, that the Managing Board indeed played such an all-encompassing role. However that may be, it remains the case that any payments facility without a strong surveillance mechanism is doomed to failure from the start. It may fail for other reasons as well, as examined in the next two sections.

a. Bilateral clearing. The pivotal goal of a regional payment mechanism is to wean countries of the straitjacket of bilateralism and guide them to multilateralism. The ultimate objective, of course, is eventually to fully integrate participants into the global trade and payment systems. Freeing partners from various bilateral arrangements (including in the form of strict barter or BTPAs with swing credit provisions) in effect moves the trade-budget constraint (see Bofinger 1990a, b), in the form of foreign-exchange availability, to the "right." It allows individual economic agents to negotiate with each other without having to be concerned all the time about the availability of an "unused quota." In that sense, a payments union increases the degree of convertibility of payments among the participants without necessarily constraining relations with outsiders. For this to work well, bilateral accounts must be multilateralized and all magnitudes must be translated into a common currency. This may entail foreign-exchange risks, whose magnitudes can be reduced. The EPU's experience cannot be repeated because the system of fixed exchange rates no longer exists. A payments union "embedded in and [deriving] its rationale from an existing supranational monetary order with relatively fixed exchange rates" (Bofinger 1990b, p. 2) would be useful, and probably more successful, than one in which no such monetary arrangement prevails. But this is not a required feature of a payments union. The necessary condition is that some group of countries is encountering intragroup current-account problems that cannot be overcome through freely floating exchange rates. Putting it another way, if the countries in question cannot divert their economically warranted intragroup trade to third markets without incurring sizably negative terms-of-trade and export-revenue effects, the only alternative to multilateralizing trade, with some payments facility, is trade destruction by "premature convertibility" (Frenkel 1990, p. 155).

b. A credit facility. There are at least two kinds of credit facilities associated with a payments union. One is the automaticity of the reciprocal granting of unlimited bilateral credit during the period that imbalances are not yet tallied and transmitted to the accounting agent. Taking advantage of the float is sometimes deemed useful (paradoxically in Polak 1991). In fact, the advantage for the debtor is at the expense of the creditor. That float should be as short as circumstances permit and, if of more than trivial duration, be associated with full interest charges.

Apart from this unlimited credit facility in-between settlements, an essential component of a payments union is the conversion of some net claims on the union into less than 100 percent currency payment. For that quotas and combinations of payments in convertible currency and loans have to be agreed upon. In case of asymmetric combinations of loans and payments, depending on either the net position with regard to the union or the degree of quota used, a capital fund needs to be constituted. This may or may not have to be utilized, depending upon the distribution of debts and credits relative to quota positions. Without such financial backing in principle, however, the risk of paralyzing the facility from the outset is too great and, in my view, really not worth running.

c. The coordination mechanism. An essential ingredient of a payments union is trade liberalization, at least within the union, so that individual economic agents can exploit their comparative advantages without having to be overly concerned about the modalities of mutual settlement, obviously within certain constraints. However, a payments union at the very least involves discrimination among partners through the monetary mechanism. By definition, payments within the union are less "hard" than payments with outsiders. This tends to favor imports from union members. To ensure minimal interference in microeconomic commercial decisions and yet administer this discriminatory payments facility, some kind of trade and/or foreign-exchange licensing needs to be instituted. The latter approach would be most constructive.

It is important to recall the policies pursued by the PETs. The inherently discriminatory features of a payments union would *not* inhibit countries with domestic convertibility from extending it. Instead of the licensing for a plethora of bilateral deals in the post-CMEA world that is currently required, the licensing of trade and payments with any reforming country in the context of the payments union would simply apply to the transactions not yet conducted in convertible currency and not yet slated to be included in such settlements. Thus, any claim to convertibility being established within the union as compared to third parties (Bergsten and Williamson 1980, Thompson 1990), while normally true for a payments union, simply fails to recognize realities in Eastern Europe.

Whereas there cannot but be relative discrimination among partners when there exists a payments union, it would run counter to the very nature of the facility to raise absolute discrimination either with partners or outsiders, except on an emergency basis. By limiting multilateralism to within-group trade and making available loans in addition to payments in convertible currency, each partner obtains a guarantee that trade liberalization at least within the union will not be inhibited as a result of the potential for prematurely depleting foreign-exchange reserves.

Clearly, countries that expect to be in surplus will temporarily have to forfeit their right to immediate full payment in convertible currency either from union partners or in diverting trade to others. Countries in that position will not be very interested in the clearing arrangement unless there is a fair expectation that they may have to avail themselves of borrowed funds from the union sometime in the near future. That is to say, any payments union with chronic or structural debtors or creditors is inherently unstable; the only exception is when there is a "captive" market, the surplus country not being able to divert its products to freer markets, and the hope of obtaining full payment in the near future. It is for that reason that throughout the volume I have emphasized that only one category of the multiple problems with managing the external payments of PETs can be dealt with through a CEPU or a similar facility.

d. Macroeconomic policy surveillance. Precisely to avoid the emergence of structural debtors and creditors, steady progress with trade liberalization needs to be enacted while adequate macroeconomic adjustments are put in train to combat excessive imbalances, regardless of sign. Only in this way can policies be kept on the reform track. This is particularly applicable to PETs, given the multiple legacies of central planning and the fragile incipient markets at best available at this juncture. Automatic stabilizers or adjustment mechanisms in these countries are not yet in place.

As examined in Chapter 6, payments imbalances with union members and outsiders are rarely of the same sign. Even if they are, their relative magnitude may be completely out of sync so that a uniform adjustment policy, either expansionary or contractionary, may correct some of the starting disequilibria but entail new imbalances of opposite sign. These can be resolved only through discriminatory macroeconomic stances. Depending upon the extent to which trade and external payments has been liberalized, discrimination or retrogression with liberalization can be prevented only if further measures are taken to free up trade constraints imposed on one set of partners. In some cases, as argued, this degree of measured progress with trade liberalization can no longer be utilized through orthodox instruments, but may have to be supplemented with decisions that in fact violate the starting conditions of the union. As such, they further discriminate against outsiders.

There is unfortunately not much that can be done about this feature of the payments union. Only a good dose of pragmatism supported by commercial and financial diplomacy can convince trading partners or the custodians of the global regimes that temporary discrimination may be a desirable short-term cost to buttress further progress toward current-account convertibility. Inasmuch as trade-policy stances are very often formulated by policy makers with short time horizons, given the pressures arising from various domestic interest groups, reconciling progress in the context of the payments union with the desirability of moving toward global multilateralism will require some delicate balancing act on the part of the Surveillance Board.

2. THE STARTING CONDITIONS OF POTENTIAL PARTICIPANTS

A solid understanding of the structures in place in the participating economies and of how they differ from the key features of third parties is very important for guiding the operations of the payments union. It is also of strategic relevance to be perfectly clear about what can and cannot be expected over the course of the life of the payments union from the replacement of bilateralism by multilateralism - some form of intra-union convertibility, if you wish.

Perhaps the most critical component of a payments union is providing some insurance for letting individual economic agents make decisions about traded quantities and prices on their own account without them having to worry about exchange rates and how to settle imbalances. Some critics (Matejka 1990) assume that this can be enforced only if effective markets exist to guide adjustments in the participants either through the trade mechanism as such or through the adoption of market-conform macroeconomic policy stances, perhaps in consultation with the Surveillance Board. Of course, this feature is in principle highly desirable. The fact is, however, that markets in the PETs are at best feeble and in some cases only incipient. In the short run, there is very little that can be done about this. Every effort should be made to enhance the preconditions for marketization while keeping adjustment costs manageable.

Another starting condition of the PETs is that they cannot or do not wish to effect their intragroup payments in convertible currency, notwithstanding policy statements to the contrary. Even countries (Poland since 1990 and Czechoslovakia since 1991) that have ostensibly committed themselves to the establishment of internal convertibility continue to be reluctant[1] to conduct their intragroup transactions in convertible currency; hence, the bewildering variety of barter deals currently being struck by virtually all pairs of former CMEA countries. This alternative to trade and payment liberalization cannot be very rewarding.

The third feature is that trade diversion even for the smaller countries of Eastern Europe can be effected only at substantial terms-of-trade and export-revenue losses. These may be sharply aggravated as a result of trade-policy stances adopted by potential convertible-currency partners, such as in Western Europe, in the case of the PETs. Even if considerable liberalization will be adopted there, the export-supply offer of the PETs can be "hardened" only gradually. There are various reasons for this state of affairs that almost tautologically hark back to the very need for "transition" in PETs.

3. Directions of desirable progress

The most immediate goal of a payments union is to replace constraints on bilateral payments with multilateral ones. As soon as possible, the objective should be balancing global payments without the imposition of trade restrictions for payments reasons. Clearly, these advantages increase with the number of participants. This leads to a paradox: The ultimate optimum size of the union is one where a union is no longer required, namely when all partners utilize convertible currency. But it is not necessary to impute an identical weight to each potential partner, as Bofinger (1990b, p. 10) apparently assumes. What matters in the first instance is that the larger share of trade of the participants in the union, regardless of their share in global trade, be conducted among themselves for other reasons than trade diversion on account of discriminatory arrangements condoned through the union. Whether the payments union is a small or large part of global trade is of secondary, not prime (Kenen 1990, Michalopoulos and Tarr 1991, Polak 1991) importance. It is not, of course, altogether immaterial. Thus, it would not be desirable to form a pay-

[1] I have been told informally that the replacement of bilateral clearing in convertible currency by payments in convertible dinars since December 1989 has been less than full, to say the least. Unfortunately, Eastern European officials and their aides are understandably reluctant to be forthcoming with details of concrete bilateral arrangements embraced at this stage.

ments union with features that diverge significantly from those prevailing in the rest of the world, when that rest accounts for the bulk of global trade.

It is of more than passing interest to bear in mind that the number of participants in a potential union can be very misleading. Simply counting the number of countries presupposes that these units have fully integrated markets upon which bilateralism in external trade and payments has been imposed. The real measure of participants, however, should be payments coming under unintegrated regimes. Thus, although a CEPU could presently include at most seven countries (Eastern Europe as defined and perhaps Albania), the interactions among any pair of these countries are conducted at heterogeneous levels. That certainly increases the number of trading circuits to be reconnected in an open multilateral environment. The latter expands also with the potential breakup of the Soviet federation and indeed Yugoslavia's, something that has recently come within the realm of possibilities.

The core objective of the EPU was, of course, to come to grips with collective imbalances against outsiders that policy makers found unsustainable at given foreign-exchange reserves. That situation is quite different from the conditions prevailing in Eastern Europe, especially countries that have made (Hungary and Poland) or are making (Czechoslovakia) substantial progress with liberalizing their trade and foreign-exchange regimes. The point is precisely that such liberalization has so far been reserved mostly for trade with full-fledged convertible-currency partners (Budzinski 1991, p. 151), essentially the members of the OECD. This forms still a small part of any PET's trade, although there has been substantial growth since 1990.

The question of why countries should resort to a payments union rather than more orthodox macroeconomic policies has baffled many a commentator. It cannot be solved solely from within a theoretical framework. In theory, if countries possess markets and are willing to adjust in any direction without debilitating the basics of the market, such as "freedom" of decision making or underpinning the pluralistic democratic regime itself, it is almost tautological that other instruments can be embraced to afford countries the means to rectify their fundamental disequilibrium on current account. Devaluation of the exchange rate in combination with the proper mix of monetary and fiscal policies should, in principle, suffice as corrective palliatives.

The fundamental problem of the PETs is now precisely that they are manifestly not - in any case, not yet - MEs and hardly have a time horizon that permits policy makers to enforce rapid structural adjustment. These societies would probably quickly destroy their exceedingly weak democratic regimes by advocating unconstrained pro-market policy commitments at this stage. Any commentator who does not, or does not wish to, understand these preconditions, is too obtuse to familiarize him- or herself with the starting conditions of the PETs, or is simply unwilling to look in greater depth at what the countries under investigation can realistically accomplish without tearing apart the social fabric of society, will come to the self-evident finding that "a fundamental balance of payments disequilibrium can always be corrected by means of monetary and fiscal policies" (Bofinger 1990b, p. 11)! To confuse matters further, Bofinger (1990b, p. 12) on the next page considers events in which the "underlying causes for unsustainable current account deficits can neither be corrected by a devaluation nor by more restrictive macroeconomic policies," but fails to specify those conditions. These would seem to be precisely the realities to be dealt with in the case of the PETs.

The PETs are economies in which automatic adjustments are still quite weak and sluggish at that. In other words, for any magnitude of adjustment required the burden would become very large, perhaps altogether intolerable, given the fragile nature of the sociopolitical processes that have been crystallizing there. It is precisely one of the purposes of the payments union to help facilitate the reforms that would in time yield automatic stabilizers and adjustment mechanisms. Once established, these should function just like in MEs.

It must simply be taken for granted that, for the time being and indeed for some years to come, all PETs without exception, even under the most favorable circumstances, will be implementing structural reforms that should abate, and eventually fully remove, the legacies from central planning. Once the market mechanism is in place, including the entire legal, institutional, fiscal, monetary, and other wherewithal for effective market operations, a critique of the payments union would and should be based on the derogation from the market framework that it under these circumstances is bound to foster. The trade-off between the desirability of fostering multilateralism and condoning discrimination through a payments facility would favor the first rather than the latter.

Not only that, for the time being solutions will have to be found for the PETs, or perhaps Eastern Europe as a whole, to assist these countries in coming to grips with their balance-of-payments problems, in keeping the reform course on track, and in helping them to alleviate the adverse impacts on society of massive structural adjustment. That these countries together in a payments union would be different in size, in macroeconomic environment, in the stage of marketization and democratization, and in their international position relative to the features of the EPU (Bofinger 1990b, pp. 15-21; Kenen 1990) are matters that simply cannot be disputed (Baneth 1991, Wagener 1991). But they should not be exaggerated when the object of the investigation is the preferred - least costly - alternative option for the PETs themselves. Granted all these realities that tend to accentuate the discriminatory character of a payments union or its weaker contribution to multilateral solutions, what can be done for these countries?

4. Comments on the CEPU and their merits

Many comments, criticisms, suggestions, and inquiries concerning the CEEU and CEPU, but especially the latter, have been conveyed in oral commentary on one paper or another presented at some international meeting. Others arose in informal discussions with individuals, who might not wish to be quoted. Many have *en passant* commented on the CEPU in the context of other papers, most of which are still in draft form or not yet available for quotation. Rather than provide an encyclopedia of attributions of one argument or another, I shall discuss groups of issues and identify commentators only when the view is available in a quotable paper and is pertinent, that is presented in a more comprehensive framework on the transition in Eastern Europe than a by-the-way.

The comments that I am familiar with fall essentially into five groups. The first one can roughly be identified with the politics of CMEA cooperation. The core questions revolve around treating Eastern Europe, or a subgroup thereof, as a "bloc," a distinct region somehow deserving a particular treatment that falls outside the mainstream of market relations eventually required to integrate these countries in the global economic context. It also imputes to me various motives as regards maintaining the CMEA "cooperation regime." These include an alleged desire to perpetuate the ossified economic structures and deliberately deny PETs from moving on with technological and structural changes that would place them in the mainstream of global economic relations (Köves 1991).

Related to the above, but decidedly less politically and emotionally charged, are points focusing on the economics of cooperation in Eastern Europe. Criticisms in this category include the stimulus for trade diversion and discrimination that a CEEU and CEPU might exert (Kenen 1990, Polak 1991). The competing (or rather duplicative) economic structures in place are held to render cooperation among these countries rather undesirable because they inhibit the emergence of intra-industry trade as the most dynamic component of commerce among most MEs. Regional cooperation would allegedly delay modernization, perpetuate obsolescence, petrify uncompetitive economic structures, and inhibit these countries from integrating themselves into the world economy (for example, Chekurov 1990, Čížkovský 1990, Inotai 1990, Köves 1991, Stankovsky 1990). More specifically, it would further prolong special preferences for the region and involve excessively discriminatory arrangements in making it work (Dăianu 1991, p. 170). Moreover, any special CMEA or post-CMEA preferences in such a scheme are deemed to be contrary to obligations under the GATT, to which most Eastern European countries are parties, have applied to gain the status of Contracting Party, or are actively interested in gaining that position as soon as politically feasible. Also, any discrimination enacted under disequilibrium exchange rates is deemed to be doomed from the start (Polak 1991).

In the course of 1990, several commentators have slowly relaxed their opposition to the desirability of creating some kind of economic union for the reforming countries in Eastern Europe, provided it would not "ossify" existing structures and not inhibit the fuller integration of these economies into the international economy. The appreciation of the positive aspects of an economic union, given the potential for trade destruction (Kádár 1991, Sosnowski 1991), is a bit curious. If it is recognized that the reforming countries in Eastern

Europe are not yet prepared to foot their intragroup trade on a convertible-currency basis, the question arises how one can ensure transferability within the union. Shifting the horizon from bilateralism to multilateral decision making and arranging for the settlement of potential deficits with the union would seem paramount. Indeed these concerns have been uppermost in my scheme of things. Yet, those advocates (including P. Kenen (1990) and J. Williamson (1990) - otherwise rather sympathetic to union formation) outrightly reject a payments arrangement.

A third category of comments focuses on the implications in a strict sense of making available funds for assisting the reformulation of intragroup cooperation in Eastern Europe. Any variation of a payments facility for the radically reforming countries is purported to make members dependent on financial aid that the west would be reluctant to grant (Bofinger 1990b). Moreover, Eastern Europe is apparently uninterested in obtaining a payments facility of the kind envisaged. In some versions of the latter critique, Eastern Europe is held to be in a position to introduce current-account convertibility for merchandise and related transactions in the very short run. They are also deemed to be able to merge themselves into the multilateral competitive environment without incurring too many negative, let alone prohibitively adverse, consequences. This easing of the adjustment burden is also taken for granted on account of the commitment to move toward convertible-currency settlement and WMPs in post-CMEA relations and let those parameters emerge from firms clearing markets on the basis of their own profitability motives. A footnote type of criticism under this heading has been that it would be far more desirable to make the PETs subject to the rules of the EMS and tie their currencies to the ECU regime at the earliest opportunity (Bofinger 1991a) - essentially applying the medicine earlier administered to the GDR also to the rest of Eastern Europe (Bergsten and Williamson 1990, p. 47).

In the same vein, Bofinger argues (1990b, p. 20) that the intermediate role of a CEPU "can be evaluated only if its members develop a clear concept for their future monetary integration with the European or international monetary arrangements." There is admittedly little doubt about what these countries covet in the medium to long run: full integration in the international monetary order in general and the EMS in particular. These ambitions may be fulfilled once stability has been regained and the worst uncertainties of the transition have been overcome (Brabant 1991f). Leaving the time frame somewhat vague at this stage should not inhibit these countries from moving steadily and as speedily as possible toward convertibility, perhaps through a cooperative strategy such as a payments facility of the CEPU type. Active involvement of the EC in both the financing and the surveillance of the CEPU would give a critical impetus to clarifying where the reforming countries of Eastern Europe will eventually fit into the global framework.

Criticisms of the more technical aspects of the CEEU and CEPU proposals cover a wide range of elements. Perhaps the most cogent is that the union would be too small to matter both in terms of the need of the participants for convertible currency and the pressures that are bound to emerge from within to make the union work. This is held to be so especially now that the former GDR for all practical purposes could no longer be involved in any type of clearing short of enacting it strictly in *Deutschmarks* (Kenen 1990). It is also alleged to be far too costly, under the circumstances, to provide an effective return on scarce assistance ECUs. Even if the cost were to be bearable, a payments union is deemed to be too slow to be of assistance, given the situation in which the PETs find themselves and the policy aspirations of the new leaderships in Eastern Europe. The cost assessment has apparently three components. One is the capital required to make the payments union function. A second is the cost involved in the technique of arranging clearing. A final one is the cost of exercising surveillance and seeing to it that policy advice is implemented in a timely fashion. As a peculiar aside, some Eastern European commentators (such as Köves 1991) have stressed that a payments union would be too expensive in part because of budgetary problems.

The final group of comments revolves around the second key component of operating a payments union. Critical is that Western Europe, as financial and spiritual sponsor of any payments scheme, would not be in a position to exert effective adjustment control. The key criticism is not about the west being unable to formulate proper macroeconomic policies for the PETs, although this too is at times invoked. Rather, it is alleged that the PETs would be unwilling to heed the policy advice and the west too wary to insist upon the policy advice being factored into the transition strategy, thereby debilitating the payments facility once the first member exhausts its quota.

There is, however, also a range of commentary that essentially rests on misunderstandings, in some cases even deliberate falsifications, of the proposals regarding a payments union that I have advanced. I shall not go into great details on these issues as the frivolity of these allegations (such as in Bofinger 1990b, p. 2) will become quite apparent to anyone taking the time to work through the mechanics of the proposal.

5. An evaluation of the criticisms

I cannot, of course, counter in detail every single argument against the creation of a CEPU or fostering a CEEU. The most relevant and, given the nature of the book, pertinent comments can be adequately dealt with by focusing on the key five components just outlined.

1. Emotional and political objections

Any accusation that the payment and cooperation proposals would be intended to prolong the "old CMEA" or seek to reconstitute that order, encourage the maintenance of "bloc-formation thinking," deliberately deny the PETs access to the EC or integration in the global economy, induce Eastern Europe to further petrify its outmoded economic structures, or withhold from the PETs the right to undertake major structural changes in line with world-market conditions must categorically be denied. The arguments brought to bear are silly at best and otherwise malicious.[2] Any motive as variation on any of the above themes attributed to the proposals for an CEEU or CEPU, singly or in combination, I simply categorically, but nonetheless very adamantly and sincerely, refute. My point of departure is quite different. Of course, I advocate intragroup economic cooperation, but primarily with reference to the economics of international trade, as argued in Chapter 3.

Even if the PETs were in a position to work off the necessary costs on the way to quick convertibility and trade diversion, it is not necessarily true that on economic grounds there would be no room left for exploring something akin to a CEEU as a means to enhancing the exploitation of prevailing static comparative advantages and buttressing rapid capitalization on the emerging dynamic comparative advantages in the region. This would require either the recognition of existing preferences and translating them into transparent market criteria. At the very least, it would call for avoiding the imposition of considerable impediments to intragroup trade, on which more in the next subsection.

2. Immediate full convertibility and global integration

Many criticisms of the proposal revolve around the proposition that the PETs aspire toward creating convertibility and integrating themselves quickly within the global economy (Michalopoulos 1990, Michalopoulos and Tarr 1990, Polak 1991), something that was not the case when the EPU was being considered (Baneth 1991); if realizable, a CEPU would be utterly superfluous. Of course, one basic point of departure (see Chapter 4) of the proposal is that none of the PETs can quickly establish full convertibility for all current-account transactions or for that matter integrate itself into the global economy without a very sharp loss in levels of living. The latter would in part result from scrapping a sizable part of the capital stock and idling a substantial share of the labor force be-

[2] This applies especially to the ridicule with which some commentators, including highly placed Hungarian policy makers in particular, have reacted to the proposal. Thus Mr. Béla Kádár, the Hungarian Minister of Foreign Economic Relations, accused me in September 1990 of trying to cling to my university chair on the CMEA! Of course, I am not aware of there existing any such chair anywhere in the west. And, for better or worse, I had then not been attached to any university at all for more than fifteen years! Another one is John Thompson's assertion (1990, p. 20) that the payments union as an attempt to revitalize cooperation would be "lethal" - a malappropriate conclusion of sorts. Others have termed the payments union "counterproductive" (Tarr 1991), something to be approached with "extreme caution" (Havrylyshyn and Tarr 1990, p. 26), or a venture that would keep alive a "traditional production system that has demonstrated its failings beyond any doubt" (Dornbusch 1990, p. 22).

cause their services are uncompetitive in global markets or they could not be utilized for lack of inputs. Among the latter, for example, provisioning of these countries with critical fuels and raw materials from other sources than the Soviet Union could be ensured only over time as the physical infrastructure (for example, oil-unloading capacities in the Baltic ports in the case of Poland) are simply not in place and thus inhibit the switching of markets in the short to medium run. If policy makers feel they have a mandate to incur such a cost quickly and they could absorb the burden, then indeed there would be no need for a CEPU. In the event, with great delight and cheer I would immediately withdraw the proposal(s).

A related comment is that the reforming countries themselves do not wish to participate in a CEPU. So be it! Clearly, countries have to examine and evaluate *all* available options realistically, including on second-best grounds. If after measured deliberation they continue to cling to the "no deal" attitude, then obviously no CEPU should be dictated. But that political attitude would not necessarily persuade outside sponsors that a different facility must be funded or policy makers of PETs that they must pursue very quickly trade and foreign-exchange liberalization. The consequences for intragroup trade and potential for diverting trade to the west will need to be taken into account too, of course.

3. A CEPU is too small and a CEEU wrong

Would trade flows among the Central European members be too small to matter? Could these countries easily trade in convertible currency among themselves, especially now that trading with the eastern part of Germany is in any case based on the *Deutschmark*, if necessary through loans (Kenen 1990), so that a payments facility would only retard the adjustment process?

Smallness in this context is often measured as the percentage of trade conducted among the potential CEPU members in their total trade. It is true that the share of trade with Central Europe for the four countries (Czechoslovakia, GDR, Hungary, and Poland) in 1989 hovered around 10 to 15 percent at most - not altogether negligible (Čičin-Šain 1991). It has been shrinking precipitously since then for reasons that are at the heart of my advocacy of a CEEU and CEPU. I contend that approaching the central question in this way cannot yield the proper answer. Placing trade among the CEPU members on a convertible-currency basis raises the demand for such exchange over and above the revenues required to maintain transactions that were already in the past conducted in convertible currency. That share manifestly amounted to much less than 100 percent of non-CMEA trade! The relevant comparison should be trade in convertible currency. In fact, trade with MEs effectively settled in convertible currency has been comparatively small, ranging between some ten percent for Bulgaria and Czechoslovakia and 25 percent for Hungary and Poland through 1989. The rest comprises trade on clearing account with other

CPEs and several DEs. Even though these accounts may have been kept in convertible currency, the fact that no payments were ever effected to settle imbalances suggests that these deals remained well removed from the transparency of "world market" conditions. In other words, at the commercial exchange rates introduced by mid-1990, the share of intra-CEPU trade relative to trade with convertible-currency partners until 1989 was anywhere between 25 and 100 percent. This is hardly a negligible rise in the transaction demand for convertible currency. Furthermore, because trade liberalization in the CEEU and/or the CEPU is bound to entail larger imbalances than experienced in the past, there is also a transitory rise in demand for precautionary purposes.

Some critics have contended that a CEPU could not be set up without participation of the Soviet Union (Bofinger 1991b, c; CEPR 1990; Daviddi and Espa 1990; Kenen 1990; Köves 1991; Lavigne 1990, 1991; Polak 1991; Williamson 1990). Politically it might well have been difficult to do so. Indeed, it would not have been very wise to deliberately exclude the USSR. From an economic perspective, however, there simply cannot be room for nonmarket relations in a CEPU, except perhaps initially. Indeed, such relations in particular form the core of the trade-liberalization policies that decision makers commit themselves to enact and the Surveillance Board needs to enforce with determination. These could not but be dysfunctional particularly for the countries bent on bearing the costs of the transition to market status. Moreover, there are signs emerging that marketization may in due course extend also to the Soviet Union or its most important successor republics. The latter would seem to be the implications of the reconceived union charter that, as now seems likely, will defer significant economic autonomy to the constituent republics. If that scheme were utterly to fail and the republics go their own way, the share of the CEPU in convertible-currency trade would be a multiple of current demand for reserves. Likewise, if Yugoslavia's dash toward convertibility were to collapse, possibly under impact of the fragmentation of the country into separate republics, the share of overall trade to be settled within a payments union would further soar.

Problems with bringing the Soviet Union into the payments scheme have also been raised because it would be a structural creditor (Bofinger 1990b, Kenen 1990, Williamson 1990), which would necessarily undermine the payments union. That conjecture is yet to be proved. It critically depends on the Soviet Union being able to maintain its supplies of fuels and raw materials to Eastern Europe and the WMP of oil. I am less sanguine than most commentators about these conditions prevailing on a permanent basis in a CEPU. That the Soviet Union would be uninterested in running surpluses with a CEPU (Kenen 1990) is also based on the doubtful assertion that it can easily market its fuels and raw materials elsewhere without depressing prices and running into transportation or severe processing problems. To switch from Saudi light to Soviet sulphuric oils, for example, a host of capital-retooling costs and security considerations need to be revolved. These cannot but inhibit the latitude of the Soviet Union in switching most of its exports to world markets, if only because of price concessions required to induce western customers to switch grades of crude.

Aside from the politics of union formation, many critics have charged that the creation of a CEEU with or without the payments facility would be wrong because it diverts trade and discriminates against outside partners. As I have argued in Chapter 3, a CEEU with a payments facility could help to avoid trade destruction for as long as the participating countries cannot or will not trade in convertible currency and they cannot divert their trade without incurring sizable negative terms-of-trade and export-revenue effects. It could not but avert trade destruction; in time it would be trade creating in the first instance for participants, but soon also for outsiders for reasons discussed in Chapter 3. Any sizable destruction of trade would lead to a contraction in levels of economic activity well surpassing what might be justified to eliminate loss-making activities. Advocating that a CEEU would avert trade destruction and help to bolster internal trade creation is not to be equated with any effort to petrify existing economic structures or trade patterns, however.

4. Inappropriateness of present trade patterns

A key criticism of any suggestion to ease the adjustment burden by facilitating gradual changes in the existing trading patterns has been that the latter are economically unwarranted and should, therefore, in any case be restructured at the earliest possible point of the transition. Prevailing trade patterns have emerged largely because of significant implicit preferences granted through mechanisms that should be suppressed in the process of marketizing these economies. In this connection, many commentators have sided with the big-bang, libertarian approach to managing the transition in PETs by arguing that what the countries need is integration in the global economy (Michalopoulos 1990), not being sucked into a "poor man's club" (Lipton and Sachs 1990a, Sachs 1990), particularly if such were to be possible only by perpetuating existing or institutionalizing new preferential arrangements, as through a CEEU.

As argued in Chapter 3, it may well be the case that upon a rationalization of the trading patterns of the PETs, a very different level, commodity composition, and geographical direction of trade would emerge. I doubt, though, that on rational economic grounds the optimal geographical division of labor for PETs would compress their intragroup trade to puny levels. I am even less convinced that taking advantage of commercial opportunities within a "poor man's club" is necessarily an undesirable way of capitalizing on comparative advantages. Surely at a time that many DMEs are exploring possibilities of reaping benefits from the establishment of joint ventures or channeling FDI into the PETs there would seem to be something fundamentally wrong about any suggestion that the countries themselves should not attempt to exploit "natural" trading opportunities offered by their neighbors.

Whether it would be undesirable to have preferential arrangements within a CEEU is a serious matter, particularly if at the same time it is argued that various east-west preferential arrangements should be put in place. I am firmly convinced, as argued in Chapter 3, that there are considerable opportunities for creating trade within Eastern Europe that have not so far been exploited because of faulty policies, institutions, and policy instruments. These could be reaped regardless of whether the postwar preferential regime is maintained. Positive discrimination *against* intragroup trade would, of course, cut into that pool of profitable trade. If substantial trade can be created and its global impact eased through regional cooperation, would it not be in the interest of both east and west to strengthen efforts to underpin intragroup trade as well?

A related comment contends that putting in place a CEEU in conjunction with a CEPU to foster regional cooperation would be trade diverting. More specifically, it is argued that trade with MEs, particularly in Western Europe, would be replaced by intragroup trade. Paradoxically perhaps, this has occurred over the past several years in part because of severe constraints on the convertible-currency payments of Eastern Europe. There is therefore room in these relations as well to restore previous levels of trade, hence the scope for trade creation. This should be further buttressed through the exploitation of the dynamic comparative advantages that the PETs are expected to generate as a result of marketizing their economies. Against this backdrop, I fail to see why a customs union among the PETs would necessarily be trade diverting at all. Indeed, the very purpose of the above-mentioned proposals would be to avert trade destruction on account of constraints on external payments or the diversion of trade to DMEs regardless of the domestic sociopolitical and economic adjustment costs in the short run. As a result of changes in comparative costs, MEs will in any case become less cost-competitive and therefore provide greater trading opportunities to other PETs. Exploitation of such opportunities on economic grounds should be encouraged.

Furthermore, what is currently going on in many PETs is that internal trade diversion is being fostered through the deliberate, if not very logical, introduction of all kinds of impediments to intragroup trade. These include typical commercial policy instruments, such as substantial customs duties on and other, less transparent, barriers to trade that previously was not at all subject to such charges. But they also extend to conventional nontariff measures as well as administrative and political impediments to discourage intragroup trade. To the extent that these measures are taken for metaeconomic reasons, *honni soit qui mal y pense* for as long as it is quite clear that adherence to such foreign-policy stances entails an economic cost that can be ill-afforded at this juncture.

That a CEEU would be against GATT rules is a poor argument, if only because commerce among the former CPEs has on the whole remained outside the GATT framework. In some of the accession agreements, including Hungary's, this "reality of the past" was in fact explicitly acknowledged in the agreement. Furthermore, a well conceived mechanism for regional economic cooperation could easily be brought under the terms of reference of article XXIV of the GATT (Williamson 1990). If in the interest of Contracting Parties, it would probably find considerable support.

Criticisms based on the budgetary implications of a CEPU or CEEU can be quickly dismissed. Certainly, there will be such financial implications of the shift in TRP regime. For several years until 1990, TRPs yielded considerable price-equalization subsidies, which accrued to the government budget of several PETs. The bulk of these "gains" arose from the effectively lower prices of Soviet oil as compared to the domestic price of oil in Hungary, for example, which came close to the WMP plus markups. Since the elimination of these subsidies is part and parcel of the terms-of-trade shift, given the switchover to current WMPs, regardless of whether there will be a CEPU or a CEEU, I shall not further discuss the issue in this context. In any case, the loss of subsidies should be solved through fiscal reform, not by seeking compensation from the Soviet Union. But that is primarily a task for domestic macroeconomic policy, not of regional or international economic cooperation.

5. TOO EXPENSIVE, UNDESIRED, AND TOO SLOW

Judging by the EPU's experience, the administrative cost of running a smooth accounting agency should be rather small. That it might take a long time to negotiate a CEPU and put it in place, if inherently desirable, is something that speaks for elaborating a CEPU proposal and negotiating its concrete features as quickly as possible, rather than jettisoning the proposal as being inherently undesirable. In fact, my advice would be to conceive the CEPU's technical arrangements in as simple a framework as possible. It should certainly be far less complex that the EPU's (see Chapters 5 and 6). Whether the CEPU would slow down the adjustment process in the member countries is something that depends on the ability of these countries to move toward full convertibility and absorb the adjustment burden. Clearly, if policy makers have a realistic mandate to do so, say, in one year it would be counterproductive to place them on, say, a five-year schedule simply to ease the burden for other PETs. The latter's concerns could, under certain conditions, be better met through bridging loans, perhaps by applying the orthodox IMF adjustment regime, although I have some reservations on that score (see Chapter 6).

Because the CEPU would be smoothed in part through a capital fund contributed from outside, it is true that for as long as the PETs cannot place their intragroup trade on a convertible-currency basis external assistance and supervision will be required to maintain their trade and ease payments. But that is precisely the purpose of the CEPU, provided the notion of moving as quickly as circumstances permit toward full participation in global trade and finance is not lost from sight. The alternative is either deflationary domestic policies to cut out import demand or reliance on external financial flows to support deficits. Clearly, the latter would be a multiple of the requirements of any

CEPU scheme. Furthermore, as so evident in the 1970s and 1980s, blanket external-financial support would not necessarily move these countries to desirable market-oriented reforms; in a number of respects that process could in fact be significantly retarded.

In this connection, a comment that the "west does not want to finance a CEPU" can be dismissed as well unless the west were prepared either to finance the PETS' adjustment process as during the 1970s, to let these economies go into a very steep economic depression, or innovate a payments facility that would combine substantial current-account financing with incisive macroeconomic surveillance. In my view, these alternatives would be undesirable for east and west alike. It is, therefore, incumbent upon the concerned observer to sort through alternative policy options that responsible western leaders (Delors 1990) may realistically entertain.

Some commentators have invoked this argument on the ground that the west would not be in a position to exercise surveillance over the reform process in the PETs. Also this is unconvincing. If the west is mounting a major assistance drive without being in a position to influence policy makers in PETs at all about how the furnished assistance will be utilized in favor of democratization and marketization, then it is a poorly conceived initiative. Surely, one cannot expect that to be the case! Political and economic decision makers should be in a position to do much better than enact measures that embody a high probability of eroding public support.

Some commentators have argued that it might be more desirable to make the PETs subject to the EMS regime than to a payments arrangement (Bofinger 1990a, b, c). Clearly, once these countries have reached a measure of macroeconomic stability and rearranged their domestic economic structures, it might well be highly desirable to fuse these economies with the EMS, if only because it would constrain policy makers of the PETs to embrace proper macroeconomic policies for domestic and external equilibrium. But bringing the PETs under the EMS at this stage, prior to fundamental stabilization being completed, would accomplish little more than putting a European veneer on the aspirations of the PETs. It certainly would contribute little, if anything, to solving the transitional problems of these economies.

8

Enlarging the European economic space

One of the key aspirations of reformers in Eastern Europe, not just economic technicians, is to (re)establish solid interdependence with the "west." In the first instance, this link refers to gaining an entry into one of the integration schemes that are on the order of the day in Western Europe. Especially the Central European countries as well as Yugoslavia have been coveting some form of association with the EC that would eventually lead up to full membership. The time-horizon qualifier in this context is as a rule understood to mean "as soon as circumstances permit." Also, the two other Balkan countries - Bulgaria and Rumania - cherish this ambition, though circumstances there are less propitious to even pursue the idea at this juncture.

Evidently, EC membership is not granted simply on economic grounds. But economics cannot be ignored if only because the transfers that are *de facto* tolerated, as well as those arranged with a view to narrowing the gaps in development levels in the various regions of the EC, could become insuperable if the PETs were to be admitted quickly. There are also costs associated with enacting labor mobility. In these calculations, considerations cannot solely be confined to claims on budgetary resources, however. Also the psychological ill-will such transfers might, and do, engender must be factored into the decision-making process. There are other economic and political criteria to be met, at least to some degree, before full membership in these trading and political blocs can realistically be contemplated.

As emphasized more than once in the preceding chapters, having something like a payments union in place for PETs can measurably shorten the duration of that "transition." At the very least, it should accelerate the speed with which currency convertibility (see Chapter 4) can be solidly anchored. Once in place, it should also smooth domestic and foreign competition for the allocation of resources in the PETs. A successful payments union will make itself superfluous approximately within the time horizon agreed upon, provided the precepts on macroeconomic adjustments that were at its roots and those developed in the course of the union's life will come to prevail. How the advocated economic and payments unions could facilitate the further integration of Eastern Europe into the global economy, especially in the all-European context, forms the core of this chapter. Initiatives enunciated from within the EC and the EFTA will be evaluated against the possibilities of the PETs individually and as a group.

The basic twin concerns of the EC at this stage are summarized in Section 1. The gap that separates the PETs from meeting these minimum requirements forms the subject of the next section. The fundamental elements of erecting markets are laid out in Section 3. Next I set forth my views on the most desirable organic evolution that in time will help bridge the still marked differences between existing PETs and these countries becoming overwhelmingly MEs. Finally, I reexamine the role of western assistance in this process, not only from the purely technical angle but also from the point of view of facilitating the Europeanization of Europe and its implications for the global framework.

1. The basic preoccupations of European integration

The European economy in its present connotation has been in the making since shortly after the conclusion of World War II. By any measuring rod, this process has not been easy. It has certainly not been characterized by steadily moving toward the goals set by the most visionary of European thinkers nearly half a century or even longer ago. The latest leap forward, at least in (Western) European precepts, was induced by concerns about coming to grips with the pervasive impression of Eurosclerosis. This sentiment prevailed in the 1970s and early 1980s, when much of Western Europe encountered demonstrable problems in enacting swift structural change, in part to weather the two oil shocks, but also to provide an impetus to technological progress and factor-productivity gains more generally. Central was the widely held impression that Western Europe was chronically falling well behind the more dynamic MEs, Japan and the United States in the first instance. To counter this trend, EC members in 1985 endorsed the white paper that advocated, finally, the resolute construction, in effect, of the Single Market by the end of 1992. All this was subsequently heeded in several political agreements. These commitments not only sought to pave the way for moving decisively forward. They also introduced seminal changes in the decision-making procedures of the EC, notably moving resolutely away from unanimity as the ruling principle in favor of majority consensus building.

To foster the "four freedoms" by integrating markets for goods, services, capital, and labor, the Commission of the EC was requested to implement no fewer than 287 directives on uniformization of chiefly institutional conditions on the continent. Their range is enormous, encompassing as they do the formal abolition of customs controls and the uniformization of quantitative restrictions, to ensuring that services will henceforth become far more mobile than they have been since the formation of the EC, and guaranteeing in effect the infrastructure for a European market (Greenaway 1991). Some measures, such as on standards, are highly technical. Others are fundamental in delineating the European space for economic, social, political, and intellectual interchanges.

There is now every likelihood that not all of these provisions will be fully in place by the end of 1992, at least not in the way in which the promoters of the Single European Market had initially envisioned the negotiating agenda. What matters here, however, are two things. One is that working continually toward the goal of the Single European Market has been the key preoccupation of the Commission of the EC, and will remain so for some time to come, together with deliberations on how to realize the EMU. Also, redefining the Euromarket cannot but effect the actual and potential competitive position of nonmember countries in that single market.

The Single Market remained on the whole the paramount, if perhaps not exclusive, challenge for Western Europe until mid-1989, when the communist societies in Eastern Europe began to unravel at a precipitous pace. This had several dimensions. It threatened stability in Western Europe as a result of a mass exodus of people, especially from the GDR to the FRG, where GDR citizens could automatically claim citizenship and avail themselves of entitlements to a range of social-welfare provisions. By extension, they could then move throughout the EC, thereby measurably burdening an already strained employment situation; lodging unwelcome claims on housing, education, and social services; and generally calling for other structural adjustments in the country of residence that would simply compound the complexibity of moving forward with unifying the Western European market.

Early efforts to dam against the rising resource claims failed. Notably the FRG in early February 1990 felt compelled to offer an economic and monetary union to the GDR by mid-1990. After rancorous exchanges on how such a union could be engineered, the prospect of erecting an economic barrier in an otherwise fairly uniform monetary zone entailed far graver problems than had been anticipated. In short order, it was felt that there was no alternative to full union between the two German states, something that was consecrated on 3 October 1990 only after several political stumbling blocks revolving around the conclusion of World War II were successfully circumnavigated. This presented the EC with a *fait accompli*, hence the task of suddenly having to assimilate yet another country into its midst. Although the implied adjustment cost would this time be cushioned through the massive financial and related transfers from the FRG, it would nonetheless negatively affect the EC's short-run flexibility.

The complexity faced in the first instance by the Commission of the EC, but one that could not but affect the life of virtually everyone closely connected with the EC, was manifold. Apart from the difficulty of moving steadily forward with the completion of the internal market by the end of 1992 and the absorption of the GDR in its midst, the Commission of the EC also had to face four other important tasks. One was predictable. The gradual accession of Greece, Portugal, and Spain to the EC over the mutually agreed period of time would continue to present impediments to be smoothed over a time frame extending well beyond 1992.

Second, although it was clear that the agenda for 1992 and its incidental adjustments would leave little, if any, room for negotiating further accessions, several countries (including Austria and Turkey, and more recently Cyprus and Malta too) formally submitted their applications for full accession. There are now signs that other EFTA members, most notably Norway and Sweden, may soon, well before the end of 1992, follow suit. Perhaps others will be lodged too before that deadline.

Third, the conclusion of a free-trade arrangement for industrial goods with the EFTA, in the context of the unified market, called for exploring the idea of a single EES. Bringing the EFTA members into the orbit of the EC without treading on delicate sovereignty issues would require patience, time, and negotiating skills. It now looks as if these efforts have not been very successful, the sovereign decision-making problems essentially constituting an insurmountable stumbling block to the EES. The alternative, as noted, is full membership of the EFTA countries in the EC. This in itself will stretch the ability of the EC to make swift decisions, unless another change in the constitutional functioning of the EC will be enacted in due course. That would, of course, strain the will and capacities of the EC to proceed toward the envisaged economic, monetary, and political union during this decade.

Finally, Eastern Europe adrift presented the EC with the task of reformulating its working horizon in terms of "all-Europe," something that had been very remote from Eurothinking for many years. It became quickly clear in the course of 1989 that the political transitions in Eastern Europe, and their subsequent disorientations and disaffections, would remain exceedingly fragile if the foundations of the underlying economies could not be buttressed and the process of moving forward with marketization propped up. One pillar should be western assistance, whose coordination especially in the context of the initiative of the Group of Twenty-four DMEs at the Paris summit of July 1989 was entrusted to the Commission of the EC. Whether Eastern Europe could eventually somehow be brought under the EC's umbrella has been causing severe headaches. No ready solution is in sight for now. The best that can be hoped for in the near term is a special association status regulated by a "European agreement" (EC 1990a, b, c, d) - Eurospeak for an association status that does *not* set a precedent for eventual full membership.

There is little doubt at this stage that some form of association with "Europe" for Eastern Europe, or major parts of it, is all but inevitable. Nonetheless, it bears to recall two key constitutional requirements for membership, as per the stipulations of the Treaty of Rome in the case of the EC, for example. These are that the candidate applying for accession be a democratic society and its economy based largely on criteria that afford economic agents the wherewithal to make their own decisions regarding the allocation of resources on the basis of market relations. Even under the most favorable of circumstances and the most flexible interpretation of these two requirements, reaching a stage where the PETs can fully meet these two conditions cannot but absorb a substantial amount of time and impose painful restructuring efforts. These will be much more convoluted and protracted in the economic domain than in the political arena, provided the incipient movement toward pluralistic decision making does not get nipped in the bud.

2. What needs to be bridged?

For all their political achievements, even the most radical PET is only now on the verge of coming to grips with the basic legacies of forty years of central planning. The highly bureaucratized administration of the macro- and micro-economy that these societies inherited has many facets. Perhaps most important is the still sluggish human response to uncertainty and fear of losing "acquired rights." The latter include job security, minimal social-welfare provisions, access to affordable medical care (including rehabilitation, convalescence, and even vacation centers), the right to education and access to the arts, price stability albeit with shortages, and slow economic progress, if at a fairly steady pace - all constants of the socialist creed. There is also widespread apprehension, even if abstracting from human reluctance and aversion to change, about the predisposition and ability of the peoples of these countries to come to grips quickly with a decidedly different decision-making environment compared with the one in which they labored for more than two generations. Without fundamentally transforming human attitudes, it will prove difficult to foster genuine democracy and reap the benefits of an ME in its own right as a key buttress for democracy. In fact, it bears to recall that these human qualities did not solely result from the installation of communist regimes. Indeed, many of the smaller Eastern European societies knew a fairly competitive market only for a brief period of time, following the painful stabilization process after World War I and before the depression of the 1930s; it never existed in the Soviet Union or pre-revolutionary Russia for that matter. Most countries can hardly be described as having become centrally planned from a well-developed market environment. Czechoslovakia may be a weak exception, though its interwar experiences hardly prepared it for the present painful transition.

Unlike the assumptions underlying most ideologies, including the Marxist-Leninist one, changing the human psyche is an arduous process. Fundamental transformations, if realizable at all, emerge only gradually over a protracted period of time. This affects not only the "spirit" in which the political revolutions in Eastern Europe can be solidified. Far more is required than intellectuals musing on this or that aspect of societal renewal. Indeed, active participation of the population at large in the societal processes must leave a more than casual imprint before steady gains from market-oriented reforms can realistically be contemplated. Whether the outcome in the political arena will be democracy on the western model is by no means certain. Becoming more closely involved in "western" affairs would certainly help to build more pluralistic societies through assimilation and emulation. But it would not suffice to carry to fruition all the conditions to be met for buttressing the reform movement.

Of the two criteria critical to being "allowed" to request accession to the EC, which are likely to be present also in accessing other European groupings, the one anchored to democratization is essentially political. I can explore its dimensions only in a rather elementary way, given the nature of this volume. I shall not even attempt to sketch the basic prerequisites of political democracy and a "modern" pluralistic society. Presumably much of Eastern Europe has made credible progress toward that state, and it is now essentially a question of consolidating the multiparty decision-making process. This includes putting in place mechanisms that will make the process irreversible - including perhaps through the privatization of some state assets. Reaching such a platform is a *sine qua non* for eventually fusing east and west into one United States of Europe. Such a transformation is an eminently political act that may materialize after centuries of divisiveness on the continent.

But a united Europe has economic facets as well. It may be instructive to ponder some of their main features and implications for they set the tone for the kind of society that can be brought into the European community of nations. The tests to pass muster are at this stage by no means defined hard and fast. Indeed, it may be just as well to contemplate, in some instances even to speculate about, what might be, minimal features to be strived for so as to facilitate the merger of east and west.

There are at least four such criteria. First, the supremacy of the rule of law needs to be constitutionally anchored. Especially after the protracted recent experiences with all-pervasive bureaucratic and Party-dominated interference in people's lives, it is now necessary to adopt legal codes that belong squarely in the mainstream of the *Rechtsstaat* typical of most DMEs, especially in Western Europe. That is not to say that these countries should simply take over, for example, the Napoleontic code lock, stock, and barrel. It does mean, however, that the principles upon which the legal infrastructure of a remade Eastern Europe can be constituted should not deviate too much from the core of the juridical systems of especially Western Europe. To ensure this, a constitution enforcing basic principles on human rights, the separation of powers, the prerogatives of the various powers, property relations, the role of political parties and free elections, the democratic process more generally, and many other items need to be fleshed out as expeditiously as circumstances permit.

Second, in view of the recent history of Eastern Europe the unconditional guarantee of human rights, even prior to the formulation of a new constitution, is especially important. At the very least, the PETs must tolerate the right to free expression in whatever form acceptable to society; entitle citizens to travel, migrate, and profess their religious beliefs without interference; and in the end recognize the inviolability of personal freedom at least to the degree it does not infringe upon the freedom of others, private citizens as well as approved societal organs. Personal freedom, therefore, may be circumscribed by communal priorities identified in the social compact. This must eventually be enshrined in a new constitution that also permits the enforcement of these rights through a fully developed juridical system of checks and balances. Indeed, providing room there for the interpretation of the constitution would be desirable too.

Third, a transition to a democratically elected government with a separation of powers among the executive, legislative, and juridical branches is highly commendable. That presupposes the recognition of the validity of multiple parties and the holding of regular elections that can be fairly contested by all. Each country must determine for itself what kind of parties will be able to survive the electoral process and in what form they will be represented in veritable parliamentary organs. The example of the western democracies may be just that. But they do not offer a patent that the eastern countries can apply without experimentation and, possibly, reconfiguration "to taste."

Finally, there is a need to recognize that the precepts of administrative planning and socialism do not blend with the interests of MEs. It is therefore necessary that the PETs liberalize their economies in major respects. This does not forcibly mean that these countries need to throw out the child with the bathwater, and forgo all planning or crimp the role of the state to near-paralysis. On the contrary, planning needs to be given a much more confined, but at the same time far more powerful, role together with redefining and enhancing the role of the state in a market environment.

The state's role as regulator, such as in preventing unfair market practices, is beyond dispute. Its potential function as owner is contested, particularly during the transition, although such cannot be avoided altogether. Much of the reluctance to accept the latter state stems from the fact that the core problems inherited from the past derived by and large from the presumed ominiscient control and intervention of the state. Most policy makers in PETs therefore believe that a resurgence of state control must be shunned at all costs. This deep mistrust of the ability of the state, or government, to function effectively as owner or operator has encumbered the search for solutions to the issue of ownership reform and led to the adoption of ill-defined, but rapid privatization as a panacea.

Regarding the role of government in the formulation and implementation of macroeconomic policies, the requirements of effective coordination and ensuring stability should reign supreme. The government's role may accordingly also extend to respecting social-welfare provisions and calls for equity that are supported through the democratic process. As far as the microeconomy is concerned, the PETs must constitutionally guarantee the validity of all property forms. To break the back of the entrenched positions of the former Party, *nomenklatura*, and managerial bureaucracy in economic affairs and to whittle the importance of monopolies some measure of privatization as well as antitrust legislation needs to be enacted as soon as feasible. But this process is strewn with pitfalls. It must, therefore, be pursued with considerable circumspection.

For the time being, however, the incipient democratic process is shaky at best. It is furthermore being buffeted by untoward domestic and external circumstances, some of which are purely economic in nature. There is, therefore, a dilemma that the western community must face up to: To fuse the eastern societies into the all-European context on the basis of fundamental western democratic principles, far-reaching transitions need to be accomplished. Many cannot be fostered within the all-European context. The choice for western assistance and support is, therefore, rather clear. Without active involvement in the transformations of Eastern Europe, these countries may face the undesirable outcome of fundamental retrenchment with reform and reneging on the weak democracy that has been coming to the fore. That is to say, as Timothy Garton Ash (1990, p. 155) so pointedly remarked in concluding his observations on the political revolutions in Central Europe:

> You can, alas, paint with a rather high degree of analytical plausibility a quite dark picture of the prospect for the former Eastern Europe in the 1990s: a prospect in which the post-communist future looks remarkably like the pre-communist past, less Central Europe than *Zwischeneuropa*, a dependent intermediate zone of weak states, national prejudice, inequality, poverty and *Schlamassel*. 1989 might then appear, to participants and historians, as just one brief shining moment between the sufferings of yesterday and those of tomorrow.

It would be a tragedy for Europe, not just the reforming countries in the east, if this prophecy were to be validated for lack of international support for easing the transition.

Whereas one could imagine democracy arising in Eastern Europe and strengthening over the course of time without it being anchored to a solid and vibrant ME, in practice this would largely remain simple intellectual musings, not reflections on what can actually be achieved in the real world. I shall, therefore, spend more time on sketching the economic requirements of bringing about vibrant MEs in Eastern Europe, primarily as the other basic precondition for lodging a credible request for accession, than on identifying the many other areas in which active, pro-reform east-west assistance could help to forestall a reenactment of the scenario of the 1930s in Eastern Europe.

3. On the transition to ME status

Whereas the construction of an ME and its proper management cannot be altogether devoid of politics, witness the case of privatization, the requirement that only MEs can be admitted into the EC under the provisions of the Treaty of Rome sets preconditions to be met before a credible accession request can be lodged. Some refer to basic institutions, while others pertain primarily to policies and policy instruments. It may seem trite to inquire briefly into what an ME really is. However, because the PETs must (re)create markets almost from the ground up, in the process remilling all - at any rate, the most essential - nuts and bolts thereof, the question is not at all rhetorical.

An underlying theme of this book has been that the transformation of the eastern economies into market-oriented societies is a far more daunting task than the reconversion of Western Europe after World War II. The latter societies had for the most part adopted wartime planning and placed controls on economic activity solely for the purpose of relentlessly pursuing the unconditional defeat of an implacable enemy. But even under nazism and its less virulent fascist strains, the basic institutions of the ME, while admittedly at times trampled upon, were kept intact. Thus, there was private property throughout Western Europe; a solid financial infrastructure remained in place, although some components, such as stock exchanges, had, of course, languished during the war; most economic activities, even those directly related to the pursuit of the war's objectives, were in fact run by private firms; the constitutional infrastructure on property rights and how to legally enforce them was never fully abolished; although the integrity of courts was tarnished in some countries, the rule of law was on the whole upheld; the tradition of profit-oriented activities and human attitudes and behavior, while confined, basically survived the rigors of the war economy; and so on. None of these features could possibly characterize the PETs at the time of the political revolutions. In many respects, little progress has since been made in that direction.

In other words, Eastern Europe must by and large still innovate the basic structures of an ME from first principles. Efficient markets do not simply spring to life on the retreat of central planners and bureaucratic controls. Among others, they require a complex infrastructure of laws, financial systems, adequate and widely disseminated information, and the gradual development of certain habits of economic behavior that arise slowly under impulse of competition, risk taking, financial probity, and other features of operating within the context of a regulated market. Furthermore, to be competitive and encourage innovation and structural change in line with shifting comparative advantages, markets require a certain size distribution of firms, a degree of openness to the world economy, and a regulatory infrastructure. Above all, the marketization of Eastern Europe requires political consensus on the broad goals of that transformation. In view of the weak political structures in place, there is also a need to secure separately a social consensus on the acceptable magnitude and distribution of the costs of the transition. Finally, a coherent blueprint of the kind of ME to be erected needs to be drawn up and agreed upon. Although the core roadblocks to marketization can be variously depicted (Nordhaus 1990, UNECE 1991c), I briefly examine here only their essential elements.

1. Creating markets with genuine prices

MEs are tautologically concerned with markets in which economic behavior is decentralized, interactions among individual agents are in the first instance geared by the price mechanism, and decisions are dovetailed either by individuals acting within the set framework or macroeconomic policy intervening to ensure compliance. These are basic preoccupations. One critical policy decision in PETs must, therefore, be the emplacement of open and competitive markets in lieu of the central allocation and rationing of resources by administrative means inherited from the *ancien régime*. This requires that prices be allowed to adjust to economic scarcities in line with mutating demand and supply.

One important prerequisite will be considerable corrective adjustment of relative prices. For brevity's sake, prices are here viewed as encompassing the terms at which alternative products, services, or production factors are traded among clearly defined owners of property rights. The concept therefore encompasses at least domestic wholesale and retail prices, rents, the exchange rate to some degree, interest rates set for monetary control, and wages. Thus, as compared to the inherited situation, relative prices of necessities in terms of luxury goods, foodstuffs against manufactures, primary products in terms of finished goods must rise; the return to capital must be raised to foster savings; the remuneration of labor (both its level and dispersion) needs to be synchronized more closely to reflect productivity; the cost of foreign exchange must be set accurately, probably through sizable devaluation; and so on. Is it desirable to leave all of these adjustments up to as yet primitive markets? or could central decision makers usefully impart basic directions for and magnitudes of the adjustments to be worked off?

Since the heart of the ME is the coordination of economic decisions via the price mechanism, considerable price liberalization should be enacted rather early in the transition. Few reformers disagree on this score. Whether the liberalization should be decreed all at once through shock therapy or phased in more gradually (perhaps by first freeing up wholesale prices and interest rates, next consumer prices, then trade prices and the exchange rate, and finally wages) are questions hotly debated in east and west alike. Price liberalization has at least two policy tangents, namely competition and inflation. One fundamental question is whether prices should be liberalized prior to enacting measures to abate the monopolistic situation in domestic markets. If not, should competition be enforced primarily by opening up the foreign-trade sectors or by fostering competition in domestic markets, including through rapid private capital formation, demonopolization, and the breaking up of conglomerates into self-contained units?

The standard recipe that is being offered to the reforming countries is to foster trade and foreign-exchange liberalization as quickly as possible to obtain both an adequate system of relative prices for traded goods and competition. The latter would whittle the rent seeking that domestic monopolies otherwise engage in upon the freeing up of domestic prices. Whether this can be accomplished quickly and in an orderly fashion depends critically on the gap between domestic and world relative prices prior to the transition. If domestic prices are pervasively distorted, moving toward scarcity pricing may be very costly in terms of idling production capacity, bankruptcies, unemployment, and inflation. These adverse impacts can be mitigated in PETs that had earlier, at the time of administrative reforms, booked solid progress with price liberalization.

An important question that arises in connection with price liberalization revolves around the tolerable magnitude of inflation and how the erosion of real incomes and wealth of households and firms should be offset, if at all. This is especially poignant when the price-adjustment process is to be propelled through effective foreign competition. Part and parcel of the societal consensus is the establishment of some fairly far-reaching social safety net. The latter may have to be strengthened if the magnitude of the adjustment cost rises in the short run to forestall price liberalization from rupturing the social consensus. But it would be utterly illusory to make claims on protecting nearly everyone against the inevitable adjustment burden; it most certainly would be futile to try to do so for its populist appeal. In fact, the limits will soon be reached once the socially more vulnerable layers of society have been taken care of.

If trade liberalization should accelerate adjustment in a competitive environment with flexible prices, but with the exchange rate on the whole remaining under the control of national policy makers, that sequencing cannot, of course, be followed. An alternative would be for central authorities to provide "guidance" to simultaneous price and trade liberalization by first resetting, in a broad sense, relative domestic prices of key inputs (say, fuels and basic ores) and very soon thereafter letting markets adjust.

If domestic conditions have not yet deteriorated into chaos, I would argue for enacting credible macroeconomic policy, including by conveying basic information to markets that has previously been hidden in central accounts. Given the incipient nature at best of the market environment, many instances of erratic overshooting would probably jolt the fragility of existing markets and infuse greater uncertainty than need be into the expectations of economic agents. Some will undoubtedly be useful inasmuch as they impart information that is difficult to generate otherwise. Others cannot but be dysfunctional and wasteful at the time of already fluid attitudes and wavering commitments.

2. Fostering competition

Markets are useful conveyors of knowledge and information. They also provide a low-cost framework for competitive transactions by economic agents acting on their own account. That is certainly the case in mature MEs. The PETs will have to foster competition with great determination by coming soonest to grips with the legacies of central planning. Most notably in this respect are the highly monopolized structures of these economies, the existence of multiproduct and -plant conglomerates with special bureaucratic ties, the highly circumscribed nature of property rights, the long-standing injunction against wealth formation in key financial and real instruments, and vast protection against foreign competition through systemic injunction or opaque trade barriers.

Regarding natural monopolies, the PETs will have to install a sufficient, yet flexible, regulatory infrastructure to forestall potentially predatory behavior. Also some externalities may have to be taken care of through government action. As concerns conglomerates and most monopolies, however, the authorities should carefully evaluate to what extent they can be functionally broken up without losing many of the potential advantages of scale accruing from vertical or horizontal integration.

In most cases, promoting effective competition at home, including through imports, quickly creates a critical stratum of competitive markets upon which further progress can be vigorously pursued. Strong emphasis must be placed on the importance of fostering private capital formation, including through state-sponsored, but nondiscriminatory, loans at favorable interest rates. This will be conducive especially to the rapid expansion of small firms.

For markets to function properly, the PETs must recreate competition. The latter requires, as Nuti (1990, pp. 18ff.) underlines, a sufficient number of autonomous and competitive firms. Subject to financial discipline and rewards, hence capable of responding to market incentives, managers must be chosen not for their political merits but primarily for their professional acumen to maximize net asset values on behalf of the ultimate owners in exchange for well-defined rewards. To attain this, the monopoly power of large specialized firms and their associations must be sharply curtailed by physically breaking them up or putting in place a sufficient regulatory framework, including on antitrust and market access. Above all, it necessitates breaking the link between the center and enterprises as regards managerial controls, incentives, and budget dependence.

Such demonopolization can be pursued variously. One way of ensuring independence of SOEs from central tutelage is by rapidly selling them off. But there are evidently other ways of achieving autonomy (Sood 1990). The elimination of the "petty tutelage" exercised by ministerial and planning bureaucracies should not necessarily dissipate state ownership for its own sake. In the smaller PETs, even after breaking up the presently existing monopolies, in the short run competition is likely to remain weak. Liberalization of the trade and foreign-exchange regimes is the only way in which sufficient competitive pressures can be brought to bear on the performance of core domestic firms. Vigorous promotion of private small and medium-sized firms can only further bolster this environment.

Particularly in the case of SOEs, government policy initially should seek to emulate as much as possible incentive schemes that have proved their worth for corporate management in MEs. Of course, SOEs should finance themselves through the commercial-banking sector at realistic, market interest rates. For that to work well, basic accounting reforms are required and bankruptcy proceedings must be instituted. Only then can it become more transparent how profitable SOEs are and to what degree management is raising the value of capital assets entrusted to it. It will then become easier to terminate fiscal and regulatory haggling between SOEs and government - incidentally, a basic prerequisite for fiscal reform. Unless a determined move is made to cut off virtually all enterprise-specific subsidies, the credibility of gradualism in the transformation process is in doubt. Perhaps a package of measures can be designed that would set a target date for the complete phasing out of such subsidies. In the interim, subsidies should be made available chiefly in a form that provides a strong incentive for management to restructure itself and thus to prepare for the "market" over a fairly short period of time.

Enforcing managerial incentives is something that needs to be done quickly, yet against the backdrop that there is little hope of changing entrepreneurial attitudes immediately or replacing old-style management. There is simply no army of well-trained, market-oriented managers standing in the wings ready to take over. That is to say, some gradualism will be required to nurse along changes in managerial behavior.

The new leaderships in Eastern Europe, often strongly supported by western gurus and proselytizers, have displayed considerable enthusiasm for the market, probably because "in economics and politics, as in religion, the new convert is often the most ardent in belief" (Galbraith 1990, p. 51). Yet, it must be recalled too that considerable market failures exist. Their adverse impact can be mitigated or forestalled only through regulatory instruments. However averse current policy makers in PETs may be toward market intervention, a corpus of antitrust legislation and regulatory laws, including for the financial infrastructure and FDI, will need to be written or simply borrowed and adapted from abroad.

3. Privatization and capital markets

A market is by definition concerned with improving resource allocation. That includes a capital stock whose various service flows need to be coordinated at least cost. In some cases, this can best - at least cost - be done through private property, which internalizes the coordination process. Other instances are preferably (in terms of efficiency) handled through alternative property forms (cooperative, corporate, or state ownership) that may be more suited to the tasks at hand. In other words, one critical task of PETs is to recognize in principle the validity of all property rights and the ability of the holder thereof to alienate them within the provisions of the law. Furthermore, it must also be accepted, not as an act of faith but primarily as one of economic logic, that in some cases the stock of capital can best be utilized by selling assets to private owners. In other cases, the usufruct of capital can best be allocated through different ownership and managerial relations. This calls for the organization of capital markets, however elementary, both for the existing stock of assets as well as for the most effective molding of new capital.

It should not be ignored that continuing further on the road to democracy requires a certain minimum of private property, for a democracy without a solid ME, while it can be imagined, would be rather unstable. Inasmuch as the ability to raise savings in the PETs is limited for now, it may be desirable to privatize quickly some portion of the capital stock through imaginative schemes other than outright cash sales and to foster the rapid accumulation of private property from new savings. Special incentives may be required to stimulate this process. One would be to make available on a nondiscriminatory basis most of the cash flow in the state sector for the erection of small private firms.

Much remains to be done to ensure that SOEs are restructured and to enhance the creation of new private firms, especially in activities other than services and arbitrage. Emerging capitalists in the PETs find the climate for conducting business rather stifling, riddled as it is with all kinds of bureaucratic and institutional impediments. Especially important is that the budding commercial-banking sector is not yet equipped to intermediate effectively between savers and newly emerging investors. Likewise, renting floor space, although many shops and buildings are vacant, and obtaining access to elementary public services (such as telecommunications) can be a trying experience. Without bolstering private initiative, the environment during the transition is less conducive to coming to grips with unemployment than it could be.

4. Trade and foreign-exchange reforms

Inasmuch as the PETs desire to integrate themselves quickly and fully into the international economy, the transition to ME status must pay special attention to the internationalization of the PET. This is desirable for other reasons too. As pointed out, the anchoring of a more effective relative price system and the rapid strengthening of competition in domestic markets also play a critical role in moving the transition forward at minimal cost. For that, measures have to be taken to liberalize the trade and foreign-exchange regimes. For one thing, the overwhelming use of export and import quotas, possibly through explicit foreign-exchange licensing, such as in the form of BTPAs, will have to be replaced by a trade regime in which normal instruments of commercial policy, foremost tariffs and exchange-rate policies, play a core role. The same applies to a plethora of opaque instruments that provided protection under central planning.

Some commentators, notably R. McKinnon (1991) and J. Williamson (1990), have suggested that very early on in the transition all nontariff protection be converted into explicit *ad valorem* tariffs restructured into several - perhaps half a dozen - cascading categories. Moreover, such protection should remain rather high, perhaps by maintaining for now the level of protection that was earlier implicit in the bewildering variety of trade-inhibiting institutions and instruments. Furthermore, the country in transition would commit itself in a precise time schedule to reduce these tariffs and eventually narrow their dispersion. The objective of such an exercise would be to forestall the collapse of large segments of industry (especially the so-called "value-subtracting" or "negative value-added" enterprises) early on during the transition.

Whereas some protection of existing economic structures could usefully be entertained, it would be counterproductive to erect formidable trade barriers for the PETs. Whereas it would permit policy makers to alter economic structures gradually, hence avoid sudden dislocations with all attendant consequences, it would also inhibit competition and the transfer of an effective system of relative prices for traded goods. Furthermore, in view of the weak central actors in the economies in transition, credibility for the phasing-out of customs duties, even if a waiver under the GATT rules for all Contracting Parties (all but Albania, Bulgaria, and the Soviet Union), could be secured, would be rather low. Moreover, it is probably an insuperable task to make explicit the degree of protection that wide segments of the planned economy have traditionally enjoyed.

Rather than aggravate price distortions and introduce levies that may be hard to repeal later on according to a set schedule, the economies in transition could resort to income transfers. This would permit sectors potentially threatened by bankruptcy to operate below real cost, yet the government would not have to support full unemployment claims. By proceeding in this way, also valuable assets that could survive on their own strength under the reformed principles, once in place, would not be lost during the transition. There is, of course, little hope that macroeconomic policy makers of the transition can neatly separate the potentially profitable firms most deserving of subsidies from others that in any case have to be fundamentally restructured or eliminated altogether. But some guidance can be taken from firms that are able to cover their variable costs under changing circumstances.

Regarding the foreign-exchange regime, the perplexing multiplicity of exchange rates must urgently be replaced by a single rate. Whether this should be fixed or flexible is one of those "either-or" choices that many economists and inexperienced policy makers are fond of. In practice, the policy question will be more about what kind of crawling peg should be entertained and at what intervals adjustments in the exchange rate should be undertaken to avoid imparting adverse credibility effects. The issues at stake are paramount to book progress toward meeting the conditions for current-account convertibility. Only under those circumstances is there a realistic chance of attracting the kind and volume of FDI that most PETs are hoping to muster. Note, however, that current-account convertibility is neither a necessary nor a sufficient prerequisite for attracting FDI, as suggested by the small number of countries, especially DEs, that have a convertible currency (see Chapter 4), yet have attracted FDI.

One key item on the agenda for transition is whether the exchange rate should be undervalued to foster exports and discourage imports or devalued by just enough to anticipate the "corrective inflation" likely to ensue from price liberalization. Should it instead be set closer to the purchasing-power level to avoid a sharp cut in the real value of wages and incomes? Whereas there are no unambiguous answers to these questions, the majority of PETs have opted for an exchange rate that is undervalued as compared to the rate that would maintain balance between demand for and supply of foreign exchange for merchandise and related transactions. But it is less clear how much that undervaluation should be. Policy makers appear to be opting for erring on the side of undervaluation.

5. Banking infrastructure and capital markets

An ME requires markets for goods, services, capital, and labor. These are not now extant in the PET and have to be created as quickly as possible. Perhaps most difficult will be the conceptualization of what a capital market is all about, what the functions of its various elements are, and how best to introduce these elements *seriatim*. Inasmuch as this is a fundamental feature of the "capitalist economy," debates on the creation of a capital market tend to treat technical matters with considerable political and ideological overtones, which are hardly germane to the effective intermediation between savers and investors.

Foremost in the creation of capital markets is a viable commercial-banking system (Brainard 1991) that can effectively intermediate between savers and investors and expeditiously clear transactions by established firms as well as newly emerging ventures. If account holders find it difficult to transfer funds, this cannot but impede smooth progress with the division of labor that is at the ME's heart. Enhanced clearing and account keeping at banks would also set the stage for the adoption of standard accounting practices throughout the economy. It may perhaps even play an active role in the investment and managerial process itself. However, owing to the weak banking capabilities in place (in terms of infrastructure, management, skills, and experience) in Eastern Europe, creating a universal-banking system could be a leap in the dark. The shift from a high degree of specialization to universal banking is very likely to strain the competence of the existing bank management as well as supervisory organs, if any. It should therefore not rank high on the initial list of priorities. Such a commercial-banking network must, of course, be allowed to function separately from the central bank, although the latter will need to ensure effective coordination to operationalize economywide monetary control.

6. Macroeconomic policy

Inasmuch as all PETs inherit macroeconomic imbalances, it is important to anchor firm stabilization policies to come to grips with these imbalances and indeed to avoid aggravating them. That must involve a reduction of budget deficits, a rise in interest rates, the pursuit of anti-inflation policies (perhaps through a tax-based income policy), holding wages in check even though inflation is eroding real incomes and wealth, and strengthening foreign competition through far-reaching trade liberalization. Budgetary and macroeconomic policies must be addressed to all economic agents, not just the nonstate entities, with a hard budget constraint.

As a key institution in formulating and implementing macroeconomic policies, the central bank needs to be entrusted with steering monetary policy in the broad sense. This includes stabilization matters and regulation of commercial-banking activity with a view to maintaining growth without overheating the economy. Analytically, stabilization can refer to coming to grips with inherited imbalances or putting in place the rudiments of monetary and fiscal policies, perhaps also price and income policies, to ensure supportive but tight policy stances. For monetary policy, targets need to be adopted and the instruments by which money supply will be controlled, such as by monitoring alternative concepts of money supply, setting a ceiling on loanable funds, and instituting the instruments by which money supply will be steered. The latter can take on various forms, but reserve requirements, differentiated interest rates, managing the exchange rate, rules on rediscounting, and so on will certainly need to be firmly rooted.

In countries with considerable instability in the macroeconomic fundamentals, the transition should accord priority to stabilization in both the stock and the flow senses. Correcting imbalances inherited from past policy failures without tackling at the same time existing imbalances in monetary and fiscal affairs is tantamount to reproducing the stock imbalances with minimal delay. In practice, coming to grips with the legacies of past policy mistakes, for example, by confiscating excess money without adopting credible current monetary and especially fiscal policies, given the rudimentary financial market in PETs, is bound to be counterproductive, as the Soviet example of early 1991 amply underlined. There would seem to be little that can be accomplished by way of economic devolution in a latent or actual inflationary situation. Key is, then, how to bring about a moderately stable economic environment.

To come to grips with instability in the stock sense, epitomized by the "monetary overhang," part of money supply (not just currency but also deposits of various maturities) will need to be sterilized through alternative measures, possibly including outright confiscation. Otherwise, price liberalization and devolution of enterprise decision making cannot but aggravate the instability that policy makers set out to correct in the first place. Incidentally, "overhang" should refer also to "forced substitution," that is activities that, under a more normal market situation, would have been conducted otherwise. If stability is restored economic agents will tend to revert back to their preferred allocation pattern. Hence stabilization in the stock sense may entail more than simply getting rid of excess currency.

There are various ways of rectifying stock imbalances. The means available include confiscation, raising the price level perhaps through runaway inflation, freezing bank deposits, selling imports at prices that reflect the exchange rate observed in the black or parallel markets, divesting state assets, creating new financial assets bearing real positive interest rates, and fostering private capital formation. Except the first two, the introduction of all elements of this stabilization package depends on the creation of new, market-oriented "institutions" and frequently the enactment of various laws. These cannot be emplaced all at once even under the most favorable circumstances. How quickly can this be done? The minimum time constraint already suggests that even putting in place the fundamentals of economic stabilization to work off inherited imbalances may call for a certain degree of structural reform, and thus requires more than simple monetary reform.

Gaining stability in the flow sense is a function of monetary and fiscal policy stances that are conducive to ensuring proper money supply and the balanced financing of mandated expenditures. There may also be a need to enact price and income policies, especially because of two other integral components of the transition: holding wage increases in check to avoid the infernal inflationary spiral and ensuring a minimal social safety net to maintain the social consensus. Initially, these policies will likely remain rudimentary at best, but the overall objective should be macroeconomic tightness.

To balance the government's budget, fiscal reforms are needed. While these cannot be emplaced in a rounded manner from the very beginning, some preliminary steps must be introduced soonest. With marketization, the state will lose more and more its absolute authority to treat net revenues of firms as its own. Further, there is an urgent need to adopt an income-based tax policy for both corporate and private sectors. These revenues may have to be supplemented with a value-added tax system and various user fees or indirect taxes.

Fiscal reform not only comprises shifts in the way government revenues are raised, but also in the pattern and extent of centrally mandated expenditures. The broad use of pricing policies for redistributive purposes will need to be severely curtailed. In their stead, tested methods for favoring certain actions through income transfers need to be substituted. It is very important to eliminate subsidies to failing firms by expeditiously enforcing bankruptcy or reorganization procedures. Rather than remaining the main instrument for the redistribution of funds typical of traditional administrative planning, the financial policy of the state will now become more limited in some sense. Providing the environment for stable economic growth will become its principal task in addition to sheer governance. The social consensus should determine which functions are to be entrusted to the state, including in steering the economy and protecting the more vulnerable layers of society, and how best to finance these assignments. How the state should perform these functions falls normally within the competence of the executive branch of government.

Stabilization in the flow sense, that is, mainly current monetary and fiscal policies, then, cannot possibly be ensured without reforming economic institutions, policies, policy instruments, and perhaps other features of the structures in place. Structural reform and stabilization policies can, therefore, be kept separate only in an analytical context, not in managing the transition of an existing economy.

Proper monetary control can be attained in several ways. The one that has proved its mettle in mature MEs is entrusting a relatively independent agent with regulating money supply. This must be adequate for economic buoyancy, yet sufficiently restrictive to discourage lending at a pace that is hard to match through production and external trade. The creation of a genuine central bank to manage monetary policy, to act as lender of last resort, and to regulate a commercial-banking sector (and later on other financial institutions) so as to hold lending within prudent bounds is indispensable. The existing central bank should cease to be, and act as, the government's treasury. Certainly, it will have to be placed in charge of the regulation of interest rates and fiduciary requirements on commercial banks and other financial institutions as they emerge. Effective control of money supply will need to be implemented.

At the same time, the other financial aspects of the traditional monobank will have to be devolved to emerging commercial banks placed under the supervision of the monetary authorities. Just like the central bank should not act as treasury, commercial banks should finance endeavors at their own risk. For that constraint to bite as soon as possible with the establishment of an independent commercial-banking sector, it is necessary to clean out the loan portfolio of the monobank and capitalize new and recapitalize existing commercial banks in a way that will not hinder these institutions from performing their intermediating functions on a strictly commercial basis (Brainard 1991).

7. Labor market

Also labor markets will need to be fostered. This is perhaps easier than the introduction of capital markets (Long and Sagari 1990) for which new institutions must be set up. Yet, at the same time it is more difficult, owing to the overprotection of labor under administrative planning and the expectation of wide layers of the population to remain substantially insulated against untoward circumstances during the transition and even beyond it.

The choice for workers between allotting time to work and leisure has by and large been free for many years. Yet, the labor market under planning remained embryonic at best. There is no question that the character, speed, and efficiency of the transition depend on the creation of labor markets. This involves not only the abolition of the job-security system and tailoring wages to effort and result. It also calls for putting in place safeguards against the most deleterious economic, social, and psychological consequences of involuntary unemployment and growing job insecurity; promoting labor mobility and retraining; and seeking a *modus vivendi* among effective labor unions, management, and government to ensure that labor rights are protected, yet not abused for whimsical reasons.

8. The social safety net

Once firms can hire and fire workers and regulate labor rewards on the basis of productivity, the need for unemployment insurance and welfare reforms will become critical to cushion the adjustment costs associated with the transition. Even though there may be agreement on the magnitude of the cost to be borne, how quickly it should be absorbed, and how equitably it needs to be distributed, the transition will inevitably have more adverse impacts on some layers of society than on others. The adversities may well exceed expectations in part because it is very difficult at the outset to be very precise about the adjustment burden. But unexpected events may further perturb any estimate.

Rather than allowing the potential for strikes and demonstrations to disrupt the fabric of the transition, it would be helpful to have in place a reserve to weather unanticipated adversities and to ensure that the transitional costs will not have to be borne solely by one - the weakest - layer of society. Indeed, one of the concomitants of stabilization policies is the imposition of controls on nominal wage gains so that they remain well below any measured increase in the cost of living or labor productivity. Also, the PETs have for decades provided minimal social security to all layers of society. In fact, many of them have been imbued with excessive attention to egalitarianism. These attitudes will undergo fundamental change only over time.

For all these and many other reasons, it is necessary to have fairly soon a safety net in place to bolster credibility of economic agents in the enunciated transformation policy. This should preferably be established prior to the launching of the transition or at least shortly thereafter. Such a social safety net has distinct components. Some try to ease unemployment, which may be conjunctural, induced by the transitory problems of enterprise restructuring and the more general economic recession that is likely to accompany the adjustment process. In addition to providing financial relief, the social safety net should embody policies to improve the functioning of the labor market, including measures to assist the unemployed soonest with their return to productive activities. Structural unemployment will need to be eased as well.

To come to grips with the adverse effects of the transition on employment at a time of budget stringency, this particular aspect of the social safety net could usefully be conceived in as comprehensive a fashion as circumstances permit. The basic motivation should be putting in place a fair and equitable labor policy that fosters market-conform behavior and instills in workers a new attitude toward the workplace. Prospects of benefiting from such a transformation in the behavior of labor with income gains, participation in profits, or perhaps obtaining access to company shares once the divestment process gets underway would have to be firmly installed.

As regards the interim measures to cope with unemployment, the social safety net should encompass effective job placement and counseling, job searches, retraining, recruitment and relocation subsidies, direct job-creation incentives to break radically with the inherited job and income security, and other measures. The package could preferably combine strict limits on the duration and magnitude of the unemployment benefits coupled with sizable expenditures on policies most conducive to activating the labor market.

Furthermore, the transition is bound to aggravate inflationary pressures, at least at the outset of the transition. This will not only tend to reduce real wages and current incomes. It will also affect monetary wealth held in local currency. Those whose incomes fall below the accepted poverty line (including the handicapped, the elderly, and children) will have to be provided for not through price subsidies, since those are to be abolished quickly, but through income transfers. Whereas the needs for support are considerable, policy makers must bear in mind that there are limited means at a time of budget pressures.

9. INSTITUTIONS OF THE MARKET

The constitutional infrastructure of the planned system differed markedly from the environment of a mature ME. Not only must all kinds of contract and bankruptcy laws be written into firm commercial and contract codes. Modern markets with their far-reaching division of labor and highly complex coordination tasks would not be able to function properly without a clear legal environment setting acceptable rules of behavior that can be enforced in courts. This is self-evident when it comes to property rights, for example. But more general, transparent civil and commercial codes ensure that all agents will have enforceable rights guaranteed by the civic infrastructure of a democracy. In addition to ensuring clear property rights, this must include company, antimonopoly, bankruptcy, and foreign-investment laws as well as financial-sector legislation. Consistency across laws needs to be ensured. Furthermore, where there is a need to fill gaps such as in the commercial code, company law, securitization, and collateralization, legislation to that effect should be introduced quickly. In addition, a corpus of managers and individuals acting as closely as possible to the stereotype of the "profit maximizer" must be nurtured. The latter importantly contribute to changing the anti-market sentiment and proclivity for egalitarianism in these societies. Building such "institutions" to the desired level of effectiveness requires a long gestation. Yet it must begin urgently. Of course, there is no need for each reforming country to draft such laws from scratch. DMEs offer several alternative codes that have served them well. Borrowing and adapting these codes, as well as other institution-building measures is quite appropriate here.

4. On the sequencing of reforms

The above key requirements of creating an ME in PETs must be fulfilled in some desirable sequence. This is not the proper place to meditate at length on the conflicts inherent in calling for comprehensive, speedy, and orderly reforms (Brabant 1990c, pp. 65-83). Suffice it to acknowledge that order is critical. As argued, transforming the PETs into MEs is fraught with hazards and uncertainty, if only because there are few experiences upon which managers of such a mutation can draw for guidance and inspiration. Nonetheless, the transition needs to be comprehensive and carried out quickly. But the order in which the various reform components are introduced is not, of course, a random matter. An ideal sequencing can be put forward only on the basis of successful experiments. Even so, the key strategy to overcome the multiple roadblocks to marketization and democratization of PETs is partly implicit in the above analyses. The proper order must set the pace and depth of feasible reform, subject to heeding societal concerns on the implied adjustment burden discussed earlier.

Given the many problems faced in improving the entire process of decision making in the PETs, a useful sequencing could be conceived in four stages, the time intervals for each essentially being dependent on concrete circumstances. Thus, if democracy were to be in jeopardy and dislodging Party bureaucrats from SOEs were to be difficult, quick privatization could help to safeguard the gains of the peaceful revolutions of late 1989. But the concomitant attraction of bolstering productive efficiency and raising budget revenue would have to be allotted a lower priority.

The first phase should aim at eliminating chronic imbalances inherited from past mismanagement. To do so, room must be created to divert pent-up demand either to new goods made available to the domestic market or to new financial instruments; monetary reform in some cases cannot be avoided. But it would be pointless to undertake any stabilization in the stock sense without at the same time putting in place the elementary mechanism to control current monetary and fiscal imbalances. Their improvement over time into key instruments of macroeconomic management depends on creating institutions and a legal framework that can mature only over time. But that should not hinder policy makers from adopting a tight monetary and fiscal policy stance at the outset of the reform process.

Very early on during the transformation, state assets may have to be renationalized to establish clear property rights. One important consideration in privatization campaigns may be a prevailing sociopolitical consensus on restituting confiscated property to former owners. This may be justified on sentimental, legal, and ethical grounds. The exceedingly complex issues invoked by restitution should not stifle the transformation process, however. The danger of hopelessly entangling the societal debate on reform, let alone the entire, still very inadequate, judicial infrastructure in endless liens for years to come should not be underrated. Perhaps more promising is a commitment to compensate those whose assets were earlier expropriated. This has complications too, notably in putting pressure on government budgets unless compensation is funded out of the proceeds of asset sales. It might be preferable simply to reserve part of the shares eventually to be given away or sold to private owners for those having a valid compensation claim. In this way, the transition process would be kept separate from the moral and legal issues involved in coming to grips with the various layers of society, both residents and foreigners, that were specifically disadvantaged under communism.

In this phase it may already be useful to recognize the full range of property rights, even though the juridical infrastructure is still being elaborated. One can in the meantime allow the gradual buildup of new property from gross state, corporate, and private savings. To help blot up excess money balances, a start should be made with the privatization of small-scale operations (such as retail, catering, and service outlets), small production units, handicrafts, housing, and the like. The authorities should ensure that this proceeds through bidding procedures open to all. If inflation has destroyed liquid wealth, generous financing at a realistic interest rate may be highly desirable because private property in this case is the most effective way of coordinating the service flow of these assets. At the start, prices are likely to be volatile. A trustee appointed with the support of parliament, to which responsibility is owed, should organize such auctions. Of course, experimentation and publicity may initially be required to overcome entrenched skepticism and inertia about state auctions. In fact, to spur on this process some variant of a giveaway may be preferred for other than economic reasons. Also broadly based land reform, perhaps along the "China theorem" (Hewett 1989), may be required so that farmers can obtain access to the residual profit of their efforts to maintain and improve the land and work it as effectively as they know how to; long-term leases that are tradeable would suffice, provided the arrangement is credible.

The next phase of the reform program should emphasize macroeconomic balance in current monetary and fiscal policies, and underpin both with the necessary infrastructure. This should be directed in the first instance at maintaining domestic equilibrium (Nuti 1990). But resources must gradually be shifted so as to regain external balance in due course as well. For that, a tight monetary policy and fiscal reform must be enacted to ensure that the government budget does not become the chronic source of inflation. This requires the rapid elaboration of a two-tier banking structure with a true central bank and effective commercial banks that intermediate between savers and investors, clear transactions smoothly, and market financial instruments that will provide the buttress for a more variegated monetary policy and the financing of government deficits. Of course, the latter will work only with a fair, credible, and reliable fiscal system.

Also in this second phase, big monopolies and conglomerates should be quickly broken up into meaningful units. Other remaining petty assets should be privatized quickly through open auctions. Finally, excepting perhaps strategic goods and public utilities, all SOEs should be turned into joint-stock companies and placed under the supervision of an impartial, professional body - a state asset-management agency. This should also supervise the transfer of property rights to state assets, including in some cases in combination with some liabilities (for instance, pension and insurance funds). At the same time, capital formation from private sources should be fostered with great determination as a basis for strengthening competition and indeed to deliver on the promises made during the revolutions (Kornai 1990a, c; Murrell 1990).

The third rung of this progression consists of enforcing competitive behavior by creating a regulatory environment and a managerial incentive scheme that ease the principal-agent problem in SOEs, even if corporatized. Gradually, such assets should be opened up to competitive bidding, for example, for leases or management contracts. The asset-management agency is charged with maximizing the return on assets and seeing to it that sufficient insurance schemes are in place to minimize the incidence of asset stripping. For that adequate managerial incentives must be put in place. At the same time, the government should continue to adhere to comprehensive stabilization, enact further fiscal and monetary reforms, dilute the power of monopolies, replace the material-technical supply system with genuine wholesale trading, and introduce market-type pricing, perhaps by first anchoring key input prices to WMPs at a realistic exchange rate. Also, the job-security system will need to be sharply relaxed and a fairly comprehensive social safety net put in place. Further, competition through trade liberalization, perhaps *de facto* current-account convertibility for merchandise transactions, FDI, and joint ventures will need to be encouraged.

Finally, once the former SOEs are behaving like competitive firms through corporatization and commercialization, the most urgent structural adjustments have been completed, domestic monetary and fiscal stability reigns, and competition is well engrained, privatization of most of the remaining SOEs through outright sale should get under way at a measured pace. This should take the form of feeding the budding domestic stock market or encouraging the formation of other components of the capital market. At least, it should open the sale of state assets to bids by domestic as well as foreign capitalists. In principle, of course, the identity of real owners should not matter provided they are bent on operating efficiently and do not seek to abuse their economic power for ulterior purposes. In reality, however, the Eastern European societies are exceedingly sensitive to the potential for selling off, let alone selling out, society's assets to foreign owners. This danger is real, given the more unsavory channels of the second economy that may act as proxies for foreign owners.

5. Economic transition and east-west assistance

How fast should the transformation of Eastern Europe be accomplished? Given that so many of the critical features of an ME are available in the PETs at best only in a very rudimentary form, one must doubt the ability of these countries to transform themselves quickly into fully functioning MEs capable of absorbing immediately large amounts of financial resources in an efficient manner, regardless of the prevailing factor-productivity gaps. That includes resources in whatever form from domestic as well as foreign origin. Foreign investment and its ancillary transfers, such as managerial skills, technology, market access, effective organization, and so on, can measurably contribute to accelerating this transformation process. But it cannot accomplish the job all by itself. For as long as asset values are ill-determined, FDI might simply seek rents. If so, it would not measurable contribute to raising the productive and allocative efficiency in PETs. This suggests two things. One is that there must be ways in which the order of priority in policy actions, including those that find support abroad, can be set, however inaccurately. Also, relative magnitudes of various foreign-assistance measures must be pinpointed.

Since changes in economic structures and behavior can materialize only over time, the arguments presented point to a more evolutionary approach to the reform process than the abrupt shock treatment championed by many observers. This poses the question of sequencing of reforms, an issue to which countless conferences have recently been devoted. Passions between partisans of shock treatment have repeatedly clashed with the more sober approach counseled by those cognizant of and concerned about the immense tasks ahead. There simply is no choice but to adhere to some sequencing. A certain order has to be brought in the various reform components to ensure that the unavoidable adjustment costs are kept to a minimum, spread over wide layers of society and some period of time, and sanctioned by some consensual decision-making process.

In addition to the logic behind this assertion, there are other considerations that weigh in. One is that those advocating a rapid reform pace are quite optimistic about the speed at which competitive markets can be erected. If correct, there would be little point in arguing the merits of any broad-based foreign-assistance program. Those subscribing to a more evolutionary approach not only see the establishment of competitive markets as a difficult process requiring time and careful state intervention. They are also concerned about the consequences in terms of upholding the political and social consensus for reform if market optimists are proved wrong. Frustrated expectations of the population at large may lead to an explosive social situation. From this point of view it is less costly to adopt the evolutionary approach and be wrong.

Second, the argument over whether reform should be rapid or gradual is sometimes obscured by the mixing up of macro- and microeconomic considerations and of long-run structural changes with macroeconomic stabilization issues. Once a reform program gains credibility, the question of gradualism versus shock therapy becomes secondary. Structural reform in countries with runaway inflation will prove to be difficult because of the uncertainty with growing inflationary expectations. Further, stabilization in most PETs will have to factor in obdurate supply-side problems that can be tackled only over several years under the best of circumstances. In this situation western assistance could be especially helpful in allowing these countries to concentrate on their structural problems by easing pervasive pressures on their external accounts, as acknowledged on 15 March 1991 in the treatment of the Polish official debt in the context of the Paris Club debt relief effort.

Probably one of the most important determinants of successful reform is whether the government is able to create and maintain credibility in its program. Economic reforms through devaluation and liberalization usually generate political resistance because the population sees the immediate costs of extensive, interrelated changes more clearly than the long-run benefits. This is especially so for the PETs, which are moving into the *terra incognita* of transition from one socioeconomic system to another, when the safety and certainty of the old are being replaced by the hazards of an emerging new society.

In most PETs, the new political landscape has only just begun to crystallize. There is, therefore, a great deal of mistrust of and suspicion about government on the part of broad layers of the population that will have to be overcome. Popular elections may help, but cannot be a panacea in the short run, given the fragility of the political process. This has been well underlined by political events since the second half of 1990. Credibility is not simply a matter of providing information or making propaganda about the ultimate benefits of reform intentions. What is needed is a coherent reform program with credible sequencing that political decision makers and the population at large can support, if only tacitly. There is, however, no simple formula of how government can best secure such credibility, except the pragmatic way.

Because of the importance of gaining credibility, sustained support for radical structural reform is required, and this might be a crucial instance for western assistance to be assembled in such a way as to reinforce the coherence and proper sequencing of reforms. The latter's preparation constitutes an area where technical assistance from western macroeconomists, especially those with knowledge of the eastern economies, could make a useful contribution. Some counseling might be required as to the proper policies to pursue and the institutions to be put in place to foster the shifts in economic behavior. For the rest, the automatic stabilizers of the market environment, once they emerge with sufficiently strength, should take care of further adjustment measures. Proper surveillance in the context of the CEPU could be a plus here.

Perhaps the greatest assistance that the west can render the PETs is to open up their economies to international competition on a fair basis. Because the export base of the PETs for now is rather thin, concentrated on products that have been treated as "sensitive" in recent trade management, the emerging MEs are at a distinct disadvantage. The potential export capacity of the PETs for some years to come is likely to remain small, by and large determined by comparatively cheap labor. This may seek to displace domestic production in DMEs, particularly the EC, something that has been resisted since the early 1970s. With comparatively buoyant prospects of Europe moving toward 1992, as well as the growth benefits of German unification, there would seem room to relax some of the traditional trade-management policies pursued in particular in the EC. I am singling out the latter not because its record has been notoriously worse than that of other DMEs, but because it is the natural trading outlet that complements the intragroup trade opportunities of PETs.

A buoyant external environment would allow the PETs to embrace resolutely outward-oriented policies as the underpinning for their transformation into competitive MEs. Taking more fully into account the repercussions of the mutations occurring in Eastern Europe in all efforts to manage the world's economy could only enhance and smooth the process of global management. Indeed, the ongoing transformations in Eastern Europe and the unprecedented promises of western assistance are bound to affect other countries and the global economic framework. In the first instance, there will be ramifications on the remaining CPEs, if only because of the far-reaching changes in the orthodox TR trade and payment regimes and the demise of the CMEA as an organization. This certainly applies to the DEs that were full members and cooperants of the CMEA. It pertains also to DEs that for one reason or another chose to maintain intimate trade ties with Eastern Europe. There will also be important changes in the east-west context, particularly in Europe, that need to be factored into the equation. In the end, the diversion of resources from west to east may constrain the financial and other forms of assistance that DMEs can sustain.

This remaking of Europe may entail negative implications in the first instance in the form of diversion of FDI and portfolio capital flows, with or without official guarantees, to the east. These may have a measurable impact on the NIEs, including the EC's southern rim. Inasmuch as the prospects of luring such capital flows into the least developed DEs have not been very good for a long time, the impact of west-to-east assistance is likely to remain negligible. However, what holds for the DEs as a whole is not necessarily relevant for individual countries, most notably the NIEs; also some other DEs may be markedly affected. With some exceptions, there is thus far little evidence that ODA sums earlier earmarked by DMEs will be diverted from south to east. But some development finance traditionally dispensed through multilateral agencies cannot but be affected by additional claims for Eastern Europe unless there were to be a sizable increase in the capital base of these multilateral agencies.

* * *

The above discussion of what is required to gradually harmonize the two parts of Europe has carried us far afield and away from the discussion of the desirability of creating economic and payments unions for Eastern Europe. But the two topics are not unrelated as the process of accelerating the assimilation of market-based and democratically oriented values in the PETs are basic ingredients to growing into Europe. Although a CEPU could conceivably reduce the transition, it cannot shortcircuit it very substantially. In other words, some organic evolution toward the market environment needs to be fostered. That could be made less painful both for the PETs and the international and regional arrangements into which they would like to merge if the PETs themselves were to adopt a cooperative strategy, such as through economic union, to ease the downside risks of adjustment in the short to medium run.

Conclusions

It is now time to wrap up the various tangles of the rather lengthy yarn spun on how Eastern Europe's prospective merger into the global economic framework could be smoothed and the adverse impacts of switching trade and payment regimes minimized. Because several countries in Eastern Europe are bent on resolutely bent on orienting their economies according to market indicators, there is now a good chance that their mutual relations can soon be footed on direct interenterprise negotiations too. For that to work well, macroeconomic authorities need to take care of the institutional framework, management of the exchange rate, and the eventual settlement of imbalances, preferably while progressing toward currency convertibility.

A subregional integration scheme propped up by a transitional mechanism for moving toward negotiated prices and settlements in a convertible currency offers an alternative to foreign-exchange constraints. Such a solution could usefully be explored in the context of the western assistance efforts for selected PETs. Several alternatives can be entertained. I have advocated here the establishment of a payments union because it would enhance intragroup cooperation, foster marketization, minimize the need for western assistance, stave off undesirable trade diversion, induce the countries to move gradually toward convertibility, and provide for macroeconomic surveillance.

All of the enumerated benefits could be obtained too by simply placing a sizable payments facility at the disposal of the reforming countries on condition that they move right away at least to domestic current-account convertibility for merchandise and related transactions. For that to work well, strong macroeconomic surveillance must be exercised, as in a payments union. Of course, such a more generous facility would require sizable outside funds. It would also be contingent on the reforming countries finding themselves in a position to adopt domestic convertibility overnight. Even if these conditions could be met, the PETs remain very dependent on trade with the Soviet Union for years to come, unless the Soviet economy were to collapse altogether and the wrangling about reform remain as convoluted and bitter as it has been since the late 1980s. Barring those outcomes, it would be constructive, for the reasons cited, to reinvigorate regional economic cooperation. Taking the failed negotiations about CMEA-wide reform as cue, the outlook for such a renewal is admittedly not very promising. This is regrettable especially for the PETs, given their existing and emerging comparative advantages. But the ultimate proof of real movement toward genuine regional integration will only crystallize when the Soviet Union aims its reform at market guidance. That is not yet in sight.

One is therefore in a quandary about what to do for as long as these "outsiders" deliberately eschew marketization. In my view, it would then be a mistake to insist upon a payments union being put in place for any but the countries seeking credible marketization. Given the comparatively small intragroup imbalances of the PETs, a clearing scheme might be set up simply to test the kind of payments disequilibria that may emerge in conjunction with rapid trade liberalization. If they were to remain small, there would be no point in insisting upon such a payments scheme. A modest three-year current-account standby loan, say, from the IMF or EC, in support of convertibility would probably suffice to help the PETs over their structural payments imbalances *vis-à-vis* each other. Those incurred with the Soviet Union, if present terms-of-trade developments hold up, would in any case have to be settled by different means, perhaps strict bilateralism with all attendant consequences for the procurement of inputs and imbalances with MEs.

I advocate the creation of a payments union with financial support from the EC and strict macroeconomic supervision exercised under the aegis of a European authority (such as the Commission of the EC, the Council of Ministers, or the European Parliament). This should be an integral appendage of some economic union among the PETs. In fact, whereas the payments problems could be weathered through a variety of facilities, engaging in greater intragroup commerce based on economic criteria is indispensable. There are multiple reasons for this stance. Clearly, prevailing comparative advantages promise sizable trade creation after some adjustment during which excessive trade contraction should be avoided. The potential for sizable trade diversion is weak at best. Provided the operations are strictly time-bound, about five years as in my scheme of things, the potential for dynamic trade diversion by encouraging the "wrong" specialization, which is admittedly real, would nonetheless seem worth risking. Also, it would be unacceptable for these countries to be granted extensive western assistance, possibly at the expense of DEs, if they were to remain reluctant to cooperate with each other. In fact, an open trading framework within some economic union would provide invaluable experience with commercial policy as well as financial diplomacy. Support for such a desirable endeavor would be forthcoming not only from the west but also from within the group. In the end, it would facilitate the integration of these countries into Europe and ultimately the global framework.

I hope to have made a cogent argument in favor of setting in train a transitional payments arrangement, although its rationale derives more from the perceived need to bolster intragroup trade on the basis of comparative advantages, as advocated in Chapter 3, than on contributing to the establishment of groupwide convertibility, as discussed in Chapter 5. It would have multiple objectives in addition to its main task, namely the accommodation of payments imbalances among the participants.

One of its most important goals would be to facilitate making steady progress toward emplacing the necessary conditions for credible current-account convertibility, at least for merchandise and related transactions. This could conceivably be achieved through a big bang. In my view (see Chapter 4), this is simply not a feasible option for most PETs. Furthermore, moving immediately to current-account convertibility is not necessarily the most appropriate way of establishing markets from the ground up, given pervasive supply rigidities and daunting institutional reform tasks.

Another important objective of the CEPU would be to create a more ambient attitude toward exploring the benefits of regional economic collaboration among countries that, at least for now, view their future to be not in the region but in integrating themselves quickly and deeply into the western economic alliance. I hope to have made it crystal clear that these two objectives do not necessarily clash or contradict each other. Integration with Western Europe, however desirable in itself, is not something that can realistically be accomplished in the near term. For one thing, most PETs themselves are not ready to compete head-on in highly contested markets. Also, Western Europe has many adjustment problems of its own before it can tackle the multiple issues arising around ushering the PETs on an equal basis into the EC, EFTA, or EES. Moreover, the PETs unquestionably have reciprocal static and dynamic comparative advantages that have not so far been exploited for lack of proper institutions, policies, and instruments. Whether the degree of intragroup trade warranted on economic grounds will be small or large, it will certainly not be zero. Exploitation thereof is desirable for both economic and political reasons.

Given the critical situation with external payments throughout Eastern Europe, reviving intragroup cooperation as a way to avert a collapse of reciprocal trade, hence a potentially debilitating economic depression, should rank high among the priorities of the transition for which active cooperative strategies can be mapped. Establishing a payments union in support of a customs or economic union for the PETs is one such top priority that has not so far received its due. There are many reasons for this. Its inherent logic and desirability may become clear once commentators conclude that the choice of the reforming countries is not between a payments union and full multilateralism, including through massive trade diversion, but between a payments union to sustain warranted intragroup trade and unbridled trade destruction. I fail to see how the latter would be desirable in and of itself, or when placed in the context of the transitional needs of the reforming countries.

Of course, the most elementary task of a payments union is to accommodate some external payments that otherwise would be difficult to clear. A cooperative strategy to come to grips with such problems through a payments union is bound to lead to failure if the balance-of-payments pressures are deeply rooted in structural imbalances. For that a coherent policy of structural change anchored to a more general - and generous - payments facility will be required. However, problems with balancing external payments that stem from the transition, including the possibly sharp rise in the transaction and precautionary demands for convertible currency, can be addressed through a cooperative mechanism anchored to a payments union, which should preferably be supported from the EC.

Clearly, a CEPU cannot possibly begin to tackle the massive problems emanating from the substantial swing in net transfers from fuel importers to fuel exporters, including in the context of relations with the Soviet Union. However, such a swing depends critically on three factors: the ability of the USSR to maintain buoyant exports, the inability of Eastern Europe to market its products in the Soviet Union, and fuel prices remaining high. With the settlement in the Persian Gulf and given the economic, political, and social chaos in the Soviet Union, the conjecture of Eastern Europe sustaining sustantial deficits with the Soviet Union in the near future is highly speculative. If it were to be borne out, however, the structural problems would have to be dealt with through other means than a simple cooperative payments facility. Recycling of petrodollars will be unavoidable. How this could be managed without repeating the mistakes of the preceding two decades is a matter that has not been addressed here. A solution without active Soviet cooperation, preferably within the context of the existing international economic organizations, would be highly desirable. Now that the Gulf crisis has subsided, the issues that first prompted me to examine the foreign-exchange problems of the PETs and to propose to set up a payments union, in the context of the western assistance efforts, remain as acute as they were in early 1990. That is the core of this book and the spirit in which, I hope, it will be read and digested.

Finally, a CEPU should aim explicitly at facilitating integration of the PETs into the global economy in general and the western integration schemes in particular. Such a regime would also assist Eastern Europe in exploring other further forms of enhancing its position in the global economic framework. This should be the ultimate aim of any effort designed to facilitate the marketization and democratization of the PETs. Both now would seem to be extraordinarily vulnerable and may get swept aside under impact of adversities among which serious foreign-exchange constraints constitute only one.

As argued many times, neither the CEEU nor the CEPU is intended as a permanent structure for the new Eastern Europe. Indeed both must be placed in the context of the transformations on the European continent. These offer excellent opportunities for reassessing the context of European integration and reinvigorating the impetus to transiting toward that state. They also impel us to look objectively at what is feasible in Eastern Europe and to what degree these countries could play a constructive role in the global economic system in general and the remaking of Europe in particular. This might call for changing the accent of, if not the preferred path toward, European integration. At least the purview from within which the EC has conceptualized its policies for the near future will need to be remodeled. In addition to recasting its pet integration scenario into a much wider framework than that predicated on what EC members in their foreign policy have adhered to for so long, dovetailing the desirable with the feasible in Eastern Europe itself may call for a new approach to all-European integration, as argued in Chapter 8.

As far as impacts on the world are concerned, it is a remarkable paradox that the global economic framework envisaged at Bretton Woods can now perhaps be implemented, but it would hardly be very relevant to the problems the world confronts going into the 1990s and beyond. Thus, all efforts to introduce special arrangements for the former planned economies in the context of the GATT are now superfluous. The real motivation underlying these efforts (see Brabant 1991g) is, of course, not. Once the PETs succeed in implanting viable markets in the broad sense, their role in the GATT, or its eventual successor International Trade Organization, will be very similar to that of the DEs at a medium level of development. Until that stage is reached, however, it would be useful to seek some accommodation for the trade-related aspects of the transition. This would be especially pertinent for delineating the characteristics of the transition to trade and foreign-exchange liberalization that has not so far been factored into scenarios of how countries can mesh themselves harmoniously into the international trade regime governed by the GATT.

Of course, many old and new issues remain to be tackled in bringing the *quasi* planned economies under the umbrella of the trade regime, perhaps as an inducement to economic reform. This applies chiefly to China and the Soviet Union at this juncture, as these countries do not yet appear ready and willing to move to full-fledged market-based decision making. The key issues at stake for these economies, as well as for the remaining small CPEs (notably Albania, Cuba, and North Korea), differ only marginally from those considered at length elsewhere (Brabant 1991g). But the latter agenda needs to be modified for countries that have been on the brink of reform, but have not yet seen fit to formulate and endorse a credible program as the backbone of the transition.

The salient problems of the former CPEs and MPEs in the Washington financial institutions were essentially confined to two. One was the issue of currency convertibility which, for as long as planning reigned supreme, was irrelevant to resource allocation in these countries. The other, and paramount, issue was how best to manage adjustment with financial support from the Fund in the case of rectifying the balance of payments or resources obtained from the World Bank Group in the case of financing structural change. In this context, most critical was the question of whether these adjustments should be engineered primarily through the reconceptualization or modification of *ex ante* plans or the lending institutions' pet recommendations for institutional and behavioral changes. In the latter event, the lenders could not avoid meddling in the reform process and associated debates.

Now that at least the radically reforming countries have opted for rapid marketization, these two obstacles take on a different character. Once the reform is firmly implanted, the reforming countries will dispose of a convertible currency and will need to manage their economies through market institutions and instruments. These may indeed call for changing the behavior of economic agents, be they households, firms, or various levels of government. Until they can successfully pass through the more difficult phases of the transition, however, the PETs face stiff foreign-exchange constraints that must be managed in part by reformulating their relationship with the Fund and the World Bank. Rather than rely primarily on demand-driven adjustment programs, the proper menu of policies that PETs could profitably explore must include a component that fosters structural change through positive supply actions. This could be done by modifying standard adjustment programs or by setting up special arrangements for the PETs, such as a discriminatory payments facility. The latter may run against the very grain of a universal institution, however. There is also doubt that these institutions will wish to modify their "proven" menus (Corbo 1990).

As regards relations on the European continent, once the PETs have firmly reached a democratic base for decision making and transformed their economies into organisms that are steered primarily through market-based decisions, there is no reason for these countries to be treated any differently from other credible applicants for accession to the EC. The lending approach of the European financial institutions, such as the European Investment Bank and the EBRD, for Eastern Europe would roughly be according to their standard criteria for other members; similarly for the emerging monetary institutions and the all-European monetary regime that may crystallize soon.

But that stage evidently depends critically on these countries passing on their own strengths, perhaps with some target economic assistance, the gauntlet emanating from the earlier phases of transition. At least when seen from the inner economic logic of the European integration perspective, there is no way in which Eastern Europe could legitimately be brought under the EC's umbrella in the near term. Likewise in the case of the financial institutions, which will have to approach the assistance to the restructuring of Eastern Europe rather gingerly. This applies even more to the eventual association of Eastern Europe with the EMS, including the possible monetary union that may come to the fore in the 1990s. Yet, credibility to reforms in Eastern Europe could be measurably enhanced by the EC and its related institutions collectively playing a godfather-type role.

This could take on various forms. One would be providing target-oriented assistance under the mandate issued by the Group of Twenty-four. The target in this case would be getting the maximum mileage out of each ECU appropriated for Eastern Europe, given that the reform programs in place are credible. Another would essentially take the form of specific assistance to facilitate fusing the interests of Eastern Europe with the EC's. The association agreements currently under negotiation (EC 1990a, b, c, d) would be one such example, but there are evidently others. Fostering intragroup economic cooperation in Eastern Europe, possibly with the financial backing of a payments union financed by the EC and supervised under its aegis, as argued in Chapters 5 and 6, would be one such alternative way by which credibility of the enunciated reform policies could be bolstered. In this, easing Eastern Europe into the framework of the EMS, once basic stabilization has been accomplished, would be very helpful (Brabant 1991f). This would provide only one peg onto which Eastern Europe could credibly hang its claim for growing into the world economy. It could be structured in such a way that the monetary regime first is stabilized, the management of the exchange rate is conceived in the context of the EMS, some loose association with the EMS is maintained, and finally full integration in the EMS is engineered.

Such a strategy of Europeanization would, of course, eventually equate the foreign trade and exchange regimes of east and west. That is to say, the EMS would include the convertible currencies of Eastern Europe, intragroup trade would be conducted according to the common rules of the EC, and externally Eastern Europe would adopt the common external tariff. Until that stage is attained, Eastern Europe has a few degrees of freedom about conceptualizing its interim trade and payment regimes.

In my view, it would be counterproductive to seek considerable protection for the reforming countries. Certainly, it would permit policy makers to alter economic structures gradually, hence avoid sudden dislocations with all attendant consequences for immiseration. But serious questions regarding the phasing-out of high customs duties, the weakening of competition from abroad, and the perpetuation of distortions in relative prices weigh heavily. Temporary income transfers would seem preferable. This would permit sectors potentially threatened by bankruptcy to operate below real costs for now.

In sum, with the prospect of marketization of a pluralistic society, there are evidently many instances in which the divide between east and west, certainly in Europe, could be closed. Eventual fusion into all-European cooperation requires actions that would quickly change the landscape of the reforming countries in Eastern Europe. This could be done in a number of instances. One that I have emphasized is the provision of support for maintaining an orderly transition in TR trade and payment regimes and fostering intragroup economic cooperation that has an inherent logic to it. But it could admittedly be achieved through different means as well.

Bibliography

Adamović, Ljubisa, "Establishing convertibility in Yugoslavia," in *Convertibility in Eastern Europe*, edited by John Williamson (Washington, DC: Institute for International Economics, 1991), forthcoming.

Agnelli, Giovanni, "The specific support of the ECU to monetary integration in Western, and to economic reconstruction in Eastern Europe," *De Pecunia*, 1990: June Special Issue, 31-36.

Allen, Mark, "Adjustment in planned economies," *Staff Papers*, 1982:3, 398-421.

Altman, Oscar L., "L'or russe et le rouble," *Economie Appliquée*, 1962:3/4, 354-72.

Assetto, Valerie J., *The Soviet bloc in the IMF and the IBRD* (Boulder, CO and London: Westview Press, 1988).

Balassa, Bela, "Economic integration in Eastern Europe" (Washington, DC, manuscript, 10 July 1990).

Baneth, Jean, "Institutional framework of reforms: a discussion," in *Reforms in foreign economic relations of Eastern Europe and the Soviet Union* (New York: United Nations publication No. E.91.II.E.5, 1991), pp. 53-58.

Bergsten, Fred C. and John Williamson, "Currency convertibility in Eastern Europe," in *Central banking issues in emerging market-oriented economies*, edited by The Federal Reserve Bank of Kansas City (Kansas City, MO: The Federal Reserve Bank of Kansas City, 1990), pp. 35-49.

Bernstein, Edward M., "Reflections on Bretton Woods," in *The international monetary system: forty years after Bretton Woods* (Boston, MA: Federal Reserve Bank of Boston, 1984), pp. 15-20.

Bofinger, Peter, "The role of monetary policy in the process of economic reform in Eastern Europe" (London: Centre for Economic Policy Research, Discussion Paper No. 457, August 1990a).

Bofinger, Peter, "A multilateral payments union for Eastern Europe?" (London: Centre for Economic Policy Research, Discussion Paper No. 458, August 1990b).

Bofinger, Peter, "The transition to convertibility in Eastern Europe: a monetary view," in *Convertibility in Eastern Europe*, edited by John Williamson (Washington, DC: Institute for International Economics, 1991a), forthcoming.

Bofinger, Peter, "A multilateral payments union for Eastern Europe?" *Banca Nazionale del Lavoro Quarterly Review*, 1991b:1, 69-88.

Bofinger, Peter, "A payments union for Eastern Europe? - a reply" *Banca Nazionale del Lavoro Quarterly Review*, 1991c:1, 99-100.

Bogomolov, Oleg T., "Integration of the Soviet Union and Eastern Europe into the world economy," in *Reforms in foreign economic relations of Eastern*

Europe and the Soviet Union (New York: United Nations publication No. E.91.II.E.5, 1991), pp. 162-6.

Bond, Daniel, "Leveling the playing field for Central European export," in *Emerging problems in intraregional trade in Eastern Europe and the Soviet Union*, edited by David Kemme (New York: Institute for East-West Security Studies, 1991), forthcoming.

Brabant, Jozef M. van, "Zur Rolle Mitteleuropas im Rahmen des Rats für gegenseitige Wirtschaftshilfe," *Osteuropa-Wirtschaft*, 1976:1, 1-20.

Brabant, Jozef M. van, *Adjustment, structural change, and economic efficiency - aspects of monetary cooperation in Eastern Europe* (New York and Cambridge, Cambridge University Press, 1987a).

Brabant, Jozef M. van, *Regional price formation in Eastern Europe - theory and practice of trade pricing* (Dordrecht-Boston-Lancaster: Kluwer Academic Publishers, 1987b).

Brabant, Jozef M. van, *Economic integration in Eastern Europe - a handbook* (Hemel Hempstead: Harvester Wheatsheaf and New York: Routledge, 1989a).

Brabant, Jozef M. van, "CMEA reform and the formulation of a constitutional framework" (presented at the conference "The radical reform of the CMEA as a precondition of cooperation with the EC - theoretical and practical questions," Sopron, Hungary, 16-20 November 1989b).

Brabant, Jozef M. van, "Regional integration, economic reforms, and convertibility in Eastern Europe," *Jahrbuch der Wirtschaft Osteuropas - Yearbook of East-European Economics*, Vol. 13/1 (1989c), pp. 44-81.

Brabant, Jozef M. van, "Ruble convertibility in the reform process - a sobering note," in *Reforming the ruble - monetary aspects of perestroika*, edited by Josef C. Brada and Michael Claudon (New York, NY: New York University Press, 1990a), pp. 133-72.

Brabant, Jozef M. van, "Wither the CMEA? - reconstructing socialist economic integration in the 1990s" (New York, manuscript, January 1990b).

Brabant, Jozef M. van, *Remaking Eastern Europe - on the political economy of transition* (Dordrecht-Boston-London: Kluwer Academic Publishers, 1990c).

Brabant, Jozef M. van, "Toward an Eastern European Payments Union: questions and answers" (New York, October 1990d, manuscript).

Brabant, Jozef M. van, "Reforming a socialist developing economy - the case of Vietnam," *Economics of Planning*, 1990e:3, 209-29.

Brabant, Jozef M. van, "On reforming the trade and payments regimes in the CMEA," *Jahrbuch der Wirtschaft Osteuropas - Yearbook of East-European Economics*, vol. 14/2 (1990f), 7-30.

Brabant, Jozef M. van, "Regional economic integration and the transition in Eastern Europe" (New York, manuscript January 1991a).

Brabant, Jozef M. van, "Economies in transition and privatization - the case of Eastern Europe," in *Changing Economic Order*, edited by W. Adriaansen and

Julien van den Broecke (Dordrecht-Boston-London: Kluwer Academic Publishers, 1991b), forthcoming.

Brabant, Jozef M. van, "Divestment of state capital in Eastern Europe and the Soviet Union," in *Great transformation in reverse*, edited by Kazimierz Poznański (Ithaca, NY: Cornell University Press, 1991c), forthcoming.

Brabant, Jozef M. van, "Socialist countries and development assistance," in *Alternatives to superpower competition in the third world - Latin America and beyond*, edited by John Weeks (New York: New York University Press, 1991d), forthcoming.

Brabant, Jozef M. van, "The demise of the CMEA - the agony of inaction," *Osteuropa-Wirtschaft*, 1991e:2, forthcoming.

Brabant, Jozef M. van, "Assistance to Eastern Europe and European economic and monetary integration," *De Pecunia*, 1991f:2, forthcoming.

Brabant, Jozef M. van, *The planned economies and international economic organizations* (Cambridge: Cambridge University Press, 1991g).

Brabant, Jozef M. van, "Renewal of cooperation and economic transition in Eastern Europe," *Studies in Comparative Communism*, 1991h:1, forthcoming.

Brabant, Jozef M. van, "Integrating the new Eastern Europe into the global economy," *Structural Change and Economic Dynamics*, 1991i:4, forthcoming.

Brabant, Jozef M. van, "The collapse of the CMEA and all-European integration," *Current Politics and Economics of Europe*, 1991j:2, 11-22.

Brabant, Jozef M. van, "The future of economic relations among the European countries in transition: a discussion," in *Reforms in foreign economic relations of Eastern Europe and the Soviet Union* (New York: United Nations publication No. E.91.II.E.5, 1991k), pp. 167-74.

Brabant, Jozef M. van, "Property rights' reform, macroeconomic performance, and welfare," in *Selected issues and strategies in the transformation of planned economies*, edited by Hans Blommestein and Michael Marrese (Paris: Organisation for Economic Co-operation and Development, 1991l), forthcoming.

Brabant, Jozef M. van, "Convertibility in Eastern Europe through a payments union" in *Convertibility in Eastern Europe*, edited by John Williamson (Washington, DC: Institute for International Economics, 1991m), forthcoming.

Brabant, Jozef M. van, "A payments union for Eastern Europe? - a comment," *Banca Nazionale del Lavoro Quarterly Review*, 1991n:1, 89-97.

Brabant, Jozef M. van, "Key problems of creating a Central European Payments Union," *Banca Nazionale del Lavoro Quarterly Review*, 1991o:2, forthcoming.

Brabant, Jozef M. van, "Obstacles in setting up a Central European Payments Union," *Recent Developments in International Banking and Finance*, Vol. 1 (1991p), forthcoming.

Brabant, Jozef M. van, "On the conditions of a Central European Payments Union," in *Emerging problems in intraregional trade in Eastern Europe and the Soviet Union*, edited by David Kemme (New York: Institute for East-West Security Studies, 1991q), forthcoming.

Soviet Union, edited by David Kemme (New York: Institute for East-West Security Studies, 1991q), forthcoming.

Brada, Josef C., "Interpreting the Soviet subsidization of Eastern Europe," *International Organization*, 1988:4, 639-58.

Brainard, Lawrence, "Strategies for economic transformation in Eastern Europe - the role of financial market reform," in *Selected issues and strategies in the transformation of planned economies*, edited by Hans Blommestein and Michael Marrese (Paris: Organisation for Economic Co-operation and Development, 1991), forthcoming.

Budzinski, Andrzej, "Economic relations of Poland with the CMEA member countries," in *Reforms in foreign economic relations of Eastern Europe and the Soviet Union* (New York: United Nations publication No. E.91.II.E.5, 1991), pp. 146-53.

Campbell, Robert W., "On the theory of economic administration," in *Industrialization in two systems - essays in honor of Alexander Gerschenkron*, edited by Henry Rosovsky (New York: Wiley, 1966), pp. 186-203.

CEPR, "Eastern Europe - payments union proposals," *CEPR Bulletin*, No. 40 (August 1990), 15-18.

Čhekurov, Vladimir, "Krizis SEV. Chto dal'she?" *Kommunist*, 1990:18, 43-50.

Čičin-Šain, Ante, "The case for an entirely new trading and clearing arrangement among former CMEA countries," in *Reforms in foreign economic relations of Eastern Europe and the Soviet Union* (New York: United Nations publication No. E.91.II.E.5, 1991), pp. 175-6.

Čížkovský, Milan, "Subregionální spolupráce ve středni Evrope - současny experiment," *Mezinárodní Vztahy*, 1990:10, 39-44.

Collignon, Stefan, "The consequences of European Monetary Union for Eastern Europe," *De Pecunia*, 1990a:2/3, 497-518.

Collignon, Stefan, "The economic consequences of a single European currency on centre-periphery relations within the Community," in *A strategy for the ECU* (London: Kogan Page for Ernst & Young and the National Institute of Economic and Social Research, 1990b), pp. 216-35.

Colombatto, Enrico, "CMEA, money and ruble convertibility," *Applied Economics*, 1983:4, 479-506.

Condliffe, John B., *The commerce of nations* (New York, NY: Norton, 1950).

Cooper, Richard N., "Commentary: currency convertibility in Eastern Europe," in *Central banking issues in emerging market-oriented economies*, edited by The Federal Reserve Bank of Kansas City (Kansas City, MO: The Federal Reserve Bank of Kansas City, 1990), pp. 141-8.

Corbo, V., "Lessons from Bank-supported adjustment programmes for Eastern Europe" (paper prepared for conference "The transition to a market economy in Central and Eastern Europe," organized by Centre for Co-operation with the European Economies in Transition and the World Bank, Paris, 28-30 November 1990).

Dăianu, Daniel, "Some thoughts on Romania's economic relations with CMEA countries," in *Reforms in foreign economic relations of Eastern Europe and the Soviet Union* (New York: United Nations publication No. E.91.II.E.5, 1991), pp. 154-61.

Dahrendorf, Ralf, *Reflections on the revolution in Europe - in a letter intended to have been sent to a gentleman in Warsaw* (New York: Times Books, 1990).

Daviddi, Renzo and Efisio Espa, "Foreign trade and monetary integration in Central and Eastern Europe" (Brussels, 28 October 1990, manuscript).

Delors, Jacques, "Some reflexions on the present EMU debate," *De Pecunia*, 1990: June Special Issue, 59-61.

Dembinski, Pawel H., "Alternative financial approaches to privatisation" (paper prepared for conference "The transition to a market economy in Central and Eastern Europe," organized by Centre for Co-operation with the European Economies in Transition and the World Bank, Paris, 28-30 November 1990).

Dembinski, Pawel H. and Jacques Morisset, "Les politiques de stabilisation du FMI: une tentative d'évaluation pour l'Amérique Latine et l'Europe de l'Est," *Revue d'Etudes Comparatives Est-Ouest*, 1990:4, forthcoming.

Diebold, William, Jr., "The Marshall Plan in retrospect: a review of recent scholarship," *Journal of International Affairs*, 1988:2, 421-35.

Dittrich, Josef, *Die Europäische Zahlungsunion als Grundlage einer europäischen Integration* (Marburg a.d. Lahn, unpublished doctoral dissertation, 1954).

Dornbusch, Rudiger, "Economic reform in Eastern Europe and the Soviet Union - priorities and strategy" (paper prepared for conference "The transition to a market economy in Central and Eastern Europe," organized by Centre for Co-operation with the European Economies in Transition and the World Bank, Paris, 28-30 November 1990).

Dubrowsky, Hans-Joachim, "Aspekte der Konvertierbarkeit sozialistischer Währungen," *Wirtschaftswissenschaft*, 1989:5, 712-34.

EC, *Accords d'association avec les pays d'Europe Centrale et Orientale: cadre général* (Brussels: Europe-documents, No. 1646/47, 1990a).

EC, "Recommendation pour une décision du Conseil autorisant la Commission à négocier un accord européen avec la Hongrie" (Brussels: European Community, mimeographed, 1990b).

EC, "Recommendation pour une décision du Conseil autorisant la Commission à négocier un accord européen avec la République de Pologne" (Brussels: European Community, mimeographed, 1990c).

EC, "Recommendation pour une décison [sic!] du Conseil autorisant la Commission à négocier un accord européen avec la République Fédérative Tchèque et Slovaque" (Brussels: European Community, mimeographed, 1990d).

Ecu Banking, *Reforms in Eastern Europe and the role of the ECU - a report by the Macro-financial Study Group of the Ecu Banking Association* (Paris: Association Bancaire pour l'ECU, 1990).

Edwards, Richard W., Jr., *International monetary collaboration* (Dobbs Ferry, NY: Transnational Publishers, 1985).

Emerson, Michael, "The economics of EMU," *Economic Insights*, 1990:6, 34-35.

Ethier, Wilfred J., "Multi-country payments in Eastern Europe - policy option from a Hungarian perspective" (Washington, DC: The World Bank, 1990, mimeographed).

Frenkel, Jacob A., "Commentary: currency convertibility in Eastern Europe," in *Central banking issues in emerging market-oriented economies*, edited by The Federal Reserve Bank of Kansas City (Kansas City, MO: The Federal Reserve Bank of Kansas City, 1990), pp. 149-56.

Galbraith, John K., "The rush to capitalism," *The New York Review of Books*, 1990:16, 51-2.

Garton Ash, Timothy, *The uses of adversity - on the fate of Central Europe* (New York: Random House, 1989).

Garton Ash, Timothy, *We the people - the revolution of 89 witnessed in Warsaw, Budapest, Berlin & Prague* (Cambridge: Granta in association with Penguin Books, 1990).

Gianviti, François, "The International Monetary Fund and external debt," *Recueil des Cours*, 1989:3, 213-86.

Gianviti, François, "Convertibility" (Washington, DC: The International Monetary Fund, office memorandum of 23 October 1990).

Gold, Joseph, "The Fund's concept of convertibility," *IMF Pamphlet Series*, No. 14 (1971).

Greenaway, David, "Implications of the EC 1992 programme for outside countries" (paper prepared for symposium on "Implications of the Single Market Act for Non-Member Countries," Geneva, 27-31 May 1991).

Havel, Václav, *Interrogatoire à distance - entretien avec Karel Hvížd'ala* (Paris: Editions de l'Aube, 1989).

Havel, Václav, "The future of Central Europe," *The New York Review of Books*, 1990:5, 18-19.

Havrylyshyn, Oli and David Tarr, "The role of trade liberalisation in transition to a market economy" (paper prepared for conference "The transition to a market economy in Central and Eastern Europe," organized by Centre for Co-operation with the European Economies in Transition and the World Bank, Paris, 28-30 November 1990).

Hewett, Ed A., "Is Soviet socialism reformable?" (Sturc Memorial Lecture, Washington, DC: The Brookings Institution, 1989, mimeographed).

Hieronymi, Otto, *Economic discrimination against the United States in Western Europe (1945-1958)* (Geneva-Paris: Droz, 1973).

Hogan, Michael J., *The Marshall Plan - America, Britain, and the reconstruction of Western Europe, 1947-1952* (Cambridge: Cambridge University Press, 1987).

IMF, *Articles of agreement* (Washington, DC: International Monetary Fund, 1978).

IMF, *Yearbook of foreign exchange restrictions* (Washington, DC: International Monetary Fund, 1990).

Inotai, András, "Mr van Brabant's paper on reforming the trade and payments regimes in the CMEA" (Washington, DC: The World Bank, office memorandum of 17 May 1990).

Jozzo, Alfonso, "One Europe - a possible role for the private Ecu in reforming monetary relations between some CMEA countries," in *EBA Newsletter*, No. 11 (1990), 30-32.

Kádár, Béla, "Economic relations with market economies in Hungary," in *Reforms in foreign economic relations of Eastern Europe and the Soviet Union* (New York: United Nations publication No. E.91.II.E.5, 1991), pp. 76-82.

Kaplan, Jacob J. and Günther Schleiminger, *The European Payments Union - financial diplomacy in the 1950s* (Oxford: Clarendon Press, 1989).

Kaplan, Jacob J., "Currency convertibility in Eastern Europe? - a review of the opinions of five experts from an IIE conference," *Economic Insights*, 1990:6, 32-33.

Kazandzhieva, Kina, "Konvertiruemost na sotsialisticheskite valuti pri sŭvremenite usloviya," *Finansi i kredit*, 1983:8, 27-37.

Kazandzhieva, Kina, "Bulgarian economic relations with CMEA countries," in *Reforms in foreign economic relations of Eastern Europe and the Soviet Union* (New York: United Nations publication No. E.91.II.E.5, 1991), pp. 121-6.

Kazmin, Andrey I. and Andrey V. Tsimailo, "Towards the convertible rouble: the case for a parallel currency," in *Convertibility in Eastern Europe*, edited by John Williamson (Washington, DC: Institute for International Economics, 1991), forthcoming.

Kenen, Peter B., "Transitional arrangements for trade and payments among the CMEA countries" (Washington, DC: International Monetary Fund, Working Paper WP/90/79, September 1990).

Knapp, Manfred, "Reconstruction and west-integration: the impact of the Marshall Plan on Germany," *Zeitschrift für die gesamte Staatswissenschaft*, 1981:3, 415-33.

Konrád, György, *Antipolitics - an essay* (San Diego-New York-London: Harcourt Brace Jovanovich, 1984).

Konstantinov, Yuriy Ya., "Konvertiruemost' rublya: kontseptual'nyy podkhod," *Voprosy ekonomiki*, 1989:9, 33-40.

Kornai, János, *The road to a free economy - shifting from a socialist system: the example of Hungary* (New York: W.W. Norton & Company, 1990a).
Kornai, János, *The affinity between ownership and coordination mechanisms - the common experience of reform in socialist countries* (Helsinki: World Institute for Development Economics Research, 1990b).
Kornai, János, "The affinity between ownership and coordination mechanisms - the common experience of reform in socialist countries," *Journal of Economic Perspectives*, 1990c:3, 131-47.
Kostrzewa, Wojciech and Holger Schmieding, "An EFTA option for Eastern Europe?" *Swiss Review of World Affairs*, 1990:10, 7-8.
Köves, András, "Hungary's eastern economic relations: a time of change," in *Reforms in foreign economic relations of Eastern Europe and the Soviet Union* (New York: United Nations publication No. E.91.II.E.5, 1991), pp. 139-45.
Krenzler, Horst G., "Die Europäische Gemeinschaft und der Wandel in Mittel- und Osteuropa," *Europa-Archiv*, 1990:3, 89-96.

Lamb, Geoffrey, "Reforming Eastern European economies," *Global Economic Policy*, 1990:1, 42-47.
Lamfalussy, Alexandre, "Foreword," in *The European Payments Union - financial diplomacy in the 1950s*, by Jacob J. Kaplan and Günther Schleiminger, (Oxford: Clarendon Press, 1989), pp. vi-xii.
Lavigne, Marie, "Economic relations between Eastern Europe and the USSR; bilateral ties vs. multilateral cooperation" (paper presented to Nato Colloquium, 4-6 April 1990).
Lavigne, Marie, "Economic relations with CMEA countries: a discussion," in *Reforms in foreign economic relations of Eastern Europe and the Soviet Union* (New York: United Nations publication No. E.91.II.E.5, 1991, pp. 177-83.

Lipton, David and Jeffrey Sachs, "Creating a market economy in Eastern Europe: the case of Poland," *Brookings Papers on Economic Activity*, 1990a:1, 75-133.
Lipton, David and Jeffrey Sachs, "Privatization in Eastern Europe: the case of Poland" (Washington, DC: Manuscript October 1990b).
Long, Millard and Silvia Sagari, "Financial reforms in socialist economies in transition" (paper prepared for conference "The transition to a market economy in Central and Eastern Europe," organized by Centre for Co-operation with the European Economies in Transition and the World Bank, Paris, 28-30 November 1990).
Luft, Christa, "Economic relations between the German Democratic Republic and the CMEA countries," in *Reforms in foreign economic relations of Eastern Europe and the Soviet Union* (New York: United Nations publication No. E.91.II.E.5, 1991), pp. 135-8.

Machowski, Heinrich, "Die Funktion der DDR im RgW," *Deutschland-Archiv*, 1973: special October issue on the GDR, 3-19.

Matejka, Harriet, "East-west European integration" (paper presented to Fourth World Congress for Soviet and East European Studies, Harrogate, 21-26 July 1990, mimeographed).

McKinnon, Ronald I., "Liberalizing foreign trade in a socialist economy: the problem of negative value-added," in *Convertibility in Eastern Europe*, edited by John Williamson (Washington, DC: Institute for International Economics, 1991), forthcoming.

Michalopoulos, Costas, "Payments arrangements in Eastern Europe in the post-CMEA era" (Washington, DC: The World Bank, office memorandum of 3 May 1990).

Michalopoulos, Constantine and David Tarr, "Trade and payments arrangements in post-CMEA East and Central Europe," in *Socialist economies in transition*, edited by Arye L. Hillman and Branco Milanovic (Washington, DC, manuscript, February 1991), forthcoming.

Milward, Alan S., *The reconstruction of Western Europe, 1945-51* (London: Methuen & Co. Ltd, 1987).

Milward, Alan S., "Was the Marshall Plan necessary?" *Diplomatic History*, 1988:2, 231-53.

Milward, Alan S., review of *The European Payments Union - financial diplomacy in the 1950s*, by Jacob J. Kaplan and Günther Schleiminger, *Economic History Review*, 1990:4, 767-8.

Murrell, Peter, "'Big bang' versus evolution: East European economic reforms in the light of recent economic history," *PlanEcon Report*, 1990:26.

Nikolov, Chavdar, "Nyakoi suvremenni problemi na konvertiruemostta i na valutnite kursove pri sotsializma," *Mezhdunarodni otnosheniya*, 1988:10, 49-54.

Nikolov, Chavdar, "Konvertiruemostta i na valutnite na stranite ot SIV: vuzhmosti i problemi," *Mezhdunarodni otnosheniya*, 1990:2, 57-68.

Nordhaus, William D., "Soviet economic reform: the longest road," *Brookings Papers on Economic Activity*, 1990:1, 287-308.

Nuti, Domenico Mario, "Stabilization and sequencing in the reform of socialist economies" (Washington, DC: The World Bank, paper for the seminar "Managing inflation in socialist economies," Laxenburg, 6-8 March 1990, mimeographed).

Nuti, Domenico Mario, "Progress in trade reforms, missing links, convertibility: a discussion," in *Reforms in foreign economic relations of Eastern Europe and the Soviet Union* (New York: United Nations publication No. E.91.II.E.5, 1991), pp. 49-52.

Oppenheimer, Peter, "Economic reforms and transitional policies: summary of discussion," in *Reforms in foreign economic relations of Eastern Europe and the Soviet Union* (New York: United Nations publication No. E.91.II.E.5, 1991), pp. 59-63.

Pant, Chandrashekar and David Tarr, "Hungary: CMEA mission back-to-office report" (Washington, DC: The World Bank, office memorandum of 23 May 1990).

Piotrowski, Janusz, "Poland's economic and trade policy in 1990 - an outline of annual report" (Warsaw: Instytut Koniunktur i Cen, 1990, No. 17, mimeographed).

Pírek, Zdenko, "Emerging problems in intra-regional trade: the case of the Czech and Slovak Federal Republic" (paper presented at the conference on "Emerging problems in intra-CMEA trade in Eastern Europe and the Soviet Union," Štiřín, Czechoslovakia, 16-18 November 1990).

Polak, Jacques J., "Convertibility: an indispensable element in the transition process in Eastern Europe," in *Convertibility in Eastern Europe*, edited by John Williamson (Washington, DC: Institute for International Economics, 1991), forthcoming.

Pons, J.-F., "The European Monetary Union and its consequences for Eastern Europe," in *EBA Newsletter*, No. 11 (1990), 16-18.

Portes, Richard, "Introduction - Economic transformation in Hungary and Poland," *European Economy*, No. 43 (1990), 13-17.

Protzman, Ferdinand, "Germany's top banker gives Europe a warning," *The New York Times*, 20 March 1991, D2.

Prowse, Michael, "How to reform eastern Europe," *Financial Times*, 22 June 1990, 21.

Rees, Graham L., *Britain and the postwar European payments system* (Cardiff: University of Wales Press, 1963).

Rodrick, Dani, "How should structural adjustment programs be designed?" *World Development*, 1990:7, 933-47.

Romainville, J., "Foreign trade, convertibility and the case for a multilateral payments system," in *EBA Newsletter*, No. 11 (1990), 28-29.

Rosati, Dariusz K., "Poland - impact of replacing CMEA trade regime by a market trade regime" (Warsaw: Instytut Koniunktur i Cen, 1990, mimeographed).

Rybalko, Gennadiy, "Valyutnyy mekhanizm: pora obnovleniya," *Ekonomicheskoe sotrudnichestvo stran-chlenov SEV*, 1989:10, 16-21.

Sachs, Jeffrey, "Eastern Europe's economies - what is to be done?" *The Economist*, 13 January 1990, 19-24.

Schill, Wolfgang, "Pioneers in establishing convertibility: the case of East Germany," in *Convertibility in Eastern Europe*, edited by John Williamson (Washington, DC: Institute for International Economics, 1991), forthcoming.

Schrenk, Martin, "Comments on Van Brabant's draft paper on CMEA" (Washington, DC: The World Bank, office memorandum of 20 April 1990).

Schrettl, Wolfram, "Summary of discussion," *Reforms in foreign economic relations of Eastern Europe and the Soviet Union* (New York: United Nations publication No. E.91.II.E.5, 1991), pp. 184-7.

Shelkov, Oleg, "K ob"edinennomy rynku: valyutnaya obratimost'," *Ekonomicheskoe sotrudnichestvo stran-chlenov SEV*, 1989:6, 24-30.

Sobell, Vladimir, "East European economies at a turning point," *Report on Eastern Europe*, 4 May 1990, 40-43.

Sołdaczuk, Józef, "Payments union of Middle - Eastern Europe with European Economic Community / a proposal for a discussion" (Bonn Conference on Security and Cooperation in Europe, 5 April 1990, mimeographed).

Sood, Anil, "Enterprise reform and restructuring in Central and Eastern Europe" (paper prepared for conference "The transition to a market economy in Central and Eastern Europe," organized by Centre for Co-operation with the European Economies in Transition and the World Bank, Paris, 28-30 November 1990).

Sosnowski, Bogusław, "Reforms in economic relations of Poland with market economies," in *Reforms in foreign economic relations of Eastern Europe and the Soviet Union* (New York: United Nations publication No. E.91.II.E.5, 1991), pp. 83-91.

Špaček, Petr, "Rozvoj vnejších funkcí socialistickych měn," *Finance a Úvěr*, 1987:11, 231-50.

Spitzer, Emil G, "Factors in stabilization programs," in *The International Monetary Fund, 1945-1965 - twenty years of international monetary cooperation; vol. II: analysis*, edited by J. Keith Horsefield (Washington, DC: The International Monetary Fund, 1969), pp. 492- 510.

Stankovsky, Jan, "The role of foreign economic relations in Eastern Europe's transition to a market economy" (paper prepared for "Workshop on East-West European Economic Interaction, Tübingen, FRG, 10-14 October 1990).

Sychev, Vyacheslav V., "Nakanune peremen," *Ekonomika i zhizn'*, 1990:33, 19.

Szabó-Pelsőczi, Miklós, "The case for an East European Payments Union" (paper prepared for the Round Table on "The future of the global economic and monetary system, with particular emphasis on East-European developments," Castle Szirák, Hungary, 29 August - 1 September 1990).

Szabó-Pelsőczi, Miklós, "The case for an East European Payments Union (EEPU)" (Bedford, NY: manuscript, February 1991).

Tarr, David, "What next for Eastern Europe after the demise of the CMEA?" (Washington, DC: The World Bank, manuscript, March 1991).

Tew, Brian, *International monetary cooperation, 1945-67* (London: Hutchinson University Library, 1967).

Tew, Brian, review of *The European Payments Union - financial diplomacy in the 1950s*, by Jacob J. Kaplan and Günther Schleiminger, *The Economic Journal*, 1990:4, 1361-3.

Thompson, John K., "Convertibility and systemic change in Central and East European Economies in Transition" (paper prepared for conference "The transition to a market economy in Central and Eastern Europe," organized by Centre for Co-operation with the European Economies in Transition and the World Bank, Paris, 28-30 November 1990).

Tokareva, Praskov'ja A., ed., *Mnogostoronnee ekonomicheskoe sotrudnichestvo sotsialisticheskikh gosudarstv - sbornik dokumentov* (Moscow: Juridicheskaya literatura, 1972, 2d ed.).

Triffin, Robert, *Europe and the money muddle - from bilateralism to near-convertibility, 1947-1956* (New Haven and London: Yale University Press, 1957).

UNECE, *Economic survey of Europe in 1989-1990* (New York: United Nations publication No. E.90.II.E.1, 1990).

UNECE, *Reforms in foreign economic relations of Eastern Europe and the Soviet Union* (New York: United Nations publication No. E.91.II.E.5, 1991a).

UNECE, *Economic Bulletin for Europe*, Vol. 42/90 (New York: United Nations publication No. E.90.II.E.37, 1991b).

UNECE, *Economic survey of Europe in 1990-1991* (New York: United Nations publication No. E.90.II.E.1, 1991c).

UNWES, *World Economic Survey, 1990* (New York: United Nations publication No. E.90.II.C.1).

Válek, Vratislav, "Czechoslovak economic relations with CMEA countries," in *Reforms in foreign economic relations of Eastern Europe and the Soviet Union* (New York: United Nations publication No. E.91.II.E.5, 1991), pp. 127-34.

Vries, Margaret G. de, "The Fund and the EPU," in *The International Monetary Fund, 1945-1965 - twenty years of international monetary cooperation; vol. II: analysis*, edited by J. Keith Horsefield (Washington, DC: The International Monetary Fund, 1969a), pp. 317-31.

Vries, Margaret G. de, "The retreat of bilateralism," in *The International Monetary Fund, 1945-1965 - twenty years of international monetary cooperation; vol. II: analysis*, edited by J. Keith Horsefield (Washington, DC: The International Monetary Fund, 1969b), pp. 297-316.

Wagener, Hans-Jürgen, "Economic relations with market economies: a discussion," in *Reforms in foreign economic relations of Eastern Europe and the Soviet Union* (New York: United Nations publication No. E.91.II.E.5, 1991), pp. 113-7.

Wandycz, Piotr S., "Recent traditions of the quest for unity - attempted Polish-Czechoslovak and Yugoslav-Bulgarian confederations 1940-1948," in *The*

People's Democracies after Prague - Soviet hegemony, nationalism, regional integration? (Bruges: De Tempel, 1970), pp. 35-93.

Wexler, Imanuel, *The Marshall Plan revisited - the European recovery program in economic perspective* (Westport, CT: Greenwood Press, 1983).

Williamson John, "Convertibility, trade policy and the payments constraint" (paper prepared for conference "The transition to a market economy in Central and Eastern Europe," organized by Centre for Co-operation with the European Economies in Transition and the World Bank, Paris, 28-30 November 1990).

Winiecki, Jan, "A Marshall Plan for Eastern Europe?" *Swiss Review of World Affairs*, 1989:11, 28-31.

Winiecki, Jan, "Obstacles to economic reform of socialism: a property-rights approach," *Annals of the American Academy of Political and Social Sciences*, 1990:1, 65-71.

Winiecki, Jan, *Resistance to change in the Soviet economic system - a property rights approach* (London and New York: Routledge, 1991).

Wood, Robert E., *From Marshall plan to debt crisis - foreign aid and development choices in the world economy* (Berkeley, CA: University of California Press, 1986).

Zhivkova, Snezhana and Ivanka Petkova, "Usloviya zu konvertiruemost na bŭlgarskia lev," *Mezhdunarodni otnosheniya*, 1990a:2, 47-56.

Zhivkova, Snezhana and Ivanka Petkova, "Grani konvertiruemosti," *Ekonomicheskoe sotrudnichestvo stran-chlenov SEV*, 1990b:4, 57-62.

Index

International Studies in Economics and Econometrics

1. T. Harder: *Introduction to Mathematical Models in Market and Opinion Research.* With Practical Applications, Computing Procedures, and Estimates of Computing Requirements. Translated from German. 1969 ISBN 90-277-0096-6
2. A.R.G. Heesterman: *Forecasting Models for National Economic Planning.* 2nd rev. and ext. ed. 1972 ISBN 90-277-0224-1
3. A.R.G. Heesterman: *Allocation Models and Their Use in Economic Planning.* 1971 ISBN 90-277-0182-2
4. M. Durdağ: *Some Problems of Development Financing.* A Case Study of the Turkish First Five-Year Plan (1963-1967). 1973 ISBN 90-277-0267-5
5. J.M. Blin: *Patterns and Configurations in Economic Science.* 1973 ISBN 90-277-0203-7
6. A.H.Q.M. Merkies: *Selection of Models by Forecasting Intervals.* Translated from Dutch. 1973 ISBN 90-277-0342-6
7. H.C. Bos, M. Sanders and C. Secchi: *Private Foreign Investment in Developing Countries.* A Quantitative Study on the Evaluation of the Macro-Economic Effects. 1974 ISBN Hb 90-277-0410-4; Pb 90-277-0439-2
8. R. Frisch: *Economic Planning Studies.* A Collection of Essays. Selected, introduced and edited by Frank Long, with a Preface by Jan Tinbergen. 1976 ISBN Hb 90-277-0245-4; Pb 90-277-1194-1
9. K.L. Gupta and M. A. Islam: *Foreign Capital, Savings and Growth.* An International Cross-Section Study. 1983 ISBN 90-277-1449-5
10. C.A. van Bochove: *Imports and Economic Growth.* 1982 ISBN 90-247-3052-X
11. O. Bjerkholt and E. Offerdal (eds.): *Macroeconomic Prospects for a Small Oil Exporting Country.* 1985 ISBN 90-247-3183-6
12. D. Weiserbs (ed.): *Industrial Investment in Europe.* Economic Theory and Measurement. 1985 ISBN 90-247-3270-0
13. J.-M. Graf von der Schulenburg and G. Skogh (eds.): *Law and Economics & The Economics of Legal Regulation.* 1986 ISBN 90-247-3377-4
14. S. Pejovich (ed.): *Socialism: Institutional, Philosophical and Economic Issues.* 1987 ISBN 90-247-3487-8
15. R. Heijmans and H. Neudecker (eds.): *The Practice of Econometrics.* Studies on Demand, Forecasting, Money and Income. In Honor of Jan Salomon Cramer. 1987 ISBN 90-247-3502-5
16. A. Steinherr and D. Weiserbs (eds.): *Employment and Growth.* Issues for the 1980s. In Honor of Albert Kervyn de Lettenhove. 1987 ISBN 90-247-3514-9
17. M.J. Holler (ed.): *The Logic of Multiparty Systems.* 1987 ISBN 90-247-3515-7

International Studies in Economics and Econometrics

18. J.M. van Brabant: *Regional Price Formation in Eastern Europe.* Theory and Practice of Trade Pricing. 1987 ISBN 90-247-3540-8
    See also below under Volume 23
19. A.M. Wesselman: *The Population-Sample Decomposition Method.* A Distribution-Free Estimation Technique for Minimum Distance Parameters. 1987 ISBN 90-247-3603-X
20. P. Coffey (ed.): *Main Economic Policy Areas of the EEC - Toward 1992.* The Challenge to the Community's Economic Policies when the 'Real' Common Market is Created by the End of 1992. 3rd rev.ed., 1990 ISBN 0-7923-0810-7
21. A. Breton, G. Galeotti, P. Salmon and R. Wintrobe (eds.): *The Competitive State.* Villa Colombella Papers on Competitive Politics. 1991 ISBN 0-7923-0835-2
22. S. Pejovich: *The Economics of Property Rights.* Towards a Theory of Comparative Systems. 1990 ISBN 0-7923-0878-6
23. J.M. Van Brabant: *Remaking Eastern Europe.* On the Political Economy of Transition. 1990 ISBN 0-7923-0955-3
24. P. Zweifel and H.E. Frech III (eds.): *Health Economics Worldwide.* 1991 ISBN 0-7923-1219-8
25. J.M. van Brabant: *Integrating Eastern Europe into the Global Economy.* Convertibility through a Payments Union. 1991 ISBN 0-7923-1352-6

KLUWER ACADEMIC PUBLISHERS – DORDRECHT / BOSTON / LONDON

MIX
Papier aus verantwortungsvollen Quellen
Paper from responsible sources
FSC® C105338

If you have any concerns about our products,
you can contact us on
ProductSafety@springernature.com

In case Publisher is established outside the EU,
the EU authorized representative is:
Springer Nature Customer Service Center GmbH
Europaplatz 3, 69115 Heidelberg, Germany

Printed by Libri Plureos GmbH
in Hamburg, Germany